EVOLUTION

THE DISGUISED FRIEND OF FAITH?

Science had pushed the deist's God farther and farther

away, and at the moment when it seemed as if He would

be thrust out altogether, *Darwinism appeared, and, under the*

disguise of a foe, did the work of a friend. It has conferred

upon philosophy and religion an inestimable benefit, by

showing us that we must choose between two alterna-

tives. *Either God is everywhere present in nature, or He is*

nowhere.

> —Aubrey Moore, "The Christian Doctrine of
> God," in *Lux Mundi*, 12th ed., ed. C. Gore
> (London: John Murray, 1891), 73, emphasis
> added.

Arthur Peacocke

EVOLUTION

THE DISGUISED FRIEND OF FAITH?

Selected Essays

TEMPLETON FOUNDATION PRESS

Philadelphia and London

Templeton Foundation Press
300 Conshohocken State Road
West Conshohocken, PA 19428
www.templetonpress.org
© 2004 by Arthur Peacocke

*Templeton Foundation Press helps intellectual leaders and others learn about science
research on aspects of realities, invisible and intangible. Spiritual realities include
unlimited love, accelerating creativity, worship, and the benefits of purpose in
persons and in the cosmos.*

Designed and typeset by Kachergis Book Design

Library of Congress Cataloging-in-Publication Data
Peacocke, A. R. (Arthur Robert)
Evolution: the disguised friend of faith? / Arthur Peacocke.
p. cm.
Includes bibliographical references and index.
ISBN 1-932031-72-3 (pbk. : alk. paper)
1. Evolution. 2. Religion and science. 1. Title.
B818.P32 2004
261.5'5—dc22
2004020728

Printed in the United States of America
04 05 06 07 08 09   10 9 8 7 6 5 4 3 2 1

Contents

Preface

My conviction has long been that critical religious thinking is most vital and creative when it faces the challenge of new ideas and new cultural settings. This has been especially true of Christian theology. One has only to think of

• the opening out of the Gospel from its Jewish setting into the wider Gentile world, as recounted and exemplified in the New Testament (the Acts of the Apostles and the various epistles, especially of St. Paul);

• the Patristic period when the Greek fathers met and overcame the challenge of neo-Platonic philosophy;

• and St. Thomas Aquinas reshaping theology when Aristotle's comprehensive scientific and philosophical works came to Europe via Islam.

Today, the pervading of all our thinking and action by the sciences constitutes the sharpest challenge to the beliefs of traditional Christianity and of other religions. This has been a preoccupation of mine since my schooldays when my incipient and ill-informed faith encountered the evidence for evolution and initiated my own long trail of integrating evolution with a transformed articulation of Christian belief. The working out of these issues has been a *leitmotif* underlying not only my own personal quest[1] but also expressed in my published books[2] on the wider interactions of science and Christian theology. My critical religious thinking on these themes has, as is customary for any thinker, inevitably not been confined to these books but has been expressed as essays, now included in this volume, which were originally presented in a wide variety of milieux and of occasions.

The word "evolution" evokes a negative reaction in only some Christian quarters—but mercifully and certainly, globally, not in most. For, not very long after Darwin produced his evidence of a plausible mechanism (natural selection) for that transformation of species which the fossil record and his researches then indicated, leading Christian thinkers in his own country were welcoming his concept of the evolution of the living world and integrating it with their understanding both of divine creation and incarnation. It is the remark, quoted after the title page, of one of these, Aubrey Moore, that is referred to in the title of this book—the question mark indicating that there is indeed a proper question needing honestly to be pursued with intellectual integrity.

The essays collected here in part 1 represent my thinking about the theological issues raised by the now completely and scientifically well-established evolution of living organisms in the natural world; and, in part 2, about how human beings should now begin to regard themselves and their own presence in the world in relation to the God creating in and through evolution. As a kind of reflection in the mirror of awareness of the created, natural processes of evolution, our thinking about God has itself "evolved" (in the sense of "unfolded") concomitantly with the reconsideration of nature and humanity stimulated by this awareness, and the essays in part 3 are concerned with this reshaping of belief. An epilogue recalls an earlier, medieval figure in English theology, Robert Grosseteste, from whose wisdom concerning education about the relation of nature, humanity, and God we can still learn much.

This book, along with all my other writings, is based on the presupposition that what the sciences tell us is true about nature cannot, in the long run, falsify what is true about human relationships to God. Indeed, because the world is created *by* God, knowledge through science of the world must enhance and clarify and, if need be, correct our understanding of God and of God's relation to the creation, including humanity.

I warmly welcome the opportunity now afforded by the Templeton Foundation Press to bring to a wider readership these essays of mine revolving around this theme of evolution, and I thank their staff, especially Joanna Hill and Laura Barrett, for their patience, cooperation, and understanding in this enterprise.

Arthur Peacocke
MAY 2004

A Note on the Language

For much of the period during which these essays were written and published, the conventions concerning gender-inclusive language were different from those that prevail now in the early part of the twenty-first century. Some of the expressions I used may be mistakenly interpreted by a contemporary reader as *non*-gender inclusive. Nothing could have been further from my intentions over my thirty years as an author in this field, as manifest in the strong arguments put forward in my early major work, *Creation and the World of Science* (Oxford: Clarendon Press, 1979, 141–44; 2nd ed., Oxford: Oxford University Press, 2004) for the attribution of feminine language to God to represent God's nature, especially in relation to divine, creative activity. I intended this as an overt correction to the use of male language to depict God. Since that time the widespread use of neologisms such as "Godself" has enabled one to avoid the use of male personal pronouns in referring to God in some constructions, and that is my current usage—always using "God" instead of "He/he" for the divine, repetitive as this often turns out to be because of the limitations of the English language.

The use of the word "man," with or without a capital M, but certainly without the definite or indefinite article, was the customary word in Britain for most of the twentieth century for referring to humanity or "humankind," for example, the *Shorter Oxford English Dictionary* (Oxford: Clarendon Press, 1974) gives as the first meanings of "man" the following: "**Man** . . . plural **men** . . . I.1. A human being . . . Now surviving in general or indefinite applications in the sense "person" (e.g., with *every, any, no,* and in the plural with *all, any, some,* etc). 2. In generic sense, without article: The human creature regarded abstractly: hence the human race or species, mankind. In *Zoology:* The human creature or race viewed as a genus of animals . . . "

Hence my earlier usage[1] in many of my essays of "man" and "men" was fully inclusive, as I intended it to be. But times and customs have changed, and I can only hope that my intentions then are not now misconstrued, because it would not have been practicable in a reprinting to alter the texts of the accompanying essays in accordance with contemporary usage.

PART I

NATURAL EVOLUTION

CHAPTER I

God's Interaction with the World

The implications of deterministic "chaos" and models from "whole-part" constraints and personal agency

At the beginning of the seventeenth century, John Donne[1] lamented the collapse of the medieval synthesis but, after that century, nothing could stem the rising tide of an individualism in which the self surveyed the world as subject over against object. This way of viewing the world involved a process of abstraction in which the entities and processes of the world were broken down into their constituent units. These parts were conceived as wholes in themselves, whose lawlike relations it was the task of the "new philosophy" to discover. It may be depicted, somewhat over-succinctly, as the asking of, firstly, "What's there?"; then, "What are the relations between what is there?"; and finally, "What are the laws describing these relations?" To implement this aim a *methodologically* reductionist approach was essential, especially when studying the complexities of matter and of

This paper was first published in *The Concept of Nature in Science and Theology, Part I*, Proceedings of the Fifth European Conference on Science and Theology, Freising, 1994, ESSSAT Studies in Science and Theology, vol. 3, ed. N. H. Gregersen, M. W. S. Parsons, and C. Wassermann (Geneva: Labor et Fides, S.A., 1997), 135–52. It is a summary and (I hope) a clarification and development of some ideas elaborated more fully in *Theology for a Scientific Age* (Oxford: Blackwell, 1990; 2nd enlarged ed., London: SCM Press, 1993; Minneapolis: Fortress Press, 1993)—denoted as *TSA* from now on. Reprinted by permission.

living organisms and the natural world came to be described as a world of entities involved in lawlike relations which determined the course of events in time.

The success of these procedures has continued to the present day, in spite of the revolution in our epistemology of the physics of the subatomic world necessitated by the advent of quantum theory. For at the macroscopic level that is the focus of most of the sciences from chemistry to population genetics, the unpredictabilities of quantum events at the subatomic level are usually either ironed out in the statistical certainties of the behavior of large populations of small entities or can be neglected because of the size of the entities involved.[2] Predictability was expected in such macroscopic systems and, by and large, it became possible after due scientific investigation. However, it has turned out that science, being the art of the soluble, has concentrated on those phenomena most amenable to such interpretations. What I intend to point to are some developments from within the natural sciences themselves that change this perspective on the natural world in a number of ways which might bear significantly on how we can conceive of God's interaction with the world.

Whole-part constraint
(or "downward/top-down" causation)

General

The notion of causality, when applied to systems, has usually been assumed to describe "bottom-up" causation—that is, the effect on the properties and behavior of the system of the properties and behavior of its constituent units. However, an influence of the state of the system as a whole on the behavior of its components units—a constraint exercised by the whole on its parts—has to be recognized. D. Campbell[3] and R. W. Sperry,[4] called this "downward" (or "top-down") causation,[5] but it will usually be referred to here as "whole-part constraint." For, to take the example of the Bénard phenomenon, beyond the critical point, individual molecules in a hexagonal "cell," over a wide range in the fluid, move with a common component of velocity in a coordinated way, having previously manifested only entirely random motions with respect to each other. In such instances,[6] the changes at the micro-level, that of the constituent units, are what they are because of their incorporation into the system as a whole, which is exerting specific constraints on its units, making them behave otherwise than they would in isolation. Using "boundary conditions" language,[7] one could say that the set of relationships between the constituent units in the complex whole is a *new* set of boundary conditions for those units. There is also, of course, the effects on a system of its total environment (ultimately, the whole universe), since no system is ever truly isolable, though the particular *system* effects can usually be distinguished from these.

It is important to emphasize again that recognition of the role of such whole-part constraint in no way derogates from the continued recognition of the effects of its components on the state of the system as a whole (i.e., of "bottom-up" effects). But the need for recognition of the former is greater since hardly anyone since the rise of reductionist scientific methodologies doubts the significance of the latter. Indeed, this lack of a proper recognition of whole-part constraint has unfortunately often inhibited the development of concepts appropriate to the more complex levels of the hierarchy of natural systems.

On a critical-realist view of the epistemology of the sciences,[8] this implies that the entities to which the theories and experimental laws refer in our analyses correspond, however inadequately and provisionally, to epistemologically nonreducible features of reality which have to be taken into account when the system-as-a-whole is interacting both with its parts and with other systems (including human observers). These new features may be deemed putatively to exist at the various levels being studied: that is, they can also have an ontological reference, however tentative.[9] It would then be legitimate to envisage the postulated reality which constitutes a complex system-as-a-whole (the "top" of the "top-down" terminology) as exerting a constraint upon its component parts, the realities postulated as existing at those lower levels—while continuing, of course, to recognize the often provisional nature of our attempted depictions of realities at all levels.

Evolution

The pattern of "causal" relationships in biological evolution is interesting in this connection. We are dealing with a process in which a selective system "edits," as it were, the products of direct physicochemical causation (i.e., changes in DNA) over periods of time covering several reproductive generations. D. Campbell[10] gives an example of this: the surfaces and muscle attachments of the jaws of a worker termite are mechanically highly efficient and their operation depends on the properties of the particular proteins of which the jaws are made. These have been optimized by natural selection. Any particular organism is only one in a series of generations of populations of termites, and it is the increasing efficacy of the proteins in constituting efficient jaws that is operative in selection and thereby determines the sequences of the DNA units. Yet when one looks at the development of a *single* organism, one observes only, with the molecular biologists, the biochemical processes whereby protein sequences, and so structures, are "read out" from the DNA sequences. Hence the network of relationships that constitute the temporal evolutionary development and the behavior pattern of the whole organism is determining what particular DNA sequence is present at the controlling point in its genetic material in the evolved organism. This is what Campbell called "downward causation."

It is not adequate to describe such complex interlocking networks of events and changes operating at different levels as *causally* connected in a sequential, constant conjunction of events. We seem rather to have here a determination of form through *a flow of information,* as distinct from a transmission of energy, where "information" is conceived of in a broad enough sense[11] to include the selective input from the environment towards molecular structures—for example, the DNA sequences in the termite jaw example. Such determinative relations may operate between two different kinds of "level" in nature. The determination of form by form requires a flow of information, in this case, between levels.[12]

The brain, mental events, and consciousness.

It is in terms such as these, relevant to our later considerations of God's interaction with the world, that some neuro-scientists and philosophers have come to speak of the relation between mental events experienced as consciousness and the physico-chemical changes at neurons that are the triggers of observable actions in those living organisms whose brains are sufficiently developed that it is appropriate to attribute to them some kind of consciousness. As John Searle has recently put it:

> Consciousness . . . is a real property of the brain that can cause things to happen. My conscious attempt to perform an action such as raising my arm causes the movement of the arm. At the higher level of description, the intention to raise my arm causes the movement of the arm. At the lower level of description, a series of neuron firings starts a chain of events that results in the contraction of the muscles . . . the same sequence of events has two levels of description. *Both of them are causally real,* and the higher level causal features are both caused by and realised in the structure of the lower level elements.[13]

For Roger Sperry and Donald Mackay, "mental events" for human beings are the internal descriptions we offer of an actual *total* state of the brain. The total brain state acts as a constraint on what happens at the more micro-level of the individual neurons; thus what occurs at this micro-level is what it is because of the prevailing state of the whole. There is, it is being suggested, operative here a whole–part constraint of one "level" upon another, from that of the brain state as a whole to that of the individual neurons. Descriptions of the total brain state in purely neurological terms would be exceedingly complex and, indeed, considering the complexity of the brain, may never be forthcoming in anything other than broad terms. The causal effectiveness of the whole brain state on the actual states of its component nerves and neurons is probably better conceived of in terms of the transfer of information rather than of energy, in the way a program representing a certain equation, say, controls the chips in a computer—but this whole area of investigation is still very much *sub judice*. (For example, is there a 1:1 correlation between brain states and mental states? Can a mental state be "realized" in a number of different brain states?)

It seems that, with the evolution of brains, this kind of whole-part constraint has become more and more significant in the evolutionary development, as the whole state and behavior of the individual organism itself plays an increasing role. This has also, as we saw, introduced an element of flexibility into the evolutionary process. Furthermore, since the brain-in-the-body is a dissipative system, it now becomes possible to envisage that the actual succession of states of the brain may prove in practice not to be describable in terms of currently available scientific concepts. This would then point to the need for some higher-level concepts (those called "mental"?) to denote and explicate sequences of events in the brain and the "whole-part constraints" operating from this level. Furthermore, as Nancey Murphy has written—"We attribute freedom to the person insofar as the states of the organism are attributable to the person as a whole, involving intentions, desires, etc. So if the brain states are not predictable [I would say "describable'] when considered solely at that [holistic] level, we have evidence that higher-level (free) processes are the determinative factor."[14]

God's interaction with the world[15] in light of these scientific considerations

Unpredictability, open-endedness, and flexibility[16]

The world appears to us less and less to possess the predictability that has been the presupposition of much theological reflection on God's interaction with the world since Newton. We now observe it to possess a degree of openness and flexibility within a lawlike framework, so that certain developments are genuinely unpredictable *by us* on the basis of any conceivable science. We have good reasons for saying, from the relevant science and mathematics, that this unpredictability will, in practice, continue.

The history of the relation between the natural sciences and the Christian religion affords many instances of a human inability to predict being exploited by theists postulating the presence and activity of God to fill the explanatory gap. However, as these gaps were filled by new knowledge, "God" as an explanation became otiose. Do we now have to take account of, as it were, *permanent* gaps in our ability to predict events in the natural world? Does this imply there is a "God of the (to us) *uncloseable* gaps"? There would then be no possibility of such a God being squeezed out by increases in scientific knowledge. This raises two theological questions: (1) "Does God know the outcome of these situations/systems that are unpredictable by us?" and (2) "Does God act within such situations/systems to effect the divine will?"

Nonquantum considerations

We will first respond to these questions *excluding quantum theory considerations*. With respect to (1), an omniscient God may be presumed to know, not only all the relevant, deterministic laws which apply to any system, but also all the relevant initial conditions of the determining variables to the degree of precision required to predict its state at any future time, however far ahead, together with the effects of any external influences from anywhere else in the universe, however small. So there could be no "eventual unpredictability" with respect to such systems for an infinite, omniscient God, even though there is such a limiting horizon for finite human beings—because of the nature of our knowledge of real numbers and because of ineluctable observational limitations. To take a particularly significant example, divine omniscience must be conceived to be such that God would know and be able to track the minutiae of the triggering fluctuations in dissipative systems, unpredictable and unobservable by us, whose amplification leads at the macroscopic level to one particular, macroscopic outcome (e.g., a symmetry-breaking) rather than an-other—consequently also unpredictable by us.

Only if we thus answered (1) affirmatively, could we then postulate that God might choose to influence events in deterministic systems in the world by changing the initial conditions so as to bring about a macroscopic consequence conforming to the divine will and pur-poses—that is, also to answer (2) affirmatively. God would then be conceived of as acting, as it were, "within" the flexibility we find in these (to us) unpredictable situations in a way that could never be detected by us. Such a mode of divine action would never be incon-sistent with our scientific knowledge of the situation. In the case of those dissipative systems whose macro-states (often involving symmetry-breaking) arise from the amplification of fluctuations at the micro-level that are unpredictable and unobservable by us, God would have to be conceived of as actually manipulating micro-events (at the atomic, molecular, and, according to some,[17] quantum levels) in these initiating fluctuations in the natural world in order to pro-duce the results at the macroscopic level which God wills.

But such a conception of God's action in these, to us, unpre-dictable situations would then be no different in principle from that of God *intervening* in the order of nature with all the problems that that evokes for a rationally coherent belief in God as the Creator of that order. The only difference in this proposal from that of earlier ones postulating divine intervention would be that, given our recent recognition of the actual unpredictability, on our part, of many natu-ral systems, God's intervention would always be hidden from us.

Thus, although at first sight this introduction of unpredictability, open-endedness, and flexibility into *our* picture of the natural world seems to help us to suggest in new terminology how God might act in the world in now uncloseable "gaps," the above considerations in-dicate that such divine action would be just as much "intervention" as it was when postulated before we were aware of these features of the world. This analysis has, it must be stressed, been grounded on the as-sumption that God *does* know the outcome of natural situations that are unpredictable by us (i.e., on an affirmative answer to [1]). It assumes total divine omniscience about all actual, natural events.

Quantum theory considerations

Consideration of the foregoing in the light of quantum theory cannot avoid the continuing current disagreements concerning the basis and significance of the quantum uncertainties which are expressed in the Heisenberg Uncertainty Principle (H.U.P.), which qualifies total predictability, however interpreted. The broad possibilities may be delineated as follows.

(i) *There are "hidden variables"*—that is, there are underlying deterministic laws, unknown to us, which govern the time-course of the precise values of the variables (momentum, position, energy, time, etc.) appearing in the H.U.P. The uncertainties, the "fuzziness," in our knowledge of the values of these variables is purely an *epistemological* limitation on our part, which would not also be one for an omniscient God. Such a God would know both these laws and the relevant initial conditions. Hence the conclusions about how God might interact with the world which were drawn in the previous section would still apply.

(ii) *No "hidden variables"*[18]—that is, the epistemological limitations expressed in the H.U.P. can never be obviated, not only in practice but also in theory, and represent a fundamental uncertainty that inherently exists in the values of the variables in question—an ontological claim that there is indeterminism with respect to these variables. The future trajectory of *any* system will always inherently have that unavoidable lack of precise predictability, given by the H.U.P. relations, with respect to these variables—it is genuinely *in*deterministic in these respects (if not in all, e.g., in the statistical properties of the ensemble). Only a probabilistic knowledge of these variables is possible for us, but this limitation is insurmountable. It represents an "in principle" limitation. This is the majority view of physicists.

If this is so, we would have to conclude that this inherent unpredictability also represents a limitation of the knowledge even an omniscient God could have[19] of the values of these variables and so of the future trajectory, in those respects, of the system. That is to say, God has so made the quantum world that God has allowed God's own *possible* knowledge to be thus limited. In this regard, then, God's omniscience is "self-limited."[20] God's knowledge with respect to H.U.P. variables in future states would be the maximum it could be compared with ours, but would nevertheless still be only probabilistic. Moreover, if the future, as I and others have argued,[21] has no ontological status—that is, does not exist in any sense—then it has no content of events *for* God to know, so it logically cannot be known even to an omniscient God, who knows all that it is possible to know. According to this view, God knows the future *definitively* only by prediction on the basis of God's omniscient knowledge of all determining laws and an infinitely precise knowledge of all initial relevant conditions; or *probabilistically* in the case of quantum-dependent events (for God cannot predict in detail the outcome of in-principle unpredictable situations, on the no-hidden-variables assumption). This conclusion about the basis of God's foreknowledge would still apply, even if it is thought God acts in the world by altering the initial conditions of a train of events to obtain the outcome God wills and so must foresee.

An easily envisaged example, related to the relations expressed in the H.U.P., is afforded by radioactive decay in which a quantum event has an observable macroscopic outcome in the decay of the atoms. In this case, the foregoing is arguing that God does not know *which* of a million radium atoms will be the next to disintegrate in, say, the next 10^{-3} seconds, but only (as we ourselves) what the average number will be that will break up in that period of time. There is no fact of the matter about which atom will decompose at a particular future moment *for* God to know. The proposal of "self-limiting" omniscience means that God has so made the natural order that it is, in principle, impossible, even for God, as it is for us, to predict the precise, future values of certain variables—which is what I take "in principle" to mean in this context. God's omniscient knowledge of the *probabilities* of these future values will, of course, always be maximal.

Hence, in the case of systems sensitive to initial conditions, the introduction of quantum uncertainty introduces an upper limit to predictability with respect to certain parameters which cannot be avoided.[22] This limit on total predictability applies to God as well as to ourselves, if there are no hidden variables. So the answer to the theological question (1) then has to be, in the light of such quantum considerations, that *God* also cannot know, beyond real limits, the outcomes of those situations, the trajectories of those systems which are also in principle (if no hidden variables) unpredictable for us beyond those same limits. God, of course, knows maximally what it is possible to know, namely the *probabilities* of the outcomes of these situations, the various possible trajectories of such systems. But this does not suffice for us to give a clear affirmative answer to question (2) to the effect that God could act in such situations or systems to implement the divine will.

On this, to some no doubt revisionary view, God bestows a certain autonomy not only on human beings, as Christian theology has long recognized, but also on the natural order as such to develop in ways that God chooses not to control in detail. God allows a degree of open-endedness and flexibility to nature, and this becomes the natural, structural basis for the flexibility of conscious organisms and, in due course and more speculatively, possibly for the freedom of the human-brain-in-the-human-body, that is, of persons. So it does help us to perceive the natural world as a matrix within which openness and flexibility and, in humanity, perhaps even freedom could naturally emerge.

Implications of "chaotic" determinism

One set of previous considerations (those concerned with the infinite decimal representation of real numbers and algorithmic complexity) implies only a long-rejected interventionism as the basis for God's interaction with the world to influence events. The other set of considerations (concerned with the H.U.P. and its consequences if there are no hidden variables) implies that God cannot know precisely the future outcome of quantum-dependent situations,[23] so cannot act *directly* to influence them to implement the divine purpose and will, as we may be tempted to postulate. It should be noted that this does not derogate at all from God having purposes which are being implemented through the propensities (to complexity, self-organization, information-processing, and consciousness) that load, as it were, the dice the throws of which shape the course of natural events.

The above discussion leads us to infer that this newly won awareness of the unpredictability, open-endedness, and flexibility inherent in many natural processes and systems does not, of itself, help directly to illuminate the "causal joint" of how God acts in the world, i.e., the nature of the interface between God and all-that-is—much as it alters our interpretation of the meaning of what is actually going on in the world. Defining the problem (à la Austin Farrer) as that of the "causal joint" between God and the world is inappropriate, for it does not do justice to the many levels in which causality operates in a world of complex systems interlocking in many ways at many levels. It is to this major feature of the world as perceived by the sciences that we must now turn.

Whole-part constraint as a model for God's interaction with the world

In a number of natural situations, interactions within complex systems constituted of complex subsystems at various levels of interlocking organization can best be understood as a two-way process. Real features of the total system-as-a-whole are constraints upon events happening within the subsystems at lower levels—events, which, it must be stressed, in themselves are describable in terms of the sciences pertinent to that lower level. In the light of this it is suggested that we can properly regard the world-as-a-whole as a total system so that its general state can be a holistic constraint[24] upon what goes on at the myriad levels that comprise it. For all-that-is displays, with wide variations in the degree of coupling, a real interconnectedness and interdependence at the quantum, biological, and cosmological levels and this would, of course, be totally and luminously clear to God in all its ramifications and degrees of coupling.[25]

I want now to explore the possibility that these new perceptions of the way in which levels within this world-system interact with each other (from higher to lower and vice versa) might provide a new resource for thinking about how God interacts with that world-as-a-whole. In making such a suggestion I am not postulating that the world *is*, as it were "God's body," but, although the world is not organized in the way a human body is, it is nevertheless a "system." The world-as-a-whole, the total world system, may be regarded as "in God,"[26] though ontologically distinct from God. For God is uniquely present to it all, all its individual component entities, in and at all spaces and all times (in whatever relativistic frame of reference[27]) and has an unsurpassed awareness of its interconnected and interdependent unity—even *more* than we can have of the unity of our own bodies. If God interacts with the "world" at a supervenient level of totality, then God, by affecting the state of the world-as-a-whole, could, on the model of whole-part constraint relationships in complex systems, be envisaged as able to exercise constraints upon events in the myriad sub-levels of existence that constitute that "world" without abrogating the laws and regularities that specifically pertain to them—and this without "intervening" within the unpredictabilities we have noted.[28] *Particular* events might occur in the world and be what they are because God intends them to be so, without at any point any contravention of the laws of physics, biology, psychology, sociology, or whatever is the pertinent science for the level of description in question.

In thus speaking of God, it has not been possible to avoid talk of God "intending," and so using the language of personal agency. For these ideas of whole-part constraint by God cannot be expounded without relating them to the concept of God as, in some sense, an agent, least misleadingly described as personal. In thus speaking, we are focusing upon *particular* events, or patterns of events, as expressive of the "purposes" (e.g., of communication) of God who is thereby conceived of as in some sense personal. Such *particular* intentions of

God must be distinguished from that perennial sustaining in existence of the entities, structures, and dynamic processes of the world which is an inherent component of all concepts of God as Creator. This sustaining is properly regarded as "continuous," an aspect of God as *semper Creator* with respect to the *creatio continua*. What is being further suggested here is that we have to envisage God as at *any* time (and in this sense only, "all the time") being able to exert constraints upon the world-as-a-whole, so that *particular* events and patterns of events can occur, which otherwise would not have done so. This is usually regarded as God's "providential" action, unhelpful as the distinction between creation and providence often proves to be.

Personal agents as psychosomatic unities— *God as "personal" agent?*

The way in which, in the preceding, we have found ourselves drawn towards the model of *personal* agency in attempting to explicate God's interaction with the world is intriguing in the contemporary context—and not only because of its biblical and traditional role. For in one particular instance of a system manifesting whole-part constraint, the human-brain-in-the-human-body, we have an immediate sense of the nonreducibility of the whole—in our "consciousness," as folk psychology calls it.[29] For, over recent decades, the pressure from the relevant sciences has been inexorably towards viewing the processes that occur in the human brain and nervous system, on the one hand, and the content of consciousness, our personal, mental experience, on the other, as two facets or functions of one total unitive process and activity.[30] We have already seen that combining a nondualist account of the human person and of the mind-body relation with the idea of whole-part constraint illuminates the way in which states of the brain-as-a-whole could have effects at the level of neurons and so of bodily action, and could actually also be holistic states of the brain-as-a-whole. Such states could be legitimately referred to in nonreducible mentalist language as a real modality of the total unitive event which is the activity of thinking that is accomplished by the human-brain-in-the-human-body.

This invoking of the notion of whole-part constraints of brain states as a whole upon the states of the "lower" level of its constituent neurons in giving an account of human agency affords, I would suggest, a new insight into the nature of human agency very pertinent to the problem of how to model God's interaction with the world. My suggestion is that a combination of the recognition of the way whole-part constraints operate in complexly interconnected and interdependent systems with the recognition of the unity of the human mind/brain/body event together provide a fruitful model for illuminating how we might think of God's interaction with the world. According to this suggestion, the state of the totality of the world-as-a-whole (all-that-is) would be known maximally only to the omniscience of God and would be the field of the exercise of the divine omniscience at God's omnicompetent level of comprehensiveness and comprehension.[31] When we act as personal agents, there is a unitive, unifying, centered constraint on the activity of our human bodies which we experience as the content of our personal subjectivity (the sense of being an "I") in its mode of willing action. God is here being conceived of as a unifying, unitive source and centered influence on events on the world.[32]

We are here courting the notion that the succession of the states of the system of the world-as-a-whole is also experienced as a succession by God, who is present to it all; and that this might be modeled after the way we presume a succession of brain states constitutes a succession in our thoughts. God would then be regarded as exerting a continuous holistic constraint on the world-as-a-whole in a way akin to that whereby in our thinking we influence our bodies to implement our intentions. This suggestion is, for me at least, entirely metaphorical, providing only a model for God's interaction with the world and thereby enabling us to conceive coherently and intelligibly how God might be conceived of as interacting with the world consistently with what we know of its nature and with the character of God already inferred on other grounds. As such, therefore, it has its limitations, indeed—as with all such attempts—an inevitably negative aspect. For, in a human being, the "I" does not transcend the body ontologically in the way that God transcends the world and must therefore be an influence on the world-state from "outside" in the sense of having a distinctively different ontological status.[33] But at least the suggested model helps us to conceive how God's transcendence and immanence might be held coherently together as a transcendence-in-immanence.

This now affords a further clue to how that continuing interaction of God with the world-as-a-whole which implements particular divine purposes might best be envisaged—namely as analogous to an input, a flow of information, rather than of energy.[34] For different, equally probable, macroscopic states of a system—and so, in the model, of the world-as-a-whole—can possess the same energy but differ in form and pattern, that is, in information content (cf. n. 11). Moreover, since God is properly regarded by most theists as in some sense "personal," this "flow of information" may more appropriately be envisaged as a means of *communication* by God of divine purposes and intentions when it is directed towards that level in the hierarchy of complexity which is uniquely capable of perceiving and recognizing it, namely, humanity.[35]

Conclusion

The foregoing suggests a way in which we could think of divine constraints (properly called "influences," to cohere with the model of *personal* agency) making a difference in the world, yet not in any way contrary to those regularities and laws operative within the observed universe which are explicated by the sciences applicable to their appropriate levels of complexity and organization. This holistic mode of action on and influence in the world is God's alone and distinctive of God. God's interaction with the whole and the constraints God exerts upon it could thereby shape and direct events at lesser levels so that the divine purposes are not ultimately frustrated. Such interaction could occur without ever abrogating at any point any of the natural relationships and inbuilt flexibilities and freedoms operative at all of the lower levels, and discerned by the sciences and ordinary human experience.

Only God in the mode of transcendence is present to the totality of all-that-is, as well as, in the mode of immanence, to the individual entities that comprise created existence. Accordingly, God's experience is of the world-as-a-whole as well as of individual entities and events within it. Only God could be aware of the distinctiveness of any state of that totality and which of its states might or might not succeed it in time (or whatever is the appropriate dimension for referring to "succession in God"). This divine knowledge would always be hidden from and eternally opaque to us, existing as we do at levels at which the conceptual language will never be available for apprehending God's own "inner" life. The best we can do, as we have already urged, is to stretch the language of personal experience as the least misleading option available to us. According to this approach, we are free to describe any particular events at our own level of existence in the natural terms available to us (e.g., in those of the sciences explaining both the "bottom-up" and whole-part effects within the natural order); and at the same time to regard at least some of those events, whether private and internal to us or public and external to all, as putatively and partially manifesting God's intentions, God's providence, and so as being communications from God. For God could have brought it about that these particular events are what they are and not something else by that overall comprehensive constraining influence which only God can exert (but does not *necessarily* do so) in a whole-part manner upon any lower-level event occurring in the totality of existing entities in order to implement divine intentions, such as communicating with humanity.

God, I am suggesting, is thus to be conceived of as all the time the continuing supra-personal, unifying, unitive Agent acting, often selectively, upon all-that-is, as God's own self purposes. We must go on recognizing—and this is essential to the whole proposal—that, in the light of our earlier discussion, it is God who has chosen to allow a degree of unpredictability, open-endedness, and flexibility in the world

God continues to hold in existence and through whose processes God continues to create; and that God, so conceived, does not intervene to break the causal chains that go from "bottom-up," from the micro- to the macro-levels.

What does this imply about the "causal joint" between God and the world? As already mentioned (n. 11), in the world we observe through the sciences, we know of no transfers of information without some exchange of matter and/or energy, however minimal. So to speak of God as "informing" the world-as-a-whole without such inputs of matter/energy (that is, as not being "intervention") is but to accept the ultimate, ontological gap between the nature of God's own being and that of the created world, all-that-is apart from God. Hence the present exercise could be regarded essentially as an attempt, as it were, to ascertain where this ontological gap, across which God transmits "information" (i.e., communicates), is most coherently "located," consistently with God's interaction with everything else having *particular* effects and without abrogating those regular relationships to which God's own self continues to give an existence which the sciences increasingly discover.

I would want to emphasize, with Kaufman[36] and Wiles,[37] that God's action is on the world-as-a-whole, but to stress more strongly than they do that this maintaining and supporting interaction is a continuing as well as an initial one; and can be general *and particular* in its effects. The freedom of God to affect the world is indeed reinforced and protected in this model. For the notion of whole-part constraint now allows us to understand how initiating divine action on the state of the world-as-a-whole can itself have consequences for individual events and entities within that world. Moreover, such divine causative, constraining influence would never be observed by us as a divine "intervention," that is, as an interference with the course of nature and as a setting aside of its natural, regular relationships.

The proposed model allows the effects of natural events, including the unpredictable ones and the outcome of freely willed human decisions, to work their way up through the hierarchy of complexity and so to contribute to the state of the world-as-a-whole. It therefore also helps us to model more convincingly the interaction, dialogue even, between human decisions and actions, on the one hand, and divine intentions and purposes, on the other. It is in such a context that the notion of God communicating with humanity can be developed in which the significance of religious experience, revelation, the incarnation, prayer, worship, and the sacraments may be grounded.[38]

In conclusion, it would seem that the unpredictabilities of nonlinear dynamic systems do not as such help us in the problem of articulating more coherently and intelligibly how God interacts with the world. Nevertheless recent insights of the natural sciences into the processes of the world, especially those on whole-part constraint in complex systems and on the unity of the human-brain-in-the-human-body, have provided not only a new context for the debate about how God might be conceived to interact with and influence events in the world, but have also afforded new conceptual resources for modeling it.

CHAPTER 2

Biological Evolution and Christian Theology—Yesterday and Today

No assessment of the relation between biological evolution and Christian theology today can be made without an adequate historical perspective. Fortunately that perspective has been greatly enriched by historical investigations in recent decades, as well represented by other contributions to this volume, and these have resulted in a significant reappraisal of the impact of Darwin and of the Darwinians on the thought of their day. Let it suffice simply to recall that evolutionary ideas, as expounded by Darwin, were widely seen as a threat to religious belief in the mid-nineteenth century, not only by their apparent impugning of the veracity of the Scriptures, as literally read, but also by their undermining of traditional ideas about the nature and origin of human beings. Instead of dwelling on this familiar confrontation, however, let us turn to some of the more conciliatory theological responses to Darwinism in the last century. For the stage has been occupied too often by those who want to stress the negative reactions of many Christians, both theologians and laypeople, to Darwinism in the Victorian era. The reconciling responses are worth recapitulating because many of them provided fruitful soil for the

From *Darwinism and Divinity,* ed. John Durant (Oxford: Blackwell, 1985), 101–30; originally presented at a conference organized by the British Society for the History of Science in the rooms of the Linnean Society of London on November 12, 1982, to mark the centenary of Darwin's death. Reprinted by permission.

growth of a more coherent and constructive approach by Christian theology to evolution. In order to face contemporary issues, it will also be necessary to sketch in some of the broad features of current evolutionary theory. Then we can return to the question that is implicit in the title, namely "What is it to be a Christian theist in a post-Darwinian world?"

Constructive reconciling theological responses to Darwin

The constructive responses of those Christian theologians who, in the phrase of Gertrude Himmelfarb,[1] wished to be "reconcilers" rather than "irreconcilers," were not based on any mood of defeatism or any sense of accommodation of Christian truth to a new and overwhelming force. Rather, they were based on a conviction that has always motivated the best and, in the long run, the most influential theology—namely that, to be intelligible and plausible to any generation, the Christian faith must express itself in ways that are consistent with such understanding of the nature of the world as is contemporarily available. For the constructive theological responses to Darwin's ideas represent a better-established way of doing theology than some of the more extreme denials that then filled the stage (and often still fill our headlines). However, the theological questions were real enough: How could one believe in Darwin's hypothesis and still hold the account of creation in Genesis to be true? How should God's action as creator be conceived in relation to an evolutionary formation of new creatures? How could one continue to use the popular argument for the existence of God, namely, that the presence of design and apparent purpose in the mechanisms of living organisms shows them to have been fashioned by a cosmic designer of an intelligence and power attributable only to a creator God? Moreover, if human beings had evolved from the animals to a higher state of intellectual and moral consciousness, how could there be any place for the supposed historic Fall, as thought to be described in the early chapters of Genesis, and much elaborated in Augustinian strands of Christianity, both Catholic and Protestant? If human higher capacities had evolved by natural means from those of animals, how could we go on supposing that they had any special ultimate value or significance? So although Darwin himself was careful never to debate these issues in public, as his own Christian belief gradually and privately ebbed away, it is not surprising that the publication of his ideas provided a new tiltyard for those who wished to enter the lists on behalf either of supposed Christian truth or of free scientific enquiry.

Because Darwin was an Englishman writing in England, and his work was first published in London, it was inevitable that the first impact of his ideas on Christian theology was upon the Church of England. But let us begin by examining the fate of his evolutionary ideas in the German and French contexts, and the response of the Roman Catholic Church.

German readers tended to see Darwin through the spectacles of Ernst Haeckel, who held a monistic worldview based on a strongly mechanistic view of evolution. For him the only viable religion was the "monistic religion of humanity," of "truth, goodness and beauty."[2] It was such a pantheistic religion of immanence which alone could form a bond with *Wissenschaft* and create a unity of God and the world. At the same time, the recruiting of Darwinism into the struggle for socialism, atheism, and free-thinking by Marx and Engels tied evolution into a package which most theologians inevitably rejected (see Daecke for a fuller exposition of this aspect of German thought). Thus German theology, insofar as it did not reject all evolutionary thought but did reject both monism and Marxism, was pushed either towards a neo-vitalism, which had its roots in an earlier Naturphilosophie, or towards an existentialist dualism of "belief" and "knowledge" in the post-Kantian tradition of Albrecht Ritschl. Those who chose the former option were deeply influenced by Hans Driesch, who saw in evolution the working of a nonmaterial factor— a vital agent or entelechie which could interlock with the material processes of living organisms as understood by physics and chemistry, and was the source of their character as living entities. Seeberg,[3] for example, saw in this a way of countering a purely mechanistic interpretation of evolutionary causality and so of "saving" the creative intervention of God. For him, as for Driesch, matter, life, and spirit were transformed by the action of an inner, active, teleological principle transcending the laws of physics and chemistry. Driesch's vitalistic concept of wholeness *(Ganzheit)* was also utilized by other theologians, such as Jacob von Uexküll,[4] who regarded the organism and its environment as parts of a concerted unity, linked together by an "immaterial factor." Arthur Titius and Karl Heim also invoked the idea of wholeness in order to unite causal and teleological explanations. In his[5] *Das Weltbild der Zukunft* (1904), Heim attempted to integrate the principle of natural selection with a natural theology. For both Titius and Heim mechanistic causality was not enough to explain evolution; an active purposefulness *(Ganzheitsfaktor)* was also necessary, and the introduction of this concept created a bond between science and religion. This emphasis on the *Ganzheit* principle brought both Titius and Heim close to vitalism, which in Heim's case sat rather uncomfortably with his understanding of God as personal. Titius developed the idea of *Ganzheit* to interpret God as the driving force of the cosmos, and he saw creation and evolution as different ways of conceiving the same divine activity (see Daecke).

For a long period after the Second World War, German theology (and with it much American and European, though not English, theology) was dominated by the impressive writings of Karl Barth, for whom the relation between the realms of nature and grace, between the sphere of the corrupt human intellect and that of the pure word of God, between the created and the creator, was simply and starkly that of a "great gulf fixed," with no possible traffic between them that man could initiate. Consequently, natural theology was relegated to the wings of the theological stage, and even a theology of nature was not much pursued. So inevitably from the mid-1940s to about the mid-1960s there was little active consideration in Barthian circles of the relation between evolutionary ideas and Christian theology. Today, however, under the pressure of environmental problems that generate the need for a theology of nature, German theology has begun to take a new interest in the findings of science in general, and of evolutionary biology in particular. Thus we have two of Germany's leading theologians, Wolfhart Pannenberg and Jürgen Moltmann, writing on these themes. Pannenberg[6] has carefully worked out the relation between theology and the natural and human sciences. In his view, when natural science and human understanding are emancipated from the specter of scientific positivism, they can regulate each other in a unified perspective in which theology deals with the all-embracing totality of meaning that is implicit in them both. According to him,[7] this entails theology asking certain questions of the natural sciences, such as, "Is there any equivalent in modern biology to the biblical notion of the Divine Spirit as origin of life that transcends the limit of the organism?" Whether or not this is the best way to formulate the question is open to debate, but it is clear that German theology has now really begun to come to grips with the actual content of evolutionary biology. Moltmann's work[8] is more confessional and political in tone, dwelling on the practical tasks of understanding and transformation. But he does take account of an evolutionary understanding of what is happening in the world. He sees the natural and biological worlds as open systems with open futures, and examines what this entails for human activity, including political action.

In France, biology was dominated in the early nineteenth century by the giant figure of Georges Cuvier, a formidable opponent of the evolutionary scheme and mechanism proposed by Jean Baptiste de Lamarck. The reaction to Darwin in France was confused by the French word *evolution* referring primarily to "individual development," while "evolution" in Darwin's sense was there referred to as *transformation* or *transformisme*. Moreover, "Ever since Ray . . . the definition of the term 'species' [Fr. *espèce*] had entailed that two different species must be *genealogically* distinct: this being so, the theory of *transformisme* could not be stated as a doctrine about 'species' at all—let alone throw light on the origin of species."[9] This semantic stumbling block, which worried the French more than the empirical English, has only been properly circumvented in the mid-twentieth-century "new taxonomy" wherein "species" are defined in a much more restricted fashion that takes account of the evolutionary process.

Undoubtedly, the chief influence in French philosophy of evolution was Henri Bergson, who was born in the same year as the publication of *The Origin of Species* and who died during the Second World War. In *Creative Evolution*,[10] Bergson invoked a vital impulse *(élan vitale)* as the cause and coordinator of the variations that produce new organs and new species. He postulated a dualism of life and spirit versus matter and regarded evolution as a process in which life and spirit diverged and unfolded from matter. Bergson differed from German neo-vitalism in that he was against "finalism," the belief that the cosmos in general (including the biological world) was moving towards a predetermined and possibly foreseeable end. For Bergson, evolution proceeded unpredictably from the one to the many. It was not a creative unification.

French Christian theology is largely Roman Catholic, and the official response of that church to Darwin may be fairly described as a cautious keeping of Darwinism at arm's length with the preserving of belief in a distinctive act of creation for the human species through two historical individuals (traditionally known as Adam and Eve). Thus the Roman Catholic church virtually "bracketed off" the whole question of evolution until the middle of the twentieth century, when the posthumous publication of the French Jesuit Teilhard de Chardin's personal synthesis of Christian faith and evolutionary philosophy stimulated a renewed debate about it. Teilhard was one of the most widely read Roman Catholic thinkers to base his thinking on evolution, which he used as a theological category and as a hermeneutical principle to transpose Christian belief out of a static worldview into one that recognized the world as being in process of becoming ("cosmogenesis"). For him, the Christian God was "a God of cosmogenesis, a God of evolution." Rejecting Bergson's emphasis on divergence, Teilhard reinstated the idea of evolution as creative unification. In spite of the plethora of living organisms, the evolutionary process had a spearhead in the human psyche and moved towards an ultimate unification in what he called the "omega point." For Teilhard, cosmogenesis had taken place in the evolution of life and spirit and potentially it could become a "Christogenesis." In his writings an emphasis on Christ as redeemer is replaced by an emphasis on Christ as evolver; and the idea of salvation is extended from that of "redemption" to embrace that of "genesis." Christ himself "saves evolution" by being its mover, animator, guide, coordinator, and uniter. It is not always clear in, for example, *The Phenomenon of Man*[11] whether the "God of evolution" and the "Christ-evolver" are vitalistic, teleological factors, or whether they represent a conjunction of two ultimate but fundamentally coincident consummations in human consciousness and the evolutionary process.

Although Teilhard's ideas were rejected by the official organs of the Roman Catholic Church, both during his lifetime and when they were eventually published posthumously, he has been extremely influential among lay Roman Catholics (and others), and possibly even in the deliberations of the Second Vatican Council (1962–65). Meanwhile the official response of the Roman Catholic Church to Darwinism in the last few decades may be summarized in the words of Alszeghi:[12]

> Documents after Pius XII touch only indirectly on the problem of evolution. Although taking account of the possibility of hominization [presumably meaning the formation of human beings or their creation] through evolution, they none the less affirm the necessity of proceeding with moderation and they insist on the fact that the question of the reconciliation of the faith with evolution cannot yet be regarded as definitely resolved. A recent allocution of Paul VI to a group of theologians characterizes evolution as no longer an hypothesis but a 'theory', and makes no other reservation for its application to man than the immediate creation of each and every human soul and the decisive importance exerted on the lot of humanity by the disobedience of Adam. . . . The Pope observes that polygenism has not been scientifically demonstrated and cannot be admitted if it involves the denial of the dogma of original sin. (16)
>
> A final factor which was to attenuate the diffidence of the Church towards evolution consisted in the deeper understanding of the Creator's special action in the formation of man. For, on the one hand, it is inadmissable that the human race should spring forth independently of the Creator; and on the other hand, the in-

terpretation of the divine intervention in a determinative manner—as an action of God which is part of the same plane of sec-
ondary causes—does not fit in with an evolutionistic vision of the
world. This obstacle has been overcome by conceiving the special
action of God as one that works through all the generations of living beings, so that everyone shares in this special but continuous
action in the great work of universal evolution. (17)

Alszeghi concludes that it is not at all likely that the ecclesiastical
magisterium would "in the concrete" declare that evolution is irrec-
oncilable with the faith.

In a significant contribution to Roman Catholic thought on evolution, Karl Rahner[13] (1966) has put forward a challenging interpretation of the incarnation of Christ. Rahner's Christology forms part of
an immensely comprehensive and profound Christian theology, and
little justice can be done to it here. Rather than attempting to summarize his position, I choose to present his ideas by some excerpts
from his work that, even out of context, may perhaps serve to indicate
the gist of an influential position within Roman Catholic theology
that adopts a positive and welcoming approach to evolutionary ideas.
We must, Rahner says,

> take into consideration the known history of the cosmos as it has
> been investigated and described by the modern natural sciences:
> this history is seen more and more as one homogeneous history of
> matter, life and man. This one history does not exclude differences
> of nature but on the contrary includes them in its concept, since
> history is precisely not the permanence of the same but rather the
> becoming of something entirely new and not merely of something
> other. (166)

Thus Rahner assumes the current evolutionary view of the world,
emphasizing the connections between matter and spirit, natural history and the history of man, that it implies. Because all is the creation
of one and the same God, he deems it self-evident for Christian theology that matter and spirit have "more things in common" than
"things dividing them." This is shown par excellence in the unity of
matter and spirit in man himself, who is not a merely temporary

composite but is fundamentally so—for the starting point is the one man in his *one* self-realization. By "spirit," Rahner means "the one man in so far as he becomes conscious of himself in an absolute consciousness of being-given-to-himself. This man does by the very fact that he is always referred to the absoluteness of reality as such and so to its one root (called God) . . . " (162, 163).

This inseparable, but irreducible, correlatedness of matter and spirit in man itself has a history; for matter develops out of its inner being in the direction of spirit, and such "becoming" must be conceived as something "becoming more"—the coming into being of more reality. This "more" Rahner describes *inter alia* as the "self-transcendence by which an existing and active being actively approaches to the higher perfection still lacking to it" (164–65). He writes:

> If man is thus the self-transcendence of living matter, then the history of Nature and spirit forms an inner, graded unity in which natural history develops towards man, continues in him as his history, is conserved and surpassed in him and hence reaches its proper goal with and in the history of the human spirit. (168)

Based on this view of the significance of the evolutionary perspective, Rahner tries

> to see man as the being in whom the basic tendency of matter to find itself in the spirit by self-transcendence arrives at the point where it definitely breaks through; thus in this way we may be in a position to regard man's being itself, from *this* view-point within the basic and total conception of the world. It is precisely this being of man, seen from this view-point, which—both by its highest, free and complete self-transcendence into God, made possible quite gratuitously by God, and by God's communication of himself—"awaits" its own consummation and that of the world in what in Christian terms we call "grace" and "glory."
>
> The first step and definitive beginning, and the absolute guarantee that this ultimate and basically unsurpassable self-transcendence will succeed and indeed has already begun, is to be found in what we call the Hypostatic Union [the union of the human nature and divine nature in the one person of Christ]. At a first approxima-

tion, this must not be seen so much as something which distinguishes Jesus Our Lord from us, but rather as some thing which must happen once, and once only, at the point where the world begins to enter into its final phase in which it is to realize its final concentration, its final climax and its radical nearness to the absolute mystery called God. Seen from this viewpoint, the Incarnation appears as the necessary and permanent beginning of the divinization of the world as a whole. (160–61)

This positive treatment of a central theological theme in relation to an evolutionary perspective by a leading orthodox Roman Catholic theologian was welcome, even if somewhat delayed, coming as it did just over a century after Darwin and Wallace announced their theory of evolution by natural selection.

Needless to say the impact of Darwinism on Christian thought was greatest in the England in which Darwin first propounded his views, though naturally the controversy soon spread throughout Britain and to the United States. Historians of the Victorian period have documented a number of particular cultural and religious features of the Darwinian debate—for example, the dominance of the argument from design within traditional natural theology, and the increasingly disturbing analysis (emanating from Germany) of the Scriptures by the criteria and methods of historical scholarship. Rather than enter into this intriguing history, study of which is revealing a greater complexity in the Christian response to Darwin and a greater flexibility and openness on the part of orthodox Christian theologians than is purveyed by the inherited mythology about this period,[14] I wish to pick out one thread in the debate. It is that quieter and, in the end, more profound response of those Christian theists who did not reject Darwin but sought seriously to incorporate the evolutionary perspective into their theological reflection.

I am referring to that part of the theological response within the Church of England that was deeply influenced by the doctrine of the incarnation. A stress on the doctrine of the incarnation, and on a sacramental understanding of the world, had been revived (by the Tractarians) in the second half of the nineteenth century. It repre-

sented a renewal in the theology of the Church of England of an earlier emphasis on the immanence of God in nature and on the sacraments as an expression and reflection of that presence of God in the
world. This goes back to the very foundations of the reformed
Catholicism of the Church of England. Some indication of the flavor
of this theology is provided by the following selected quotations.
Some thirty years after the publication of the *Origin*, Aubrey Moore
wrote:

> The scientific evidence in favour of evolution, *as a theory* is infi-
> nitely more Christian than the theory of "special creation." For it
> implies the immanence of God in nature, and the omnipresence of
> His creative power. Those who oppose the doctrine of evolution in
> defence of a "continued intervention" of God, seem to have failed
> to notice that a theory of occasional intervention implies as its cor-
> relative *a theory of ordinary absence.*[15]

The same author also wrote in the collection *Lux Mundi* (1891):

> The one absolutely impossible conception of God, in the present
> day, is that which represents him as an occasional visitor. Science
> has pushed the deist's God further and further away, and at the mo-
> ment when it seemed as if He would be thrust out all together,
> Darwinism appeared, and, under the disguise of a foe, did the work
> of a friend. . . . Either God is everywhere present in nature, or He
> is nowhere.[16]

In the same volume, in an essay entitled significantly "The Incarnation in Relation to Development," J. R. Illingworth wrote:

> The last few years have witnessed the gradual acceptance by Chris-
> tians of the great scientific generalisation of our age, which is
> briefly if somewhat vaguely described as the Theory of Evolution.
> . . . It is an advance in our theological thinking; a definite increase
> of insight; a fresher and fuller appreciation of those "many ways" in
> which "God fulfills Himself."

Illingworth saw Christ as the consummation of the evolutionary
process:

[I]n scientific language, the Incarnation may be said to have introduced a new species into the world—the Divine man transcending past humanity, as humanity transcended the rest of the animal creation, and communicating His vital energy by a spiritual process to subsequent generations of men.[17]

Charles Gore, the editor of that same controversial volume, later in his 1891 Bampton Lectures affirmed that:

from the Christian point of view, this revelation of God, this unfolding of divine qualities, reaches a climax in Christ. God has expressed in inorganic nature, His immutability, immensity, power, wisdom; in organic nature He has shown also that He is alive; in human nature He has given glimpses of His mind and character. In Christ not one of these earlier revelations is abrogated; nay, they are reaffirmed; but they reach a completion in the fuller exposition of the divine character, the divine personality, the divine love.[18]

In the twentieth century one of the most positive attempts to integrate evolutionary biology into Christian theology was made by Tennant,[19] who rejected the traditional pessimism about man, as it had been developed from the Bible by the combination of Genesis with the Pauline epistles. Instead, Tennant appealed from the Scriptures, understood in the light of tradition, to the evidence of the evolutionary process. In the original man, he argued, the moral consciousness awakened only slowly: there was no question of some catastrophic change for the worse in his relationship with God, nor was there, at a later stage in man's development, a "radical bias towards evil" because of the Fall. It was as true to say that God was still making man as to say that God had made him. Similarly, the origin and meaning of sin were to be sought in the process of becoming. This emphasis on the "process of becoming" was also a major strand in the philosophy of Whitehead.[20] The theologians Temple[21] and Thornton[22] were contemporaries of Whitehead and were deeply influenced by him; like Tennant, they drew upon the tradition of evolutionary interpretation that went back to *Lux Mundi*.

The last name I want to mention in this specifically Anglican tradition is that of Charles Raven, formerly Regius Professor of Divinity in the University of Cambridge, and one whom his biographer, Dillistone[23] dubbed as "naturalist, historian, theologian." Raven's whole life was devoted to integrating the evolutionary perspective of biology with his Christian theology, for he embraced evolution wholeheartedly and believed that it could serve as the conceptual framework for religious expression.[24] He strove to enhance the place of the life sciences in man's understanding of the universe, then largely dominated by physics, and pioneered in emphasizing the need for ecologically wise policies of conservation. The living world was for him the many-splendored sacrament of the activity and presence of the living God. His last words from the pulpit, which I was privileged to hear, expressed with characteristic eloquence his vision of the unity of Christian insight and aspiration with a perspective on the cosmos that was deeply informed by the natural sciences and above all by that of evolution. Such a vision pervades this "immanentist" tradition of Christian theology in Britain, and this may help to explain why the ideas of Teilhard de Chardin and of Whiteheadian "process theology" have been generally less significant for an indigenous tradition that was already integrating science and religion, but not under the sway of one dominating metaphysic.

In contrast, process theology is that particular development of American natural theology which, utilizing the metaphysical system of Whitehead, incorporates both the idea of the natural world as "in process of becoming" and an emphasis on organicism. The process theologians have taken more seriously than almost any others in recent decades the problem of explicating God's action in a world for which all is describable in terms of law-like evolutionary processes. In process thought, God in His "primordial nature" is regarded as providing "aims" for all actual occasions, the ideals which they are striving to become, and in this aspect God is the envisager and fund of universals—he is eternal, absolute, unchangeable. In his "consequent nature" he is responsive love and is temporal, relative, dependent, and constantly changing in response to new unforeseen happenings. Process theology is closely interlocked with pan-psychism, a view of the world which sees mental and physical aspects in all entities and events. Although I find the postulate of pan-psychism to be flawed,[25] there is no doubting the seriousness with which process theology takes the evolutionary perspective. Process thought has had considerable influence, particularly as developed by Charles Hartshorne at Chicago, and it has subsequently proliferated elsewhere, especially at the Center for Process Studies at Claremont, California. It is still the dominant form of natural theology in America today.

An even more complete welding of theology and evolutionary ideas occurs in the "scientific theology" of Ralph Burhoe. Burhoe regarded the sciences of human nature and the increasingly accepted role of religion in human evolution as capable of providing the major religious traditions with the means of interpreting themselves in harmonious relation both to science itself and to one another. He even went so far as to claim that it makes "little difference whether we name it [the power that created the earth and life] natural selection or God, so long as we recognise it as that to which we must bow our heads or adapt."[26]

However, science never stands still, and there is a continuous need to rethink our understanding of the relation of nature, man, and God as our perceptive upon the natural world changes, so we turn to consider contemporary

Biological evolution

Some features of contemporary evolutionary theory which will have to be taken into account in formulating any viable Christian theological response are as follows.

Evolution—"Fact" or "Theory"?

Much play has been made by "creationists" of the proposal that the evolutionary account of biological relationships is "only a theory." There are a number of confusions locked up in such a view. Any scientific account of the past has to be based on inferences from present-day observations. On such reckoning the whole of historical geology and much of modern cosmology is "only a theory." However, inferences of this kind can lead to near-certainty, and then it becomes proper to speak of these inferences as describing what actually happened. The idea of biological evolution refers principally to the past, and, in its general form, simply affirms the existence of genetic relations between the different organisms we now see on the Earth or know from fossils to have been there in the past. The relationship inferred is that, to use Darwin's phrase, of "descent with modification," *by whatever mechanism*. That the mechanism is natural selection is another matter and must be substantiated by other means. Whatever controversies there may be about the mechanism and speed of evolution, there is no dispute among biologists about the *fact* of evolution itself.

It is true that when Darwin propounded his theory the evidence for evolution was circumstantial rather than direct. But twentieth-century biochemistry, notably in its phase of "molecular biology," has now demonstrated fundamental similarities at the molecular level between all living organisms from bacteria to man. Not only is nucleic acid (DNA or RNA) the prime carrier of hereditary information in all living organisms, but the code that translates this information from base sequences in DNA, via messenger RNA, to amino acid sequences in proteins (and thence to their structure and function) is the *same* code in *all* living organisms. This code is arbitrary with respect to the relations of the molecular structures involved and its universality is explicable and comprehensible only as the result of evolution: the code now universally operative is the one which happened to be present in the living matter that first successfully reproduced itself fast enough to outnumber all other rivals. Molecular biology has provided another independent and powerful confirmation of evolutionary relations through its ability to compare the amino acid sequences in proteins with the same chemical function (e.g., cytochrome C) in widely different organisms. The striking fact is that such comparisons entirely and independently confirm (and often illuminatingly amplify) the evolutionary relationships previously deduced on morphological and paleontological grounds. (For example, such studies have provided direct biochemical evidence concerning the degrees of re-latedness between man and the other living primates.)

Again and again, the evolutionary hypothesis (if that is what we still prefer to call it) has survived the test of consistency with observations of a kind unthinkable even four decades ago when the "modern synthesis" of neo-Darwinism first emerged. This does not preclude controversy about the tempo of, mode of, and constraints upon evolution, but it renders it entirely reasonable for us to base our philosophy and theology on what we can presume to be the "fact" of biological evolution, including that of man, who is regarded as being entirely within the world of nature with respect to both the biological and molecular aspects of his existence relevant to his origins.

Cosmic evolution

Darwin himself, T. H. Huxley, and the first generation of Darwinists saw biological evolution in the context of a much wider cosmic process embracing the development of the solar system and of the galaxy. Today we can place biological evolution in a cosmic context that involves a continuous development of the forms of matter from the original "hot big bang," through atoms and molecules, to those complex structures that could self-reproduce their pattern of organization and can be properly designated as "living." This gives us a new incentive to reflect on the cosmic significance of the process of evolution. We now know that it is not confined simply to the development of life, but that the potentiality of matter to develop new forms of organization, according to the prevailing conditions, stretches back beyond the beginning of living forms, and may well stretch on into the future beyond their eventual demise on the surface of the Earth.

Chance, law, and the origin of life

Until the late twentieth century, chance and law (necessity, or determinism) have often been regarded as alternatives for interpreting the natural world. But the interplay between these principles is more subtle and complex than the simple dichotomies of the past would allow. Jacques Monod[27] did indeed contrast the "chance" processes which bring about mutations in the genetic material of an organism with the "necessity" of their consequences in the law-abiding, well-ordered, replicative mechanisms that constitute an organism's continuity as a living form. However, there is no reason that the randomness of molecular event in relation to biological consequence has to be raised to the level of a metaphysical principle, as Monod tended to do. In the behavior of matter on a larger scale many lawful regularities arise from the combined effect of random microscopic events. The involvement of chance at the level of genetic mutation does not preclude these events manifesting law-like behavior at the higher levels of organisms, populations, and biosystems. Rather, it would be more consistent with observation to assert that the full gamut of the potentialities of living matter could be covered only through the agency of the rapid and frequent randomizations that are possible at the molecular level of DNA. This role of chance is what one would expect if the universe were so constituted that exploration of all the potential organized forms of matter (both living and nonliving) were to occur.

Since Monod wrote *Chance and Necessity*, there have been developments in theoretical biology that cast new light on the interrelation of chance and law in the origin and development of life.[28] The Nobel Laureate Ilya Prigogine and his colleagues at Brussels have been able to show that there exists a class of open systems, "dissipative structures," which can maintain themselves in an ordered steady state far from equilibrium. Under certain conditions they can undergo fluctuations that are no longer damped, as they are near to equilibrium, but are amplified so that the system switches to a new ordered state in which it can again become steady. It turns out that many plausible "proto-living" systems, which must have involved complex networks of chemical reactions, are likely to undergo such changes. Thus it is now possible to regard as highly probable the emergence of ordered, self-reproducing molecular structures. To this extent, the emergence of life was inevitable, but the form it was to take remained entirely open and unpredictable.

Similar conclusions have been reached by another Nobel Laureate,

Manfred Eigen: ". . . the evolution of life, it is based on a derivable physical principle, must be considered an inevitable process despite its indeterminate course . . . it is not only inevitable 'in principle' but also sufficiently probable within a realistic span of time."[29] These studies demonstrate that the mutual interplay of chance and law is creative, for it is the combination of the two which allows new forms to emerge and evolve. If this is so, it looks as though evolution proceeds not like an engineer working from scratch but rather by "tinkering, *bricolage*," that is, working on what already exists, "managing with odds and ends."[30] In other words, natural selection appears to be opportunistic. Nevertheless its end result is the kind of complex conscious life that we see in the higher mammals, including the primates and man.

From astrophysics and cosmology there has also emerged a renewed understanding of the close relation of the possibility of the existence of life, and therefore of human life, to the fundamental parameters and laws of the cosmos. This raises the intriguing question of whether or not this universe, in a run of possible universes, just happens to be the one which can generate within itself creatures who can observe it and report on its own character and nature! This is the Chinese-box puzzle that lurks inside the so-called "anthropic principle."

Continuity and emergence in human evolution

As the investigations of man's biochemistry, physiology, nervous system, and behavior patterns burgeon, striking similarities and continuities are more and more being observed between what had previously been regarded as uniquely human characteristics and parallel characteristics of the higher mammals, especially the primates. But it is also becoming increasingly apparent that there is a distinctive transition in passing from the most intelligent primates, or dolphins, to human beings. The most Herculean efforts of devoted investigators rarely seem to be able to train a highly domesticated chimpanzee beyond the level of that of an eighteen-month-old child. Distinctive transitions have, of course, occurred at other stages in evolution and have given rise to the notion of "emergence"—the recognition that, with the development of new forms of life, there arise new modes of existence, new activities, and new kinds of behavior, and that new modes of investigation and new conceptual language are required for their proper and appropriate understanding. All will agree that there has been a general increase in the complexity of the organization of living systems through time. Moreover, it is clear that evolution has occurred concomitantly with increasing levels of consciousness and that in man self-consciousness emerged. In this connection, the judgement of the evolutionary biologist G. G. Simpson is pertinent:

> Man has certain basic diagnostic features which set him off most sharply from any other animal and which have involved other developments not only increasing this sharp distinction but also making it an absolute difference in kind and not only a relative difference of degree. . . . Even when viewed within the framework of the animal kingdom and judged by criteria of progress applicable to that kingdom as a whole and not peculiar to man, man is thus the highest animal.[31]

Because of our ability to transmit culture in mankind, evolution has become "psycho-social" as Julian Huxley used to put it; that is to say, in the case of man we have a creature that shapes its own evolution by willingly shaping its own environment. With man biology has become history.

The problem of reduction

Most molecular biologists would now agree with Sidney Brenner when he wrote of the upshot of their endeavors: "I think it is now quite clear what the enterprise is about. We are looking at a rather special part of the physical universe which contains special mechanisms none of which conflict at all with the laws of physics."[32] No conflict at all with the laws of physics—agreed; but does this mean that all accounts of biological systems are to be subsumed into physics? Does the triumph of molecular biology really imply the final victory for a reductionist interpretation of biology? Is the ultimate aim of biology, in the words of Francis Crick "to explain *all* biology in terms of physics and chemistry"?[33]

Here we come up against an important issue raised by modern biology not only for theology but for philosophy in general. This is the question of reductionism. This is too large a question to examine here; but the pertinent point is that it is possible to be anti-reductionist (that is, against the kind of reductionism defined by Crick) without being a vitalist. The anti-reductionist position requires no mystical affirmations of the existence of "nonnatural" forces or agencies operating in living organisms. But it does require a recognition of the need for autonomous concepts and theories at each level of complexity of the natural world, including the biological. There simply are not just grades of "reality" such that atoms are the "most real," biological entities less so, and persons the least (for a fuller discussion, see Beckner,[34] Peacocke,[35] and Wimsatt[36]).

Ecology

One feature of the contemporary biological scene has been a rediscovered awareness of the ecological integration of living systems. "It is hard to be a reductionist ecologist" according to Dr Norman Moore, an eminent ecologist, and this increasingly important branch of biology—amazingly unfashionable even two decades ago—certainly qualifies as one in which the study of composite wholes is essential. For ecology is the study of the interdependence of all living forms within their physical, organic, and social environment. This interconnectedness of living systems on the surface of the Earth and their interaction with their physical environment can be regarded as one expression of a more general unity and interdependence of all things and events in the cosmos.

The role of behavior in evolution

The statistical interplay between genetic mutation and environmental pressures as the sole mechanism of evolutionary change has appeared increasingly inadequate to some biologists. This mechanism, even in its most sophisticated contemporary form, represents evolution as an "unfolding" of the basic internal genetic programme of the organism, a programme that is already present in the genes. However, some biologists have urged that "unfolding" is an inappropriate metaphor for development. For example, the geneticist Richard Lewontin[37] stresses that organisms are consequences of themselves, that is, of their state at any given moment, with all its dependence on historical accidents—as well as of their genotype and environment. Thus the evolution of organisms cannot be understood as a movement towards a fixed point; organisms are not climbing an "adaptive peak" with a fixed summit but rather, Lewontin suggests, walking on a trampoline that changes with the impact. In so speaking, Lewontin is close to an earlier stress of Sir Alister Hardy[38] on the role of behavioral patterns in evolution. This debate still continues, and we have not heard the end of it yet. But it is worth drawing attention to it, to show that even amongst biologists a purely mechanistic account of evolution has its critics among those who favour more holistic and "compositionist" interpretations.

What is it to be a Christian theist in a post-Darwinian world?

The previous section has indicated, all too briefly, how our perspective on human life is altered by evolution (and the change would be even greater if advances in psychology, sociology, and anthropology were also included). But religion in general, and Christian theology in particular, has its own distinctive perspective which may best be indicated by reminding ourselves of the actual character of the experience of human beings of their life in the natural and social worlds. As far as we can tell, *Homo sapiens* is the only organism that asks itself questions about the meaning of its existence, questions like the penetrating title of the famous story by Tolstoy, "What do men live by?" This is a question about man's needs. Of course, man has biological needs, and the pursuit of their satisfaction has shaped human history. But even when these basic needs have been met, man is not necessarily happy. For he has a restlessness which stems from his failure to satisfy other needs which he seems not to share with other animals. Human beings need to come to terms with their awareness of their own death, to come to terms with their finitude, to learn how to bear suffering, to realize their potentialities, and to determine their own directions. It is to the satisfaction of needs such as these that the religious quest of mankind has always directed itself, and this is true a fortiori of what I prefer to call the Christian experiment. These fundamental questions about human existence have to be raised because it is as a response to them that the Christian experience has developed and the theological enterprise has unfolded as reflection upon this experience. But our particular world is informed and dominated by the evolutionary perspective that we have expounded. So "What is it to be a Christian theist in a post-Darwinian world"?

To ask such a question is to ask how Christian theology is to be related to scientific knowledge, and there are many answers to that particular question. In another context, I have delineated at least eight different ways in which modern science and Christian faith can interact in relation to their intellectual content and epistemology.[39] Like most scientists, I am a skeptical, qualified realist with respect to my scientific knowledge; and since I take this same stance with respect to theological affirmations, my approach is to regard science and theology as interacting approaches to the same reality.[40] I want to affirm that both the scientific and the theological enterprises are explorations into the nature of reality. The former is widely assumed, but less frequently the latter. I heartily endorse the initial and controlling statement in the report of the Doctrine Commission of the Church of England on *Christian Believing*, which opens as follows: "Christian life is an adventure, a voyage of discovery, a journey, sustained by faith and hope, towards a final and complete communion with Love at the heart of all things."[41] Let me therefore indicate the lines along which I think Christian theology and evolutionary ideas may be incorporated into a coherent view of nature, man, and God. Inevitably, this can be only a mere sketch of a style of theological reflection that takes seriously the evolutionary perspective.

Nature, man, and God

Nature. The sciences of the twentieth century have confirmed what many in the nineteenth century believed, but without adequate evidence, and what in the eighteenth century was only intimated, namely, that the whole cosmos is in a state of evolution from one form of matter to another, and that a significant point in this evolutionary process has occurred on the surface of the Earth where the conditions were such that matter was able to become living. This process is of a kind that it does not require the postulate for its occurrence of any factors external to the world itself. Our understanding of matter has been enormously enhanced as a result of this perspective, for matter turns out to be capable of organizing itself into self-reproducing systems that are capable of receiving signals and storing and processing information from their environment. Gradually, and only along certain lines in this development, matter in the form of living organisms manifests behavior to which we attribute consciousness, and self-consciousness when it takes the form of the human-brain-in-the-human-body. These manifestations are as real at their own level as any chemical reaction or subatomic interaction at theirs. Self-consciousness cannot lightly be set on one side, and by the very nature of the activity itself cannot but appear to us as being one of the most significant features of the cosmos. Paradoxically, man's arrival as a product of nature must give us pause in thinking we know all about what matter is "in itself," for it shows the potentialities of matter in a new light.

Man. We have already seen that man is to be conceived as a part of nature. Yet in his self-consciousness he transcends nature, perceiving the outside world and parts of his body as objects for his understanding and attention. In man, part of the world has become conscious of itself and consciously responds to its surroundings; in man a new mode of interaction in the world is introduced. Oddly, however, this product of evolution, unlike any other, is strangely ill at ease in its environment. Man alone amongst living creatures individually commits suicide. Somehow, biology has produced a being of infinite restlessness, and this certainly raises the question of whether human beings have properly conceived of what their true "environment" is. In the natural world, new life can arise only from the death of the old, for the death of the individual is essential to the possibility of new forms evolving in the future. To man this is an affront and he grieves over his suffering and his own personal demise.

God. The postulate of God as creator of all-that-is is not, in its most profound form, a statement about what happened at a point in time. To speak of God as creator is a postulate about a perennial or "eternal," that is to say, timeless, relation of God to the world—a relation which involves both differentiation and interaction. God is differentiated from the world in that he is totally other than it. "God" is postulated in answer to the question "Why is there anything at all?" He is the "ground of being" of the world: that without which we could neither make sense of the world having existence at all, nor of its having that kind of intellectually coherent and explorable existence which science continuously unveils. All of this is included when we say that God in himself must be "transcendent."

This affirmation has had to be held in tension with a sense of God's immanence in the world; for if the world is in any sense what God has created and that through which he acts and expresses his own inner being, then there is a sense in which God is never absent from his world and he is as much in his world as, say, Beethoven is in his Seventh Symphony during a performance of it. What is happening today is that our reinforced understanding of the world as continuously in process of creating new kinds of entities, new modes of existence—supremely, as we have seen, in the biological and human worlds—is leading us to reaffirm the conception of God as continuously creative, as *semper Creator*. Creation is continuous—it is a *creatio continua*. The ongoing cosmic processes of evolution are God himself being creator in his own universe. If I had to represent on a blackboard the relation of God and the world, including man, I would not simply draw three spheres labeled respectively "nature," "man," and

"God" and draw arrows between them to represent their interrelation. Rather, I would denote an area representing nature and place that entirely within another area representing God, which would have to extend to the edges of the blackboard and, indeed, point beyond it. When I came to depict man, I would have to place him with his feet firmly in nature but with his self-consciousness (perhaps represented by his brain?) protruding beyond the boundary of nature and into the area depicting God.

The view I have just been describing is sometimes denoted by the inelegant word "pan-en-theism." The basic affirmation here is that all-that-is, both nature and man, is in some sense in God, but that God is more than nature and man and there is more to God than nature and man. God in his being transcends, goes beyond, both man and nature. Either God is in everything created from the beginning to the end, at all times and in all places, or he is not there at all. What we see in the world is the mode of God's creativity in the world. The analogy with Beethoven's Seventh Symphony as an expression of Beethoven's own inner creative being is, I think, a fair one. In the actual processes of the world, and supremely in human self-consciousness, God is involving himself and expressing himself as creator. However, since man has free will we have also to recognize that God put himself "at risk," as it were, in creatively evoking in the natural world a being who has free will and who can transcend his perceived world and shape it in his own way.

The relationships between nature, man, and God

God and nature. In speaking of God as creator, and as *semper Creator*, we have inevitably been thinking of God's relation to all-that-is. But there is more to be said. We now see in a new way the role in evolution of the interplay between random chance micro-events and the necessity which arises from the stuff of this world having its particular "given" properties. These potentialities a theist must regard as written into creation by the creator himself in order that they may be unveiled by chance exploring their gamut. God as creator we now see as somewhat like a composer who, beginning with an arrangement of notes in an apparently simple tune, elaborates and expands it into a fugue by a variety of devices. In this way the creator may be imagined to unfold the potentialities of the universe that he himself has given it, selecting and shaping by his providential and redemptive action those that are to come to fruition—an improviser, we may suggest, of unsurpassed ingenuity.

We have found that the processes of the universe are continuous and that in them there are emergent new organizations of matter-energy. Such new levels of organization require epistemologically nonreducible concepts to articulate their distinctiveness. Any new meaning which God is able to express in such new levels of organization is thus not discontinuous with the meanings expressed in that out of which it has emerged. So we anticipate continuity, with new meanings emerging out of the old, subsuming them, perhaps, but not denying them. Both continuity and emergence are inherent features of the observed world. The processes of that world are also open-ended and so we have to develop the notion of God as "exploring" in creation, of actualizing all the potentialities of creation, of improvising fugally all the derivations inherently possible from the tune he originally called (for a cogent discussion, see Bartholomew[42]).

God and man: in the light of the scientific perspective

Evolved man seeks meaning and intelligibility in the world; that is (from a theological point of view), he seeks to discern the meanings expressed by God in his creation. These are meanings which, alone among created organisms, man has evolved to be capable not only of consciously discerning but also of freely appropriating to give purpose and meaning to his life. Although God is not more present at one time or place than at others, nevertheless man finds that in some sequences of events in nature and history God unveils his meaning more than in others. Though in one sense God as creator acts in all events, not all events are received as "acts of God." Some events will be more revealing than others. In any survey of events we have to recognize the existence of a natural hierarchy (or, rather, hierarchies) of complexity. The aspect of God's meaning expressed by any one level in these hierarchies is limited to what it alone can itself distinctively convey. The meanings of God unveiled to and for man will be the more partial, broken, and incomplete the more the level of creation being examined departs from the human and personal, in which the transcendence of the "I" is experienced as immanent in our bodies. Thus although God is, in some sense, supra-personal, we may well expect that in the personal—in history, in personal experience, in personal encounter—we shall find meanings of God unveiled in a way that is not possible at the impersonal levels of existence with which we have hitherto been principally concerned. For the more personal and self-conscious is the entity in which God is immanent, the more capable it is of expressing God's supra-personal characteristics, and the more God can be immanent personally in that entity. The transcendence-in-immanence of man's experience raises the hope that uniquely in man there might be unveiled, without distortion, the transcendent-creator-who-is-immanent; that is, that in man (in a human being, or human beings) the presence of God the creator might be revealed with a clarity and in a glory not hitherto perceived.

Nature, man, and God in a Christian perspective. There is in the long tradition of Christian thought, going back to Jesus' own actions and words, a way of relating the physical and the personal worlds which avoids any stark dichotomy between them, seeing them rather as two facets of the same reality. This way of thinking is generally denoted by the word "sacramental." In the Christian liturgy, things in the universe—bread, wine, water, oil sometimes—are taken as being both symbols of God's self expression and as instruments of God's action in effecting his purposes. This mode of thinking can be extended more widely to the universe as a whole, which can then be seen as both a symbol of God's self-expression, and thus a mode of his revelation of himself, and also the very means whereby he effects his purposes in his own actions as agent. In the twentieth century this view was expressed particularly by William Temple.[43] It provides, I think, a deeper perspective on the world described by the sciences than the sciences alone can afford—a perspective in which the world's continuous and

seamless web of self-development, of self-organizing by its own inherent properties, generates forms of matter that are capable of being
persons and perceiving meaning, those meanings, indeed, with which
the creator imbued his creation.

Conclusion

In the history of the people of Israel, God was always raising up
apparent scourges, such as Cyrus, that were in reality blessings in disguise leading his people through the trauma that would alone enable
them to apprehend new truths. So it is too with evolutionary biology
which in the words of Aubrey Moore[44] for Christian theology "under
the disguise of a foe, did the work of a friend." For it has brought to
light again and reinvigorated an older, immanentist aspect of the
Judeo-Christian doctrine of creation that was in danger of being sub-
merged. It is this strand in that doctrine which, in the *Logos* terminology of John 1, is the basic conceptual framework in Christian theology for articulating, however inadequately, its distinctive doctrine of
the Incarnation, of the "Word of God" becoming "flesh" of man.

Contemporary evolutionary biology continues to raise new questions and so continues to provide a stimulus for that rebirth of images
without which any living theology soon becomes, in a rapidly changing cultural milieu, the mere inner musings of a religious ghetto. Thus
Christian theology continues to be vastly indebted to that view of the
transformations of the living world into which Darwin initiated us.

CHAPTER 3

Chance, Potentiality, and God

In 1972, Jacques Monod's reflections on recent advances in biology were published in English, as *Chance and Necessity*.[1] In this work, which has had an immediate impact on current thought, he delineates what he perceives to be the philosophical and theological consequences of, in particular, the molecular biology generated by the discovery of the structure of DNA in 1953. If this were to be a sermon which I was to contribute to a new volume of holy writ, of which Professor Monod was to be the chief apostle, then I could do no better than take as my text words from the book of Lord Bertrand Russell, both for their realism and their haunting beauty:

> That Man is the product of causes which had no prevision of the end they were achieving; that his origin, his growth, his hopes and fears, his loves and beliefs, are but the outcome of accidental collocations of atoms; . . . all these things, if not quite beyond dispute, are yet so nearly certain that no philosophy which rejects them can hope to stand. Only within the scaffolding of these truths, only on the firm foundation of unyielding despair, can the soul's habitation henceforth be safely built.[2]

For this passage represents the abyss into which both Russell and Monod peer and the noble courage with which they respond to it, as they both "whistle in the dark." Although Monod writes from the

From *The Modern Churchman* 17 (New series) (1973): 13–23; and in *Beyond Chance and Necessity*, ed. J. Lewis (London: Garnstone Press, 1974), 13–25. Reprinted by permission.

vantage point afforded by the pinnacle of modern molecular biology, I believe the dark prospect he perceives has long been apparent to earlier generations in the Anglo-Saxon world—for example, Tennyson's *In Memoriam* reveals an anguish at the severance between the moral and material world quite as acute as that of Russell, some eighty years later. Be that as it may, the principal keystone of Monod's work raises in this Anglo-Saxon reader a reaction somewhat *déjà vu*. This keystone is the contrast between the "chance" processes which bring about mutations in the genetic material of an organism and the "necessity" of their consequences in the well-ordered, replicative, interlocking mechanism which constitutes that organism's continuity as a living form. More specifically, mutations in DNA are the results of chemical or physical events, and their location in the genome are entirely random with respect to the biological needs of the organism. Those that are incorporated into the genome of the organism (i.e., if they are not lethal) are only permanently so incorporated if, in interacting with its environment, the differential reproduction rate of the mutated form is advantageous. So put, and I think I have been fair to Monod, this is already something of a gloss on neo-Darwinism orthodoxy—as I shall have cause to mention later. But, even if we take it as it stands, it cannot be said to add anything very new *in principle* to the debates of the last one hundred years. For the essential crux in these debates was, and is, that the mechanism of variation was causally entirely independent of the processes of selection, so that (as I have said) mutations were regarded as purely random with respect to the selective needs of the organism—and were so regarded long before the molecular mechanism of transmission, and alteration, of genetic information was unravelled in the last two decades. However, that mechanism *has* now been elucidated, and Monod describes it beautifully and clearly in its setting in the total functioning of living organisms.

The general conclusion he draws is, not surprisingly, like that of Russell in that he sees man, and so all the works of his mind and culture, as the products of pure chance and the ore without any cosmic significance. The universe must be seen not as a cosmos, that is, a directionally ordered whole, but as a giant Monte Carlo saloon in

which the dice have happened to fall out in the way which produced
man. There is, according to Monod, no general purpose in the universe and in the existence of life (and so none in the universe as a
whole). It need not, it might not, have existed—nor might man.
Therefore any system of philosophy or religion which presupposes
any plan or intention in the universe is founded on a fallacy, now
fully exposed by the molecular-biological account of DNA and its
mutations. The only attitude which is adoptable in the face of this is
one of "objectivity," as he calls it—which he regards as nonemotive
and not prejudiced in favor of man over other natural phenomena.
The adoption of this "principle of objectivity" puts out of court all
systems of thought which try to show that there is any sort of harmony between man and the universe and that man is a predictable, if
not indispensable, product of the evolution of the universe. Those systems of thought, which this "principle of objectivity" of Monad re-
jects, include, of course, "vitalism" (said to be represented in its "metaphysical" form by Bergson and in its "scientific" form by Elsässer and
Polanyi) and all forms of cosmic "animism," which sees a purpose being worked out in at least some aspect of the universe. This spurned
"animism" is a remarkable collection, for it includes dialectical materialism (notably the ideas of Engels, who draws most of Monod's
fire), Judeo-Christianity (especially in any Teilhardian form), and a
large part of Western philosophy. All exponents of these, he says, have
constructed *a posteriori* ideological edifices designed to justify preconceived ethico-political theories. Needless to say, the philosophers[3]
have descended upon Monod in all their wrath—not without some
wry smiles from the various kinds of Christian spectators of the game
left at the turnstiles! It is not surprising that the philosophers are also
scornful of those sections of the book where he imputes the naturalistic fallacy (that of trying to derive "ought" statements from "is"
statements) to all "animist" philosophers, which in his language means
all philosophers except those who now adopt his "principal of objectivity"—for what "is," according to Monod, is the product of chance
and indifferent to man and his aspirations. But, what is interesting to
me and what is nobly expressed in his own special style is that

Monod is deeply concerned for man's future and also that he recognizes man as a unique product of evolution, with his brain and ability to communicate by language; and he urges, with great force, that man must choose a system of values, since man as an individual person and as a society has to live, and to live means to act, and to act is to choose (shades of Sartre). The system of values which he espouses is based on his "ethic of knowledge," which is set in a mould of ideas distinctly existentialist, and he has, on both counts, been criticized by professional philosophers on this side of the Channel.

Nevertheless, when the philosophers have had their say, the chief attraction of Monod's book to those of a scientific temper of mind is that it starts from the most accurate view of the physical and biological world available to us—namely, that afforded by natural science—and tries to understand man's significance in the world thus perceived. This seems to me to be an absolutely necessary exercise and let none of my criticisms, already given or those to come, of Monod's position be allowed to diminish at all my applaud at the attempt—especially as I am now about to launch my own ship from the same home port. I will in the end find myself navigating towards a different destination, but at least I recognize Monod as a fellow voyager on these rough and dangerous seas. I now turn to an account of the particular course I prefer to steer in these troubled waters by looking again at

The scientific perspective on matter and man

In the last one hundred years the perspective of the sciences concerned with the origin and development of the physical and biological worlds has, or should have, altered our attitude to the natural surroundings which human minds appear to transcend as subjects. For our familiar environment of stone, water, air, earth, grass, birds, animals, and so on are seen in this perspective no longer to be a kind of stage for the enactment of the human drama but to share with man common molecular structures and to be stages in a common continuous development in time.

Although this continuity of man with the organic world had some-times been accepted in principle,[4] it was only just over one hundred years ago that the scientific evidence for man's relation to other species began to appear, and it is only in the last few decades that the emergence of primitive living organisms from inorganic matter could be outlined in any fashion which had a scientific basis in the new knowledge of biological evolution and of molecular biology and in new insights into the development of the physical cosmos.

The broad picture is familiar enough: how the nuclei of atoms more complex than hydrogen (which is the simplest atom and ap-pears to be the basic material of the universe, for it occurs every-where) are held together; how these atoms can combine to form molecules of a complexity increasing from the diatomic H_2 mole-cules up to those large molecules, containing tens of thousands of atoms, which constitute the enzymes and genetic material (DNA) of living organisms; how these macro-molecules interlock structurally and functionally with small molecules in an aqueous matrix so as to have the characteristics of living matter in cells; how living organisms, containing such cells, have developed in time on the surface of the planet Earth, itself the outcome of vast processes in immense con-glomerations of matter on an astronomical scale.

However, there is one stage in this development on which I wish to refocus, since it occupies a key position in Monod's thesis—namely the randomness of the molecular events on which natural se-lection is based. The whole context of the fundamental idea of natu-ral selection of living organisms has been amplified, since Darwin and Wallace, by our knowledge of the existence of genetic factors, "genes," located in cell nuclei and constituted by molecules of DNA. This DNA, whose molecular patterns *are* the genes, are subject, as al-ready mentioned, to sudden changes ("mutations") as a result of irra-diation or chemical events, and these molecular changes are random with respect to the biological needs of the organisms. It is this which so impresses Monod that he regards all living forms, including man, as the products of "chance." For the processes of natural selection (which are now increasingly seen to be much more subtle than previ-

ously thought, involving a complex interplay of heredity, environment, mutation, and behavior) that favor the survival of particular
mutated organisms can only operate among the spectrum of possibilities provided by the random chemical events at the level of the
DNA. Unlike Monod, I see no reason why this randomness of molecular event in relation to biological consequence has to be raised to
the level almost of a metaphysical principle in interpreting the cosmos. For in the behavior of matter on a larger scale, many regularities,
which have been raised to the peerage of "laws," arise from the combined effects of random microscopic events which constitute the
macroscopic (e.g., Boyle's Law and its dependence on molecular kinetics and all of statistical thermodynamics). It would be more accurate to say that the full gamut of possible forms of living matter could
only be explored through the agency of the rapid and frequent ran-
domization which is possible at the molecular level of the DNA. This
view leads to a quite different interpretation from that of Monod. After all, the random molecular events in DNA have occurred in a system which has the properties it has because its constituent atoms and
molecules have *their* characteristic properties. In other words, the
emergence of the immense variety of living forms manifests the potentialities of matter. That it does so through an exploration of all
available possibilities by random molecular events does not seem to
me to be in itself a sufficient basis for any apotheosis of "chance."
Thus biological evolution no more qualifies for description as a
"chance" process than any other. There is, nevertheless, a particularity
about biological evolution since, once a variation has been favored in
an organism in a habitat in a particular location, the future variations
which will then be favorable to that organism will be the result of the
interplay of these variations past and present with the climatic and
other factors (including other creatures) in its particular environment.
The imprinting of the new variation yields gains in viability at the
expense of channeling and limiting future possibilities. Because of this
channeling effect of contingent circumstances, it is quite likely the
case that *all* possible modes of organization of matter have not yet
been elicited even by this random running through of the available

possibilities, so that one cannot exclude the possibility of other forms of matter, both living and nonliving, occurring in other parts of the universe. However, all observations suggest that the component parts of these hypothetical structures will obey the laws we have been able to observe on and from the Earth. Moreover, the existence of this hypothetical possibility need not detract us from considering the significance of the manifestation of those potentialities of matter that we have been able to observe on the Earth and notably in its biosphere. It is worth recalling some of the features of this cosmic development or "evolution" (in the strict, *O.E.D.* sense of "an appearance [of events, etc.] in due succession").

The whole of the present variety of living organisms, and of all of those species long since extinct, can be tracked back in a continuous line to those one, or a few, ordered aggregates of molecules which first acquired the ability to replicate themselves and grow by incorporating surrounding molecules. A "materialistic" view of our existence and of that of all living organisms is apparently justified, if linked with an important qualification which is that we recognize that the most significant of the "properties of matter" is that, organized in certain ways, it has the characteristics we call living and, indeed, human too. The primordial nebular cloud of hydrogen—or of its sub-nuclear "particulate" predecessors—has developed into living organisms and into man, with all his special qualities, achievements, and potentialities for sublimity and degradation. *If* we are prepared to recognize that matter, the stuff of the universe, has this character and that the continuity I have described is from hydrogen atoms to the personalities and creative genius of men at their most developed, then it would still be legitimate to call the process "materialistic."

Each transition (e.g., the origin of life) within the cosmic development can be seen, in the light of our present-day scientific knowledge, to proceed in accordance with regularities in parallel observations we can make in or infer from our present experimental and theoretical investigation of the world we know. Briefly, we can say the cosmic development has proceeded by natural "law," using this term simply to denote the ordered and regular character of the knowledge which scientific investigation yields by the methodologies it has established. It is important to stress that the cosmic development presents us with an ordered behavior of matter which is not abrogated, so it seems to me, by its depending on the random, chance character of the micro-events which underlie the regularities of many kinds of macro-observation (e.g., the naturally selected phenotypic changes following on a random chemical modification of DNA or Boyle's Law on the random collisions of gas molecules).

The cosmic development is, moreover, apparently a process in which new forms of organization of matter emerge. The description of evolution as displaying "emergence" is often also used to point to the difficulty of fully explaining the mode of being of the newly appearing form in terms of its immediate, and certainly of its distant, predecessors. It is important to realize that it is reasonable to affirm and recognize this emergent character of the cosmic development, as for example Polanyi[5] does, without thereby intending to postulate in any sense any special super-added force or principle ("élan vital," "entelechy," "life force") which somehow mysteriously distinguishes living organisms from their nonliving components. For the principle applies equally (as Polanyi rightly argues, it seems to me) to the logical (not contingent) impossibility of reducing the principles of operation of, for example, a steam engine to the physics and chemistry of each of its components considered separately.

New properties, functions, and abilities have genuinely emerged in the successive stages of the cosmic development, and this may now be taken as a datum of our thinking. The laws, principles, and categories of thinking and vocabulary needed to describe each stage of this process will be particular to and characteristic of it. In this sense, chemistry is not "nothing-but" physics, especially not the physics of the nucleus; nor is biology "nothing-but" physics and chemistry; nor is human psychology and sociology "nothing-but" biology. All these ascriptions, which aspire to subsume the more developed form in terms of the intellectual concepts and experimental approaches which have succeeded at the lower and especially the immediately preceding levels, constitute, in my view, a mistaken analysis of the modes of investigation which each level of organization of matter renders necessary for its understanding.

Even allowing for our natural anthropomorphism, there are nevertheless good grounds for emphasizing that man represents a point of biological development in which many tendencies have reached a pre-eminently high level, e.g., ability to expand into new environments, adaptability, complexity of structure and behavior, protected reproduction and care of the young, awareness of and flexible reaction to the environment, socialization, individualization, and communication by language. These are purely biological criteria, and if we are to interpret the whole cosmic development honestly, then we are bound to look at all the facts. Yet a full description of human beings who have emerged in the universe goes beyond their purely biological features, even if these are as highly developed as those just listed (but let us note that man's linguistic ability is now widely regarded as so separated from that of the highest primate as to be unique). One's assessment of the nature of man has a determinative influence at this point. Thus the challenge of the presence of man in the universe as the outcome of evolution evokes various responses among scientists. To Monod it is a stark fact but in itself not significant as regards the nature of the cosmos, for he regards man as the consequence of mere "chance" events at the molecular level of the DNA of his living progenitors and bases his view of man's significance on a particular interpretation of and emphasis on this role of "chance." But to other scientists it is a false modesty, verging on intellectual perversity, "to renounce, in the name of scientific objectivity, our position as the highest form of life on earth and our own advent by a process of evolution as the most important problem of evolution," as Polanyi affirms[6]—in concurrence with Eccles, Hinshelwood, Dobzhansky, Hardy, Thorpe.

For to take seriously, as scientists *qua* scientists ought, the presence of man as the outcome of the cosmic evolution of matter, is to open up many questions which go far beyond the applicable range of languages, concepts, and modes of investigation developed by the natural sciences for describing and examining the less developed and less complex forms of matter which preceded the emergence of man. For if the stuff of the world, the primeval concourse of hydrogen atoms or sub-nuclear particles, has as a matter of fact and not conjecture become man—man who possesses not only a social life and biological organization but also an "inner," self-conscious life in relation to others, which make him personal—then how *are* we properly to speak of the cosmic development if after aeons of time the atoms have become human beings, persons? Moreover, paradoxically and significantly, knowledge of the process by which they have arrived in the world seems to be confined to human beings. We alone reflect on our atomic and simpler forebears and we alone adjust our behavior in the light of this perspective. To ignore the glory, the predicament, and the possibilities of man in assessing the trend and meaning of the cosmic development would be as unscientific as the former pre-Copernican account of the universe, based as it was on the contrary prejudice. Apparently, by a continuous development under the control of the regular processes of natural laws, new forms of matter have creatively emerged out of the nuclear particles and atoms of several thousand million years ago and have now in man become conscious of themselves. From man's consciousness, new creativities of a specifically human kind have erupted, notably in men of genius but, just as significantly, also in the very real individual creativity of each human being within his own social environment—a creativity which, however humble, far transcends that of the highest animal.

Thus the perspective of science on the world raises acutely certain questions which by their very nature cannot be answered from within the realm of discourse of science alone.

1. What sort of cosmos is it if the original primeval mass of hydrogen atoms has (maybe by pure randomness, which is just the surest way of trying out all the possible permutations and combinations) eventually manifested the potentiality of becoming organised in material forms such as ourselves which are conscious and even *self*-conscious, can reflect, and love and hate, and pray, have ideas, can discourse with each other, can exhibit the creative genius of a Mozart or Shakespeare, or display the personal qualities of a Socrates or Jesus of Nazareth?

2. How can we explain the existence of such a cosmos of *this* particular character, outlined above? It seems to me that any explanation (not cause in the cause-effect sequence of our space-time) of the existence of such a cosmos to be plausibly adequate must be one that grounds this existence in a mode of being which is other than the cosmos so described and which transcends mental activity as much as mental activity transcends physical processes. Such a cosmos-explaining-entity must be *not less* than personal or mental in its nature. Its (his/her) existence would make it more comprehensible how matter could possess the potentiality of the mental activity evidenced in man than would the designation of "chance" alone (à la Monod) as a sufficient explanation of the cosmos. The role of randomness in natural processes does not of itself preclude the possibility of the existence of such an entity which, as Aquinas would say, "men call God." So we come explicitly to the question of

God and the cosmos

To the Christian theologian, the question of God is prior to the question of man and matter. The essentially new element which the scientific perspective inevitably introduces into the theistic concept of creation in its classical form is the realisation that the cosmos which is sustained and held in being by God (this sustaining and holding itself constituting "creation") is a cosmos which has always been in process of producing new emergent forms of matter. It is a world which is still being made and, on the surface of the Earth at least, man has emerged from biological life and his history is still developing. Any static conception of the way in which God sustains and holds the cosmos in being is therefore precluded, for the cosmos is in a dynamic state and, in the corner which we as men can observe, has evolved conscious and self-conscious minds who shape their environment and choose between ends.

That the world was in a flux and change, with all its corollaries for the destiny of the individual man, has been reflected upon since the ancient Greeks. But that the matter of the world developed in a particular direction to more complex and ultimately thinking forms was not established knowledge. The people of Israel, and following them, the Christian Church, have traditionally believed in the providential hand of God in human history, with the nonhuman world being regarded simply as the stage for that drama. Science now sees man as part of "nature" and both together as subject to continuous development. If the emergence of new forms of matter in the world is in some way an activity of God, then this creative action must be regarded as God's perennial activity and not something already completed and entirely in the past. The scientific perspective of a cosmos in development introduces a dynamic element into our understanding of God's relation to the cosmos which was previously obscured, although never excluded.

The convergence of the lines of thought which see God (usually designated, in this context, as "Holy Spirit") as immanent in the cosmos in general, in man in particular, and as consummated in Jesus and in the community expressing his spirit, is, I would suggest, peculiarly consonant with the scientific perspective. For in that scientific perspective we see a cosmos in which creativity is ever-present, in which new forms of matter emerge and in which, with many fruitless directions, nevertheless in the end there emerged man, mind, human society, human values, in brief, what people call the "human spirit." These two perspectives from, on the one hand, the Hebrew and Christian experience and, on the other, the gamut of the sciences, mutually illuminate each other. Each has its own autonomy and justification but, if both are recognized, a combined insight into the cosmic development is then afforded in which, it seems to me, the features elaborated by the sciences are in harmony with the experiences which cluster around particular events in history and which theological language expounds. The Christian theological interpretation complements and develops the scientific account in the significance it attributes to these events in human history. Moreover, the theological perspective, if accepted, gives meaning to the present, and a sense of direction for the future to a world still regarded as in process and as the matrix of new emergent forms of human life.

The theological perspective itself is correspondingly reshaped by this consideration of the scientific account of the cosmic development. For the theological account will now be seen to be most meaningful and to correspond best with the scientific one when it emphasizes that God is immanent, that his action in the world is continuously creative, and that the coming of Christ and the role of the Church are to be understood in such dynamic terms, rather than in the more classical and static images of earlier theological exposition. The two perspectives are complementary, for the scientific provides the necessary grounding in material reality which the theological requires, and the theological provides the means whereby contemporary man in his community can consciously participate and find both personal and corporate meaning in a cosmic process which, without the Christian perspective, would appear impersonal and even inimical. The first Christians found themselves inevitably using language which was an extension of that applied to persons and so corresponded to the highest they knew, about that power of God (as "Holy Spirit"), which through Jesus had possessed them. In accordance with this, and indeed, as a kind of extension of it, the Christian understanding is that the meaning of the cosmic process revealed by science is ultimately to be expressed in personal terms in the sense that the language of human personality is the least misleading for describing the direction in which the process moves.

However, the contemporary Christian theist in stressing the immanent creativity of God in the cosmos must recognize that it is by the "laws" and through the regularities of nature that God must be presumed to be working. This recognition is linked with the important understanding that matter is of such a kind and the regularities which it manifests are of such a kind that creativity, in the sense of the emergence of new forms of matter, is a permanent potentiality whose actualization depends on circumstances. This potentiality is not injected into the cosmos from "outside" either by God, or by a Life Force, élan vital, or other supposedly "supernatural" agency. If God is in the world-process of matter at all, God is in it all through, in all its potentialities, whether actualized or not, and he continues to hold it in being by his will with these potentialities and not otherwise. It has long been recognized, and emphasized especially by the late C. A. Coulson, that to postulate a "God of the gaps" who is supposed to intervene to bridge the gap between, for example, the living and nonliving is not only a tactical error on the part of theists (for science has a habit of bridging these gaps from its own resources!) but is to mistake entirely the relation between God and the cosmos. For, with hindsight, it seems almost an impertinence for us not to allow God to be creative in God's own way through the stuff of the cosmos and its regular mutual interrelationships, or the "laws" it obeys, and to assert that God had both brought matter into existence and had to intervene from time to time to help it on to the next stage, presumably divinely willed—for example, the transition from nonliving to living, or the special creation of individual species, notably man himself. It now seems more consistent to urge that God has been creating all the time through eliciting all the possibilities of the matter which he had brought into existence endowed with certain potentialities and governed by the laws of its transformations; and that this exploration of potentialities rests on the statistical coverage available to random events at the micro-level.

Hence Christians have no interest in finding evidence for any form of vitalism, as they and their critics have frequently supposed. To postulate a "special creation" of species or that God injected "life" into the universe or that God somehow directly and personally directs the processes of biological evolution by means other than that inherent in the nature of matter and its "laws" are all errors on *Christian* premises. The old theistic "argument from design," in spite of its evocative power, foundered on its inability by itself to show that the concept of an omnipotent architect and designer generated by reflection on the natural order actually had an object; and it was later vulnerable to the further criticism, based on biology, that what appealed to be the result of design, and so of the intention of a designer, in the biological world could, in principle at least if not always in detail, be more readily explained in terms of the operation of natural selection. Now, however, the sciences afforded a wider perspective and a sequence which itself can evoke, like religious language, a situation to which we respond by commitment and which, in its oddity, points to the appropriate logical status for the word "God," thus: baryons, nucleons, atoms, molecules, inorganic matter, nucleo-proteins, living matter, cells, cellular assemblies, fishes, mammals, conscious organisms, primates, *Homo sapiens*, Stone Age men, the inventor of fire, the inventor of the wheel, intelligent, self-conscious persons—and so on, and so on, taking many different lines of human excellence until the sequence evokes a disclosure and a commitment to values, "the light dawns," "the ice breaks," as the late Ian Ramsey characteristically used to say.[7]

Earlier, I suggested that Monod and I were at least fellow voyagers setting out from the same home port of the scientific perspective on the world. The course I have steered approaches a very different landfall from that of Monod, and there are many features of the coast I would like to have pointed out, had I had space. I am not pretending that the journey by the route I have indicated will be any less stormy, indeed some nights may be darker, but, if we had time to travel this route further, I would suggest that a gleam of light could be discerned on the horizon, perhaps even that "day spring from on high" which was promised us. Either way, his or mine, our duty is clear—it is that first enjoined on self-conscious thinking man by Plato through the mouth of Socrates: "Our duty is to take whatever doctrine is best and hardest to disprove and embarking upon it as upon a craft, to sail upon it through life in the midst of dangers."

CHAPTER 4

Complexity, Emergence, and Divine Creativity

The significance of the DNA structure: reductionism and emergence

As my good fortune would have it, when I had completed my doctoral apprenticeship and was for the first time pursuing research entirely of my own devising in my first university post, it was mainly centered on what we now call DNA. In the late 1940s, DNA had been identified as the principal carrier of the genes, but it was still not certain even that it was a large molecule—and although it was known to contain nucleotides linked together in chains of uncertain length, its double-helical structure was unknown. Suffice to say that, after 1952, its discovered structure revolutionized biology and has now become part of general public awareness. What gradually especially impressed itself on me as a physical biochemist participating in this community of discovery is that it is a clue to many important issues in the epistemology and relationships of the sciences—for the first time we were witnessing the existence of a complex macromolecule the *chemical structure* of which had the ability to convey *infor-*

In *From Complexity to Life: On the Emergence of Life and Meaning*, ed. Niels Henrik Gregersen (Oxford and New York: Oxford University Press, 2003), 187–205. Originally presented at a research symposium on "Complexity, Information, and Design," held in Santa Fe, New Mexico, October 14–16, 1999, under the auspices of the John Templeton Foundation. Reprinted by permission.

mation, the genetic instructions to the next generation to be like its parent(s).

In my days as a chemistry student, I had studied the structure of the purine and pyrimidine "bases" which are part of the nucleotide units from which DNA is assembled. All that was pure organic chemistry, with no hint of any particular significance in their internal arrangement of its atoms of carbon, nitrogen, phosphorus. Yet here, in DNA, we had discovered a double string of such units so linked together through the operation of natural processes that each particular DNA macromolecule had the new capacity, when set in the matrix of the particular cytoplasm evolved with it, of being able to convey hereditary information. Now the concept of "information," originating in the mathematical theory of communication, had never been, and could never have been, part of the organic chemistry of nucleotides, even of polynucleotides, that I had learned in my chemistry degree work. Hence in DNA, I realized, we were witnessing a notable example of what many reflecting on the evolutionary process have called *emergence*—the entirely neutral name[1] for that general feature of natural processes wherein complex structures, especially in living organisms, develop distinctively new capabilities and functions at levels of greater complexity. Such emergence is an undoubted, observed feature of the evolutionary process, especially of the biological. As such, it was the goad that stimulated me to wider reflections: first, epistemological, on the relation between the knowledge that different sciences provide; and second, ontological, on the nature of the realities which the sciences putatively claim to disclose—in other words, the issue of reductionism. I am convinced that this has to be clarified in any discussion of complex systems and of their general significance.

There is, as we well know, a polemical edge to all this. For Francis Crick, one of the co-discoverers of the DNA structure, early threw down the gauntlet in these matters by declaring that "the ultimate aim of the modern movement in biology is in fact to explain *all* biology in terms of physics and chemistry."[2] Such a challenge can be, and has been, mounted at many other interfaces between the sciences other than that between biology and physics/chemistry. We have all witnessed the attempted takeover bids, for example, of psychology by neurophysiology and of anthropology and sociology by biology. The name of the game is "reductionism" or, more colloquially, "nothing-buttery"—"discipline X, usually meaning 'yours,' is really nothing but discipline Y, which happens to be 'mine.'"

After the discovery of the DNA structure, there was an intense discussion between the new "molecular" biologists and "whole-organism" biologists about whether or not Crick's dictum could be accepted. By and large, whole-organism biologists insisted[3] on the distinctiveness of the biological concepts they employed and on their irreducibility to purely physicochemical ones. The controversy was, in fact, only one aspect of a debate which had been going on previously among philosophers of science concerning the possible "unity of the sciences," a notion that implied the hegemony of physics in the hierarchy of explanation.

All could, and by and large did, agree on the necessity for *method-ological* reduction, that is, the breaking down of complex systems into their units to begin to understand them and the interrelation of the parts so obtained. That was not the issue. What was at stake was the relation between our knowledge of complex systems and their ontology, between how they are known and how they are conceived actually to be.[4] *Epistemological* reduction occurs when the concepts used to describe and explicate a particular complex system are reducible[5] to, translatable into, concepts applicable to the entities of which the complex is composed. The claim by many biologists, for example, is that many biological concepts are not so reducible.

Ontological reduction is more subtle, being about what complex entities *are*. One form of this simply recognizes, uncontroversially these days (no one claims, for example, to be a vitalist concerning living organisms in the sense of Driesch and Bergson), that everything in the world is constituted of whatever physics says is the basic constituent of matter, currently quarks. That is to say, most thinkers are, in this respect, monists concerning the ontology of the world and not dualist, vitalist, or supernaturalist. However, to say that diverse entities are all made up of, are "nothing but," the same basic physical constituents is

clearly inadequate, for it fails to distinguish and characterize their specific identities and characteristics, that is, their specific ontology.
Hence it has come to be widely recognized that this form of basic ontological assertion is inadequate to the complexities of the world, understanding of which can be illuminated by these considerations concerning the varieties of reduction.

It will be enough here to recognize that the natural (and also human) sciences more and more give us a picture of the world as consisting of a complex hierarchy—or, more accurately, hierarchies—a
series of levels of organization and matter in which each successive
member of the series is a whole constituted of parts preceding it in
the series.[6] The wholes are organized systems of parts that are dynamically and spatially interrelated. This feature of the world is now
widely recognized to be of significance in coordinating our knowledge of its various levels of complexity—that is, of the sciences which
correspond to these levels.[7] It also corresponds not only to the world
in its present condition but also to the way complex systems have
evolved in time out of earlier simpler ones.

What is significant about the relation of complex systems to their
constituents now is that the concepts needed to describe and understand—as indeed also the methods needed to investigate—each level
in the hierarchy of complexity are specific to and distinctive of those
levels. It is very often the case (but not always) that the properties,
concepts, and explanations used to describe the higher-level wholes
are not reducible to those used to describe their constituent parts,
themselves often also constituted of yet smaller entities. This is an
epistemological assertion of a nonreductionist kind, and its precise
implications have been much discussed.[8]

When the epistemological nonreducibility of properties, concepts,
and explanations applicable to higher levels of complexity is well established, their employment in scientific discourse can often, but not
in all cases, lead to a putative and then to an increasingly confident attribution of a distinctive *causal efficacy* to the complex wholes that
does not apply to the separated, constituent parts. Now "to be real,
new, and irreducible . . . must be to have new, irreducible causal pow-

ers."[9] If this continues to be the case under a variety of independent procedures[10] and in a variety of contexts, then an *ontological* affirmation becomes possible—namely, that new and distinctive kinds of realities at the higher levels of complexity have *emerged*. This can occur with respect either to moving, synchronically, up the ladder of complexity or, diachronically, through cosmic and biological evolutionary history. This understanding accords with the pragmatic attribution, both in ordinary life and scientific investigation, of the term "reality" to that which we cannot avoid taking account of in our diagnosis of the course of events, in experience or experiments. Real entities have effects and play irreducible roles in adequate explanation of the world.

I shall denote[11] this position as that of *emergentist monism*, rather than as "nonreductive physicalism." For those who adopt the latter label for their view, particularly in their talk of the "physical realization" of the mental in the physical, often seem to me to hold a much less realistic view of higher-level properties than I wish to affirm here—and also not to attribute causal powers to that to which higher-level concepts refer.

If we do make such an ontological commitment about the reality of the "emergent" whole of a given total system, the question then arises how one is to explicate the relation between the state of the whole and the behavior of parts of that system at the micro-level. The simple concept of chains of causally related events ($A \rightarrow B \rightarrow C \ldots$) in constant conjunction (à la Hume) is inadequate for this purpose. Extending and enriching the notion of causality now becomes necessary because of new insights into the way complex systems, in general, and biological ones, in particular, behave. This subtler understanding of how higher levels influence the lower levels, and vice versa, still allows application in this context of the notion of a kind of "causal" relation between whole and part (of system to constituent)—never ignoring, of course, the "bottom-up" effects of parts on wholes which depend for their properties on the parts being what they are.

The relation of wholes and parts in complex systems

A number of related concepts have in recent years been developed to describe the relation of wholes and parts in both synchronic and diachronic systems—that is, respectively, both those in some kind of steady state with stable characteristic emergent features of the whole and those that display an emergence of new features in the course of time.

The term *downward-causation*, or *top-down causation*, was, as far as I can ascertain, first employed in 1974 by Donald Campbell[12] to denote the way in which the network of an organism's relationships to its environment and its behavior patterns together determine in the course of time the actual DNA sequences at the molecular level present in an evolved organism—even though, from a "bottom-up" viewpoint of that organism once in existence, a molecular biologist would tend to describe its form and behavior as a consequence of the same DNA sequences. Campbell instances the evolutionary development of efficacious jaws made of suitable proteins in a worker termite. I prefer to use actual complex systems to clarify this suggestion, such as the Bénard phenomenon: at a critical point a fluid heated uniformly from below in a containing vessel ceases to manifest the entirely random "Brownian" motion of its molecules, but displays up and down convective currents in columns of hexagonal cross-section. Moreover, certain autocatalytic reaction systems (e.g., the famous Zhabotinsky reaction and glycolysis in yeast extracts) display spontaneously, often after a time interval from the point when first mixed, rhythmic temporal and spatial patterns, the forms of which can even depend on the size of the containing vessel. Many examples are now known also of dissipative systems which, because they are open, a long way from equilibrium, and nonlinear in certain essential relationships between fluxes and forces, can display large-scale patterns in spite of random motions of the units—"order out of chaos," as Prigogine and Stengers[13] dubbed it.

In these examples, the ordinary physicochemical account of the interactions at the micro-level of description simply cannot account for these phenomena. It is clear that what the parts (molecules and ions, in the Bénard and Zhabotinsky cases) are doing and the patterns they form are what they are *because* of their incorporation into the system-as-a-whole—in fact, these are patterns *within* the systems in question. This is even clearer in the much more complex, and only partly understood, systems of gene switchings on-and-off and their interplay with cell metabolism and specific protein production in the processes of development of biological forms. The parts would not be behaving as observed if they were not parts of that particular system (the "whole"). The state of the system-as-a-whole is affecting (i.e., acting like a cause on) what the parts, the constituents, actually do. Many other examples of this kind could be taken from the literature on, for example, self-organizing and dissipative systems and also economic and social ones.

We do not have available for such systems any account of events in terms of temporal, linear chains of causality as usually conceived (A→ B→ C→ ...). A wider use of "causality" and "causation" is now needed to include the kind of whole-part relationships, higher-to lower-level, which the sciences have themselves recently been discovering in complex systems, especially the biological and neurological ones. Here the term *whole-part influence* will be used to represent the net effect of all those ways in which the system-as-a-whole, operating from its "higher" level, is a causal factor in what happens to its constituent parts, the "lower" one.

Various interpretations have been deployed by other authors to represent this whole-part relation in different kinds of systems, though not always with causal implications.

Structuring causes

The notion of whole-part influence is germane to one that Niels H. Gregersen has employed[14] in his valuable discussion of autopoietic (self-making, self-organizing) systems—namely, that of *structuring causes*, as developed by F. Dretske[15] for understanding mental causation. They instance the event(s) that produced the hardware conditions (actual electrical connections in the computer) and the word-processing program (software) as the "structuring causes" of the cursor movement on the screen connected with the computer; whereas the "triggering cause" is, usually, pressure on a key on the keyboard. The two kinds of causes exhibit a different relationship to their effects. A triggering one falls into the familiar (Humean) pattern of constant conjunction. However, a structuring cause is never sufficient to produce the particular effect (the key still has to be pressed); there is no constant relationship between structuring cause and effect. In the case of complex systems, such as those already mentioned, the system-as-a-whole often has the role, I suggest, of a structuring cause in Dretske's sense.

Propensities

The category of "structuring cause" is closely related to that of *propensities*, developed by Karl Popper, who pointed out that "there exist weighted possibilities which are *more than mere possibilities*, but tendencies or propensities to become real"[16] and that these "propensities in physics are properties *of the whole situation* and sometimes even of the particular way in which a situation changes. And the same holds of the propensities in chemistry, biochemistry and in biology."[17] The effects of random events depend on the context in which they occur. Hence Popper's "propensities" are the effects of Dretske's structuring causes in the case that triggering causes are random in their operation (that is, *genuinely* random, with no "loading of the dice").

For example, the long-term effects of random mutations in the genetic information carrier, DNA, depend on the state of the environment (in the widest sense, so including predators) in which the phenotype comes to exist. This "environment" acts as a structuring cause. Hence a mutation that induces an increase, for example, in the ability of the whole organism to store information about its surroundings might (not necessarily *would*, because of variable exigencies of the environment) lead to the organism having more progeny and so an advantage in natural selection. This is an example of what I regard as a propensity in biological evolution. In this perspective, there are propensities in biological evolution, favored by natural selection, to complexity, self-organization, information processing and storage, and so to consciousness.

Boundary (limiting) conditions

In the discussion of the relations between properties of a system-as-a-whole and the behavior of its constituent parts, some authors refer to the *boundary conditions* that are operating (e.g., Polanyi[18]). It can be a somewhat misleading term ("limiting condition" would be better), but I will continue to use it only in this wider, Polanyian sense as referring to the given parameters of the structural complex in which the processes under consideration are occurring.

A more recent, sophisticated development of these ideas has been proffered by Bernd-Olaf Küppers:

> [T]he [living] organism is subservient to the manner in which it is constructed. . . . Its principle of construction represents a boundary condition under which the laws of physics and chemistry become operational in such a way that the organism is reproductively self-sustaining. . . . [T]he phenomenon of emergence as well as that of downward causation can be observed in the living organism and can be coupled to the existence of specific boundary conditions posed in the living matter.[19]

Thus a richer notion of the concept of boundary conditions is operative in systems as complex as living ones. The simpler forms of the idea of "boundary condition," as applied, for example, by Polanyi to machines, are not adequate to express the causal features basic to biological phenomena. Indeed, the "boundary conditions" of a system will have to include not only purely physical factors on a global scale but also complex intersystemic interactions between type-different systems.

There is a sense in which systems-as-a-whole, because of their distinctive configuration, can constrain and influence the behavior of their parts to be otherwise than they would be if isolated from the particular system. Yet the system-as-a-whole would not be describable by the concepts and laws of that level and still have the properties it does have if the parts (e.g., the ceric and cerous ions in the Zhabotinsky case) were not of the particular kind they are. What is distinctive in the system-as-a-whole is the new kind of interrelations and interactions, spatially and temporally, of the parts.

Supervenience

Another much-debated term which has been used in this connection, especially in describing the relation of mental events to neurophysiological ones in the brain, is *supervenience*. This term, which does not usually imply any "whole-part" causative relation, goes back to Donald Davidson's employment of it in expounding his view of the mind-brain-body relation.[20] The various meanings and scope of the term in this context had been formulated and classified by J. Kim[21] as involving: the supervenient properties' *covariance* with, *dependency* on, and *nonreducibility* to their base properties. One can ask the question: "[H]ow are the properties characteristic of entities at a given level related to those that characterize entities of adjacent levels? Given that entities at distinct levels are ordered by the part-whole relation, is it the case that properties associated with different levels are also ordered by some distinctive and significant relationship?"[22]

The attribution of "supervenience" asserts primarily that there is a necessary covariance between the properties of the higher level and those of the lower level. When the term "supervenience" was first introduced, it was neutral with respect to causal relations—of any influence of the supervenient level on the subvenient one. Later, supervenient causality was even denied (so Kim). Its appropriateness is obscure for analyzing whole-part relations, which by their very nature relate, with respect to complex systems, entities that are in some sense the same. For, in the context of the physical and biological (and, it must also be said, ecological and social) worlds, the mutual interrelations between whole and parts in any internally hierarchically organized system often, as I have shown, appear to involve causal effects of the whole on the parts.

The mind–brain–body relation and personhood

Much of the discussion of the relation of higher to lower levels in hierarchically stratified systems has centred on the mind–brain–body relation, on how mental events are related to neurophysiological ones in the human-brain-in-the-human-body—in effect, the whole question of human agency and what we mean by it. A hierarchy of levels can be delineated, each of which is the focus of a corresponding scientific study, from neuroanatomy and neurophysiology to psychology. Those involved in studying "how the brain works" have come to recognize that

> [p]roperties not found in components of a lower level can emerge from the organization and interaction of these components at a higher level. For example, rhythmic pattern generation in some neural circuits is a property of the circuit, not of isolated pacemaker neurons. Higher brain functions (e.g., perception, attention) may depend on temporally coherent functional units distributed through different maps and nuclei.[23]

The still intense philosophical discussion of the mind–brain–body relation has been, broadly, concerned with attempting to elucidate the relation between the "top" level of human mental experience and the lowest, bodily physical levels. In recent decades it has often involved considering the applicability and precise definition of some of the terms used already to relate higher to lower levels in hierarchically stratified systems. The question of what kind of "causation," if any, may be said to be operating from a "top-down," as well as the obvious and generally accepted "bottom-up direction," is still much debated in this context.[24]

When discussing the general relation of wholes to constituent parts in a hierarchically stratified complex system of stable parts, I used "whole-part influence"[25] and other terms and maintained that a nonreductionist view of the predicates, concepts, laws, and so on applicable to the higher level could be coherent. Reality could, I argued, putatively be attributable to that to which these nonreducible, higher-level predicates, concepts, laws, and so on applied, and these new realities, with their distinctive properties, could be properly called "emergent." Mental properties are now widely regarded by philosophers[26] as epistemologically irreducible to their physical ones, indeed as "emergent" from them, but also dependent on them, and similar terms have been used to describe their relation as in the context of nonconscious, complex systems. I have argued[27] that what happens in these systems at the lower level is the result of the *joint* operation of both higher- and lower-level influences—the higher and lower levels could be said to be jointly sufficient, type-different causes of the lower-level events. When the higher-lower relation is that of mind/brain-body, it seems to me that similar considerations should apply.

Up to this point, I have been taking the term "mind," and its cognate "mental," to refer to that which is the emergent reality distinctive especially of human beings. But in many wider contexts, not least that of philosophical theology, a more appropriate term for this emergent reality would be "person," and its cognate "personal," to represent the total psychosomatic, holistic experience of the human being in all its modalities—conscious and unconscious; rational and emotional; spiritual; active and passive; individual and social; and so on. The concept of personhood recognizes that, as Philip Clayton puts it,

> [w]e have thoughts, wishes and desires that together constitute our character. We express these mental states through our bodies, which are simultaneously our organs of perception and our means of affecting other things and persons in the world. . . . [The massive literature on theories of personhood] clearly points to the indispensability of embodiedness as the precondition for perception and action, moral agency, community and freedom—all aspects that philosophers take as indispensable to human personhood and that theologians have viewed as part of the *imago dei*.[28]

There is therefore a strong case for designating the highest level— the whole, in that unique system that is the human-brain-in-the-human-body-in-social-relations—as that of the "person." Persons are *inter alia* causal agents with respect to their own bodies and to the surrounding world (including other persons). They can, moreover, report on aspects of their internal states concomitant with their actions with varying degrees of accuracy. Hence the exercise of personal *agency* by individuals transpires to be a paradigm case and supreme exemplar of whole-part influence—in this case exerted on their own bodies and on the world of their surroundings (including other persons). I conclude that the details of the relation between cerebral neurological activity and consciousness cannot in principle detract from the causal efficacy of the content of the latter on the former and so on behavior. In other words, "folk psychology" and the real reference of the language of "personhood" are both justified and necessary.

Divine creativity

We have become accustomed in recent years to hearing of the "epic of evolution" so often that sometimes our ears have become dulled to just how remarkable it is. If something akin to human intelligence had been able to witness the original "hot big bang" some twelve or so billion years ago, would it ever have predicted from the properties of the quarks, the laws of quantum theory and of gravity, and the nature of the four fundamental forces that the process would complexify and self-organize over the aeons in at least one small range of space-time to become persons who can know not only the processes by which they have emerged but also each other and could be creative of truth, beauty, and goodness? It is to the significance of this that we must now turn.

I have been recounting in the foregoing the scientific perspective on a world in which over the course of space-time new realities have emerged by virtue of the inherent properties of basic matter-energy to complexify and self-organize[29] into systems manifesting new properties and capabilities. These emergent capacities include, we have seen, mental and personal ones and, I would add, spiritual ones— by which I mean the capacity to relate personally to that Ultimate Reality that is the source and ground of all existence. For the very existence of all-that-is, with that inherent creativity to bring persons out of quarks just described, is for me and all theists only explicable by postulating an Ultimate Reality which is: the source and ground of all being and becoming; suprapersonal; suprarational; capable of knowing all that it is logically possible to know and of doing all that it is logically possible to do; and unsurpassedly instantiating the values which human mental and spiritual capacities can discern, if only fail-ingly implement. In English the name for this Reality is "God"—and that usage I will follow from this point.

The question at once arises of how to conceive of the relation of God to all-that-is (the "world"). In more classical terms, how do we conceive of God as *Creator*? The physics of the earlier part of the last century (that is, the twentieth!) showed—as in the famous equation e = mc²—that matter, energy, space, and time are closely related cate-gories in our analysis of the world; so that God must be conceived of as giving existence to, as creating, all time and space as well as matter and energy.[30] So whatever "divine creation" is, it is not about what God can be supposed to have been doing at 4004 BCE or even 12 billion BCE! Divine "creation" concerns the *perennial* relation of God to the world. For we have to conceive now of God giving existence to all entities, structures, and processes "all the time" and to all times as each moment, for us, unfolds. They would not be if God was not. Augustine, of course, perceived this sixteen centuries ago with respect to time when he famously affirmed the impossibility of asking what God was doing "before" creating the world and addressed God thus: "It is therefore true to say that when you [God] had not made any-thing there was no time, because time itself was of your making."[31]

What we now see today, in the light of the whole epic of evolution and our understanding of complex systems, is that the very processes of the world are inherently creative of new realities. We therefore conclude that God is creating all the time in and through the com-plexifying and self-organizing processes to which God is giving con-tinuous existence in divinely created temporal relations ("time"). God is not a has-been Creator but always and continuously Cre-ator—*semper Creator*, and the world is a *creatio continua*, as traditional theology has sometimes expressed it.

This is far from being a recent concept, for it is implicit in the traditional concept of God's *immanence* in the world. It is noteworthy that, just four years after Darwin published *The Origin of Species*, the Church of England clergyman and novelist Charles Kingsley, in his evolutionary fairy tale *The Water Babies*, depicts Tom, the boy chimney sweep, looking at Mother Earth in puzzlement, for she is apparently *doing* nothing. "Tom to the mother of creation: 'I heard that you were always making new beasts out of old.' 'So people fancy,' she said. 'I make things make themselves.'"[32] And Frederick Temple, later the Archbishop of Canterbury, affirmed in his 1854 Bampton Lectures that "God did not make the things, we may say, but He made them make themselves."[33]

The understanding of cosmic and biological evolution illuminated by new insights into the capacities of complex systems with their self-organizing capabilities and the philosophical framework of an emergentist monism all converge to reinstate the concept of God not only as necessarily *transcendent*—"other" in ultimate Being to be Creator at all—but also as *immanent:* in, with, and under the processes to which God is giving existence. Indeed, these very processes are to be conceived of *as* the activity of God as Creator, and a *theistic* naturalism then becomes imperative. The Christian theological tradition in fact already has imaginative and symbolic resources[34] to enrich this notion:

• creation seen as the self-expression of God the Word/*Logos.*

• God's *Wisdom* as imprinted in the fabric of the world, especially in human minds open to "her."[35]

• God as the "one in Whom we live and move and have our being" (Paul at Athens in the account of Acts 17:28—a key text in the current reconsideration of "pan*en*theism" as denoting God's relation to the world).

• the tradition's understanding of the sacramental.[36]

• in the Eastern Christian tradition, the world as the milieu in which the "uncreated Energies" of God operate.[37]

It is implicit, and is increasingly emphasized recently[38] in the understanding of God's creating, that the world is not only dependent on God for its very existence but also that this God-given existence is autonomous in developing its own possibilities by its own inherent, God-endowed capacities and laws. Although the world is in one sense "in" God, as panentheistically understood, yet God is ontologically distinct from it—there is an ontological gap everywhere and at all times between God and the world. Hence creation is a self-limiting activity of God rendering Godself vulnerable, for in it God takes the risk of letting everything be and become itself, and this in human persons, who are free and autonomous, means allowing them to be capable of falsity as well as truth, ugliness as well as beauty, and evil as well as good. God, it appears, literally suffers this to happen for the world to be creative, capable of developing through complexification and self-organization new forms of existence, one of which, *Homo sapiens*, is capable of freely chosen, harmonious, personal relations with God's own self.

God is not a magician who overrules by intervening in the creative processes with which God continuously endows and blesses the world—though God is eternally present to it. The future is open, not set in concrete, and does not yet exist even for God to know or determine, but God will, uniquely, be present to all futures and will be able to respond to those personal beings who have evolved to have the capacity freely to respond to God.

The nature of such relationships of persons to God may, like the general scenario of creation outlined in this chapter, also be illuminated by our understanding of the emergence of new realities in complex, especially self-organizing, systems. For in many situations where God is experienced by human persons, we have by intention and according to well-winnowed experience and tradition complexes of interacting personal entities, material things, and historical circumstances that are epistemologically not reducible to concepts applicable to these individual components. Could not new realities—and so new experiences of God for humanity—be seen to "emerge" in such complexes and even to be causally effective?

I am thinking,[39] for example, of the Christian Church's Eucharist (Holy Communion, the Mass, "the Lord's Supper"), in which there exists a distinctive complex of interrelations between its constituents. The latter could be identified, *inter alia* (for it is many-layered in the richness of its meanings and symbols), as follows:

1. Individual Christians are motivated by a sense of *obedience* to the ancient, historically well-authenticated command of Jesus, the founder of their faith, at the actual Last Supper to "Do *this* . . . "— that is, to eat the bread and to drink the wine in the same way he did on that occasion and so to identify themselves with his project in the world.

2. Christians of all denominations have been concerned that their communal act is properly *authorized* as being in continuity with that original act of Jesus and its repetition, recorded in the New Testament, in the first community of Christians. Churches have differed about the character of this authorization but not about its importance.

3. The physical "elements," as they are often called, of bread and wine are, of course, part of the matter of the world and so are representative, in this regard, of the created order. So Christians perceive in these actions, in this context and with the words of Jesus in mind, that *a new significance and valuation of the very stuff of the world* is being expressed in this action.

4. Because it is bread and not wheat, wine and not grapes, which are consecrated, this act has come to be experienced also as a new evaluation of the work of *humanity in cocreating with God in ordinary work*.

5. The broken bread and poured-out wine was explicitly linked by Jesus with his anticipated self-sacrificial offering of himself on the cross, in which his body was broken and blood shed to draw all toward unity of human life with God. Christians in this act consciously acknowledge and identify themselves with Jesus' *self-sacrifice*, thereby offering to reproduce the same self-emptying love for others in their own lives and so to further his purposes of bringing in the reign of God in the world.

6. They are also aware of the promise of Jesus to be present again in their recalling and remaking of the historical events of his death and

resurrection. This "making-present" *(anamnesis)* of the Jesus who is regarded as now fully in the presence of—and, in some sense, identified
with—God is a unique and spiritually powerful feature of this communal act.

7. There is creatively *present* the *God who is transcendent, incarnate,*
and *immanent*. Here do we not have an exemplification of the emergence of a new kind of reality, since this complex situation is epistemologically not reducible? For what (if one dare so put it) "emerges"
in the eucharistic event *in toto* can only be described in special nonreducible terms such as "real presence" and "sacrifice." A new kind of
reality is attributable to the eucharistic event, for in it there is an
effect on both the individual and on the community that induces distinctively Christian personhood and society (of "being ever deeper
incorporated into this body of love"[40]). So it is not surprising there is
a branch of study called "sacramental theology" to explicate this special reality and human experience and interpretations of it. Since God
is present "in, with, and under" this holistic eucharistic event, in it
God may properly be regarded as distinctively acting through it on
the individual and community.[41]

I have taken this as one example, but I propose that the principle
involved in trying to make clear what is special about this particular
spiritual situation is broadly applicable[42] to many other experiences of
theological concern and interest, both historical and contemporary.
For this last reason, in conjunction with the broader exhilarating theistic perspective I have been trying to expound, it seems to me that
the new sciences of complexity and of self-organization provide a
fruitful release for theology from the oppression of excessively reductionist interpretations of the hierarchy of the sciences and a making
accessible of theological language and concepts to the general ex-
changes of the intellectual life of our times—a milieu from which it
has been woefully and misguidedly excluded for too long.

Would it be too much to suggest that these new, emergentist
monist insights into the inbuilt creativity of our world through its
complexifying and self-organizing capacities open up a vista of conti-

nuity between the physical, the mental, and the spiritual which could, in this new century, break down the parallel barricades mounted in the last, both between the "two cultures" of the sciences and the humanities—and between the experiences of nature and of God, the sciences, and religion?

PART 2

HUMANITY EVOLVING IN THE PRESENCE OF GOD

CHAPTER 5

Articulating God's Presence
In and To the World Unveiled by
the Sciences

The WORLD is unknown, till the Value and Glory of it is seen; till the Beauty and the Serviceableness of its part is considered.

— *Thomas Traherne, ca. 1670[1]*

Thomas Traherne's deeply sacramental—and, eventually we shall have to say, "panentheistic"—vision of the world, especially as expressed in the golden prose of his *Centuries*, was historically coincident in England with the quite differently motivated insights of his great contemporary, Isaac Newton. Traherne died in 1674, some thirteen years before the publication of the *Principia* gave a defining impetus to the scientific revolution in its modern form, bringing with it the widespread recognition of the universe as lawfully embedding rational principles discoverable by experiment. The implications of Newton's scheme led his contemporaries, notably Robert Boyle, to envisage the universe in terms of a mechanistic clockwork and his

Paper presented at a consultation sponsored by the John Templeton Foundation at St. George's House, Windsor Castle, Berkshire, England, December 6–8, 2001, and subsequently published in *In Whom We Live and Have Our Being: Panentheistic Reflections in God's Presence in a Scientific World,* ed. Philip Clayton and Arthur Peacocke (Grand Rapids: Eerdmans, 2004), 137–54. Reprinted by permission.

successors in the eighteenth century to an excessively transcendent perception of God as creating the world, as it were, "outside" of the divine life—in spite of an ancient immanentist strand in Christian theology. Inevitably "Creation" came to be seen by many as an event in which God brought into existence (in time) an autonomous world, which was then free to run according to its divinely endowed laws, so that God tended to become the redundant Clockmaker, or absentee Landlord, of deism.

Many developments in science itself have led to a radical transformation of that mechanical picture of the natural world; these in turn have led to a profound reconsideration by Christian theists (and others) of how, in the light of the sciences, to conceive of God's relation to the world as it is now perceived to be and to be becoming.

To discern the direction that must be taken in this new exploration of God's relation to the world, it is necessary briefly to recount the relevant features of the scientific perspectives.

The world of science

A synchronic scientific perspective

First, the world as it is, in a kind of "still shot." The underlying unity of the natural world is evidenced in its universal embedded rationality, which the sciences assume and continue to verify. In the realm of the very small and of the very large—the subatomic and the cosmic—the extraordinary applicability of mathematics in elucidating the entities, structures, and processes of the world continues to reinforce that it is indeed one world. On the one hand, the early twentieth-century unification of space-time-matter-energy within one mathematical framework by Einstein anticipated current attempts to unify also the four fundamental forces operating in the world. On the other hand, the diversity of this world is apparent not only in the purely physical—molecules, the Earth's surface, the immensely variegated systems of the astronomical heavens—but even more strikingly in the biological world. New species continue to be discovered in spite of the destruction caused by human action.

This diversity has been rendered more intelligible in recent years by an increased awareness of the principles involved in the formation and constitution of complex systems. There is even a corresponding "science of complexity" concerned with theories about them. The natural (and human) sciences more and more give us a picture of the world as consisting of complex hierarchies—a series of levels of organization of matter in which each successive member is a whole constituted of parts preceding it in the series. The wholes are organized systems of parts that are dynamically and spatially interrelated. This feature of the world is now widely recognized to be significant in relating our knowledge of its various levels of complexity—that is, the sciences that correspond to the different levels.

The concepts needed to describe and understand—and also the methods needed to investigate—each level in the hierarchy of complexity are specific to what is distinctive about it. Sociological, psychological, and biological concepts are characteristic of their own levels and quite different from those of physics and chemistry. It is very often the case (but not always) that the properties, concepts, and explanations used to describe the higher-level wholes are not logically reducible to those used to describe their constituent parts. Thus sociological concepts are often not logically reducible to—that is, translatable into—those of individual psychology (e.g., the difference between communities of more than three, three, and two); psychological concepts are not reducible to those of the neurosciences; biological concepts to those of biochemistry, etc. Such nonreductionist assertions are about the status of a particular kind of knowledge (they are "epistemological") and are usually strongly defended by the practitioners of the science concerning the higher level of complexity. When the nonreducibility of properties, concepts, and explanations applicable to higher levels of complexity is well established, their employment in scientific discourse can often, but not in all cases, lead to a putative, and then to an increasingly confident, attribution of a distinctive causal efficacy to the complex wholes that does not apply to the separated, constituent parts. It has often been argued that for something to be real, new, and irreducible, it must have new, irreducible causal powers. If this continues to be the case for a complex under a variety of independent procedures and in a variety of contexts, then new and distinctive kinds of realities at the higher levels of complexity may properly be said to have "emerged." This can occur with respect either to moving up the ladder of complexity or, as we shall see, through cosmic and biological evolutionary history. This understanding accords with the pragmatic attribution, in both ordinary life and scientific investigation, of the term "reality" to that which we cannot avoid taking account of in our diagnosis of the course of events, in experience or experiments. Real entities have effects and play irreducible roles in adequate explanations of the world.

All entities, all concrete particulars in the world, including human beings, are constituted of fundamental physical entities—quarks or whatever it is that current physics postulates as the basic building constituents of the world (which, of course, includes energy as well as matter). This is a "monistic" view that everything can be broken down into fundamental physical entities and that no *extra* entities are thought to be inserted at higher levels of complexity to account for their properties. I prefer to call this view "emergentist monism," rather than "nonreductive physicalism." In addition to the incoherence in the latter view (notably pointed out by J. Kim[2]), those who adopt it, particularly in speaking of the "physical realization" of the mental in the physical, often seem to me to hold a much less realistic view of the higher-level properties than I wish to affirm here—and also not to attribute causal powers to that to which the higher-level concepts refer.

If we do make such a commitment about the reality of the emergent whole of a given total system, the question then arises of how one is to explicate the relation between the state of the whole and the behavior of parts of that system at the micro-level. The simple concept of chains of causally related events ($A \rightarrow B \rightarrow C \ldots$) in constant conjunction is inadequate for this purpose. Extending and enriching the notion of causality now becomes necessary because of new insights into the way complex systems in general, and biological ones in particular, behave.

It has become increasingly clear that one can preserve the reality, distinctiveness, and causal powers of higher levels relative to lower ones while continuing to recognize that the higher complexes are complex assemblies of the fundamental building blocks currently being discovered by physicists. No new entities are being *added* to the constituent parts for such parts to acquire the new distinctive properties characteristic of the wholes. For example, in the early twentieth century it was proposed that something had to be added to matter to explain the difference between living organisms and the inorganic. Such "vitalism" is now universally rejected by biologists. Even more significantly with respect to human beings, one can affirm the distinctiveness of the language of the "mental" as not, in principle, reducible to that of the neurophysiological without asserting the existence of an entity, the "mind," in a realm other than that of the physical world.

The new challenge then becomes how it is that what we have regarded as physical entities can in the human-brain-in-the-human-body-in-society be so organized to become a thinking self-conscious person. Persons are better regarded, it transpires, as psychosomatic unities with physical, mental, and spiritual capacities—rather than physical entities to which a "mind" and/or a "soul/spirit" have been added. This is in fact the biblical understanding, as H. Wheeler Robinson expressed in a famous epigram: "The Hebrew idea of personality is an animated body and not an incarnated soul."[3] Talk about the "soul" or "spirit" of human beings as entities, and especially as naturally immortal ones, no longer represents the best explanation of the emergence of spiritual capacities in the light of what we now know about the kind of complexity that constitutes a human being. Dualism of that kind seems to be incommensurate with any picture of the world consistent with scientific observations. This does not, of course, undermine the reality and validity of mental and spiritual activities and capacities. Those Christians who have affirmed not the natural immortality of the "soul/spirit" but the biblical doctrine of resurrection of the whole person can welcome this development.

A diachronic scientific perspective: the "epic of evolution."

The foregoing describes only one way of perceiving the natural world through the sciences. For since the time of Newton and his eighteenth-century deist successors, our whole perspective on the world has been transformed through studies in geology, biology, and cosmology—indeed, in all those sciences which may be dubbed as "historical" insofar as they are inevitably concerned with the processes that have been occurring in the past throughout the universe, on the surface of the Earth, and in its living organisms. By inferring to the best explanation of the succession of states of these systems from the relevant data, we are now possessed with a remarkably coherent picture of the origin and development to the present state of the universe, planet Earth, and of life on the Earth. This account is a naturalistic, intelligible, and well-evidenced story of the development over the last 12 billion years or so of the observable universe from a primal concentration of mass-energy expanding with space in time to the present observable universe, including Earth. This story joins up with the contemporary epic of evolution which describes how inorganic matter on the Earth has acquired the property of self-copying particular patterns in complex structures—and so to be living—and through the processes of natural selection, perhaps supported by some other natural factors facilitating complexification, has generated the multiple diverse forms of past and present living creatures on the Earth, including *Homo sapiens*. The general sweep of the story is too well-known to need repeating here. But certain features must be stressed, for these were quite unknown until a century and a half ago—or were at the most but dimly intuited—by those who developed classical Christian (and indeed Muslim and Jewish) theism in relation to the world as it was then understood.

The nexus of causality is unbroken and now requires no *deus ex machina*, no "God of the gaps," to explain *inter alia* the cosmic development, the formation of planet Earth, the transition from inorganic to living matter, the origin of species, and the development of complex brains that have the capacity to be aware. Much remains unknown and obscure, but the sequences are supported increasingly by hard science and new observations that become available as technology enhances the subtlety and power of scientific instrumentation. The picture is one of all-pervasive, incessant change. Although the Second Law of Thermodynamics entails an inexorable overall increase in entropy (and so of randomness and disorder) in the universe as a whole, it is now understood, both in terms of irreversible thermodynamics and of stochastic kinetics, how new complex structures can arise even within homogeneous physicochemical systems, especially when they involve a flux of matter and/or energy. In fact studies of complex systems of many kinds (e.g., sets of light bulbs, cell formation in liquids, snow crystal growth, gene complexes, immune systems, neural nets, conglomerations of economic centers) show that, when certain rules apply to the relationships prevailing between their constituent units, and when there are fluxes of matter/energy, they can self-organize[4] into surprisingly few and recurring patterns. Indeed, it is proposed that such factors are involved[5] in the appearance of more complex living organisms. Through the operation of natural selection favoring those developments which increase descendants' chances of survival, biological evolution evidences a propensity[6] towards an increase in complexity, information processing and storage, consciousness, sensitivity to pain, and perhaps even self-consciousness, which is a prerequisite for human social development and the cultural transmission of knowledge down the generations. Moreover, the operation of random factors (e.g., mutations in DNA) within the constraints of some wider lawlike system (e.g., the environment exerting a selection effect) is not at all inconsistent with the whole process manifesting purposes, such as those of a creator God.[7] Yet it is significant for how we understand God as Creator to note that this process of "things making themselves" is a purely naturalistic one, built into the very nature of the systems and of their constituents. As T. W. Deacon recently expressed it, "in an evolutionary emergent account of natural "design," the creative dynamic is understood to be *immanent* in the world rather than external to it, and this can be extended to subjective issues as well."[8]

The processes of the world by their inherent properties manifest a spontaneous creativity in which new properties emerge. One can even agree with Deacon when he also asserts that

> The subjective experience of being a locus of incessant novel self-organised mental activities is consistent with evolution-like emergence of spontaneously ordered neural activity. . . . Emergent phenomena, including subjective states and relationships, are not contingent in form because they are highly constrained by this self-organising holistic dynamic that gives rise to emergence. So, although emergent subjective states and relationships may in some sense be contingent products of the material world, this does not entail that their realised forms are either arbitrary or merely relative.[9]

It is this situation that any understanding of the creativity of God, the Giver of Existence to all-that-is and all-that-is-becoming, must now take into account—not reluctantly but as a new illumination of the divine activity. It is but a further elaboration and development of the "emergentist monism" which was required in our "synchronic" consideration of the relations within the hierarchies of complexity in the world as it now *is*—and, we now have to add, as it is *becoming*.

These new scientifically originating perspectives on the world, including humanity, and on its processes in time urgently press upon us the need for theological reconstruction.

Theological reconstruction

Clearly the deistic conception of a God external to nature—dwelling in an entirely different kind of space and being of a "substance" sufficiently different that it could not be involved continuously in the created order—does not cohere with these new insights into the world and its processes. As an Anglican theologian expressed it as long ago as the 1880s, "Darwinism appeared and, under the disguise of a foe, did the work of a friend. . . . Either God is everywhere present in nature, or He is nowhere."[10] Both a later Archbishop of Canterbury, Frederick Temple, and Charles Kingsley[11] in *The Water*

Babies (1863), could express the idea that "God makes things make themselves." Recent concepts of self-organization would indeed have been welcomed by these authors, but unfortunately their insights, although appropriated by many theologians (in Britain, at least) in the earlier part of the twentieth century, were overshadowed by the influence of Barthian neo-orthodoxy, with its repudiation of "natural theology" in the mid-century. Today the impact of the perspectives of the sciences impels us to develop further those earlier insights prompted by theological reflection on "Darwinism." The following gives an account of those themes which are becoming prominent and pressing for reconsideration.

Immanence: a theistic naturalism

God must now be seen as creating in the world, often through what science calls "chance" operating within the created order, each stage of which constitutes the launching pad for the next. The Creator is unfolding the created potentialities of the universe through a process in which its possibilities and propensities become actualized. God may be said to have "gifted" the universe, and goes on doing so, with a "formational economy" that "is sufficiently robust to make possible the actualization of all inanimate structures and all life forms that have ever appeared in the course of time."[12]

We have to emphasize anew the immanence of God as Creator "in, with, and under" the natural processes of the world unveiled by the sciences in accord with all that the sciences have revealed since those debates in the nineteenth century. At no point do modern natural scientists have to invoke any nonnatural causes to explain their observations and inferences about the past. The processes constitute a seamless web of interconnectedness and display emergence, for new forms of matter and a hierarchy of organization of these forms appear in the course of time. New kinds of reality emerge successively, each with its own specific environment, with its specific boundary conditions and with specific adjacent possibilities open to it in its specific situation.

Hence there is inexorably impressed upon us a dynamic picture of the world of entities, structures, and processes involved in continuous and incessant change and in process without ceasing. This picture impels us to reintroduce a dynamic element into our understanding of God's creative relation to the world—an element which was always implicit in the Hebrew conception of a "living God," dynamic in action, but often obscured by the tendency to think of "creation" as an event in the past. God has again to be imagined as continuously creating, continuously giving existence to what is new. God is creating at every moment of the world's existence through perpetually giving creativity to the very stuff of the world.

All of this reinforces the need to reaffirm more urgently than at any other time in Christian (and Jewish and Islamic) history that in a very strong sense God is the immanent Creator creating through the processes of the natural order. The processes are not themselves God, but the *action*[13] of God as Creator. God gives existence in divinely created time to a process that itself brings forth the new—thereby God is crea*ting*. This means we do not have to look for any alleged extra gaps in which, or mechanisms whereby, God might be supposed to be acting as Creator in the living world.

A musical analogy may help: when we are listening to a musical work, say, a Beethoven piano sonata, there are times when we are so deeply absorbed in it that for the moment we are thinking Beethoven's musical thoughts with him. Yet if anyone were to ask at that moment (unseemingly interrupting our concentration!), "Where is Beethoven now?"—we could only reply that Beethoven-as-composer is to be found only in the music itself. Beethoven-as-composer was or is—for this could have been said even when he was alive—other than the music (he "transcends" it) but his communication with us is entirely subsumed in and represented by the music itself: he is immanent in it and we need not look elsewhere to meet him in that creating role. The processes revealed by the sciences are in themselves God acting as Creator, and God is not to be found as some kind of *additional* influence or factor added on to the processes of the world God is creating. This perspective can properly be called "theistic naturalism" and is not deism *redivivus,* for it conceives of

God as *actively* and (in the light of an analogy developed below) *personally* creating through the processes of the world.

Panentheism

The scientific picture of the world has pointed to a perspective on God's relation to all natural events, entities, structures, and processes in which they are continuously being given existence by God, who thereby expresses in and through them God's own inherent rationality. In principle this should raise no new problems for classical Western theism which has maintained the ontological distinction between God and the created world. However, classical theism also conceived of God as a necessary "substance" with attributes and posited a space "outside" God in which the realm of the created was located—for one entity cannot exist in another and retain its own (ontological) identity when they are regarded as substances. Hence, if God is also so regarded, God can only exert influence "from outside" on events in the world. Such intervention, for that is what it would be, raises acute problems in the light of our contemporary scientific perception of the causal nexus of the world being a closed one. Because of such considerations, this substantival way of speaking has become inadequate in the view of many thinkers. It has become increasingly difficult to express the way in which God is present to the world in terms of "substances," which by definition cannot be internally present to each other. This inadequacy of Western classical theism is aggravated by the evolutionary perspective which, as we have just seen, requires that natural processes in the world need to be regarded *as such* as God's creative action.

We therefore need a new model for expressing the closeness of God's presence to finite, natural events, entities, structures, and processes; and we need the divine to be as close to them as it is possible to imagine, without dissolving the distinction between Creator and what is created. It is therefore not surprising that many contemporary theologians,[14] especially those with a scientific background, have resorted to the idea of "pan*en*theism": "The belief that the Being of God includes and penetrates the whole universe, so that every part of it exists in Him, but (as against Pantheism) that His Being is more than, and is not exhausted by, the universe."[15] One recalls the description of God in the speech at Athens attributed to St. Paul, who is depicted as quoting a Greek poet to the effect that God is the one of whom it may be said, "in him we live, and move, and have our being."[16] Since God cannot, in principle, have any spatial attributes, the "in" (Gk. *en*) expresses an intimacy of relation and is clearly not meant in any locative sense, with the world being conceived as a "part of God." It refers, rather, to an ontological relation so that the world is conceived as within the Being of God but, nevertheless, with its own distinct ontology. It is as if the world has a mode of being created by, but distinct from, God. Jürgen Moltmann, drawing on the kabbalistic notion of *zimsum* (meaning a "withdrawing into oneself"), has argued that this creative act of God involves a self-limitation by Godself.[17] In order to create a world other than Godself and in that sense "outside":

> God must have made room beforehand for a finitude *in himself*. It is only a withdrawal by God into himself that can free space into which God can act creatively. . . . (86, italics added)

> God does not create merely by calling something into existence, or by setting something afoot. In a more profound sense he [God] "creates" by letting-be, by making room, and by withdrawing himself. . . . (88)

> But if creation *ad extra* takes place in the space freed by God himself, then in this case the reality outside God still remains *in* the God who has yielded up that "outwards" in himself. Without the difference between creator and creation, creation cannot be conceived of at all; but this difference is embraced and comprehended by the greater truth . . . : the truth that God is all in all. (88–89)

In these quotations in defense of panentheism, Moltmann is clearly using "space" in an ontological sense—as in that vision of St. Augustine of the "the whole creation" as if it were "some sponge, huge but bounded . . . filled with that unmeasurable sea" of God, "environing and penetrating it through every way infinite . . . everywhere and on every side."[18]

The language of Moltmann and the striking image of St. Augustine both use the "in" (the *en* of pan*en*theism) to express the idea of the world, including humanity, as enveloped by God without it losing its true distinctiveness and as a way of intensifying the traditional belief in God's immanence in the world. It is this kind of panentheism, emphasizing the coinherent presence of God and the world, which I wish to espouse here—rather than one that allows any kind of identity of the world with God, even in the form of the "world as a part of God." The latter too easily merges into pantheism and weakens the necessary emphasis on God's ultimate transcendence of all-that-is (the "more than" in that definition of panentheism quoted earlier). The "in" metaphor has advantages in this context over the "separate-but-present-to" terminology of divine immanence in Western classical theism. For God is best conceived of as the circumambient Reality enclosing all existing entities, structures, and processes; and as operating in and through all, while being "more" than all. Hence, all that is not God has its existence within God's operation and Being. The infinity of God includes all other finite entities, structures, and processes; God's infinity comprehends and incorporates all.

The pan*en*theistic model as propounded here is intended to be consistent with the monist concept that all concrete particulars in the world system are composed only of basic physical entities, and with the conviction that the world system is causally closed. There are no dualistic, no vitalistic, no supernatural levels through which God might be supposed to be exercising *special* divine activity. In this model, the proposed kind of interactions of God with the world system would not be from "outside" but from "inside" it. That's why the world-system is regarded as being "in God."

These panentheistic interrelations of God with the world System, including humanity, I have attempted to represent in figure 1. This is a kind of Venn diagram representing ontological (including logical) relationships; the infinity sign represents not infinite space or time but the infinitely "more" of God's Being in comparison with everything else. The diagram has the limitation of being in two planes so that the "God" label appears dualistically to be (ontologically) outside the world; although this conveys the truth that God is "more and other" than the world, it cannot represent God's omnipresence in and to the world. A vertical arrow has been placed at the center of this circle to signal God's immanent influence and activity *within* the world. It may also be noted that "God" is denoted by the (imagined) infinite planar surface of the page *on* which the circle representing the world is printed. For, it is assumed, God is "more than" the world, which is nevertheless "in" God. The page underlies and supports the circle and its contents, just as God sustains everything in existence and is present to all. So the larger dashed circle, representing the ontological location of God's interaction with all-that-is, really needs a many-dimensional convoluted surface not available on a two-dimensional surface— something like St. Augustine's sponge?—though we continue to recognize the limitation of this inevitably locative model, as of all others.

In this model, there is no "place outside" the infinite God in which what is created could exist. God creates all-that-is *within* Godself. This can be developed into a more fruitful biological model based on mammalian, and so human, procreation. The classical Western concept of God as Creator has placed too much stress on the externality of the process—God is regarded as creating rather in the way the male fertilizes the female from outside. But mammalian females nurture new life within themselves, and this provides a much-needed corrective to the purely masculine image of divine creation. God, according to panentheism, creates a world other than Godself and "within herself" (we find ourselves saying for the most appropriate image—yet another reminder of the need to escape from the limitations of male-dominated language about God).

A further pointer to the cogency of a panentheistic interpretation of God's relation to the world is the way the different sciences relate to each other and to the world they study—the hierarchy of sciences from particle physics to ecology and sociology. The more complex is constituted of the less complex, and all interact and interrelate in systems of systems. It is to this world discovered by the sciences that we have to think of God as relating. The "external" God of classical Western theism can be modeled only as acting upon such a world by intervening separately at the various discrete levels. But if God incorporates both the individual systems and the total system-of-systems within Godself, as in the panentheistic model, then it is more conceivable that God could interact with all the complex systems at their own holistic levels. God is present to the wholes as well as to the parts.

At the terminus of one of the branching lines of natural hierarchies of complexity stands the human person—the complex of the human-brain-in-the-human-body-in-society. Persons can have intentions and purposes that can be implemented by particular bodily actions. Indeed, the action of the body as a whole in its multiple levels just *is* the intended action of the person. The physical action is describable, at the bodily level, in terms of the appropriate physiology, anatomy, etc., but also expresses the intentions and purposes of the person's thinking. The physical and the mental are two levels of the same holistic psychosomatic event.

Personal agency has been used both traditionally in the biblical literature and in contemporary theology as a model for God's action in the world. "We" as thinking, conscious persons appear to transcend our bodies while nevertheless remaining immanent in their actions. This psychosomatic, unified understanding of human personhood partly illuminates the use of a panentheistic model for God's relation to the world. For, according to the model, God is *internally* present to all of the world's entities, structures, and processes in a way analogous to the way we as persons are present and act in our bodies. This model, in the light of current concepts of the person as a psychosomatic unity, is then an apt way of modeling God's personal agency in the world as in some sense "personal."

As with all analogies, models, and metaphors, qualifications are needed before we too hastily draw a parallel between God's relation to the world and our relation as persons to our bodies. The *first* is that God who, it is being suggested, relates to the world like a personal

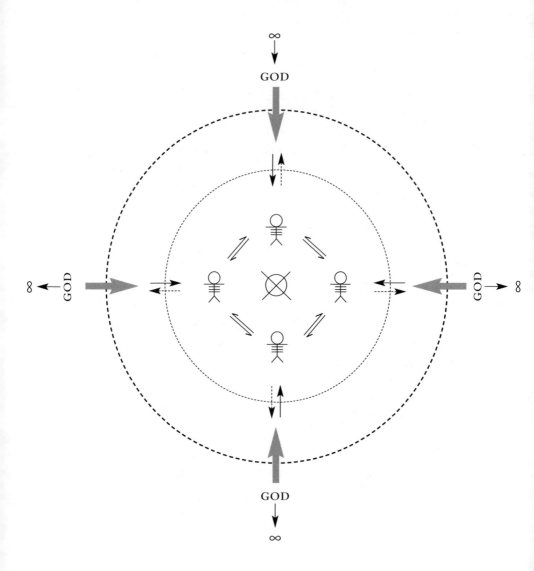

FIGURE 1. Diagram representing spatially the ontological relation of, and the interactions between, God and the world (including humanity).

Key

GOD God represented by the whole surface of the page, imagined to extend to infinity (∞) in all directions

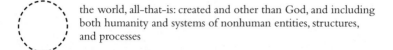 the world, all-that-is: created and other than God, and including both humanity and systems of nonhuman entities, structures, and processes

the human world: excluding systems of nonhuman entities, structures, and processes

God's interaction with and influence on the world and its events.

a similar arrow to the preceding one but perpendicular to the page: God's influence and activity within the world

- - - ▶ human agency in the nonhuman world

——▶ effects of the nonhuman world on humanity

⇌ personal interactions, both individual and social, between human beings, including cultural and historical influences

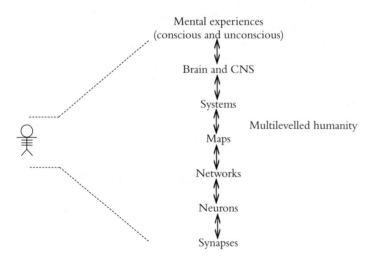

Mental experiences
(conscious and unconscious)
↕
Brain and CNS
↕
Systems
↕   Multilevelled humanity
Maps
↕
Networks
↕
Neurons
↕
Synapses

Apart from the top one, these are the levels of organization of the human nervous system depicted in Patricia S. Churchland and T. J. Sejnowski, 'Perspectives on Congitive Neuroscience', *Science*, 242 (1988): 741–45.

agent is also the one who creates it, gives it existence, and infinitely transcends it. Indeed, the panentheistic model emphasizes this in its "more than the world." However, our capacity for intentional (and other) thinking is a natural emergent within the world of brains-in-bodies, and *we* do not create our own bodies.

The *second* qualification of the model is that, as human persons, we are not conscious of most of what goes on in our bodies' autonomous functions such as breathing, digestion, and heart beating. Yet other events in our bodies are conscious and deliberate. So we distinguish between these functions, but this can scarcely apply to an omniscient God's relation to the world—God knows all that it is logically possible to know, hence God's knowledge of the world would include all patterns of events in it, namely: (1) those, relevant to the panentheistic analogy developed here, which are analogous to autonomic functions in human bodies and which constitute God's general providence in continually and actively giving existence to the world's entities, structures, and processes; and (2) and those patterns of events in human bodies that implement particular intentions and may therefore be held to be analogous to any implementation of any particular divine intentions. The separate discussion of how (2) could occur continues intensively,[19] and without any general consensus, but note that both kinds of patterns of events would be observed as natural, meaning here consistent with the scientific accounts. The *third* qualification of the model is that, in so using human personal agency as analogous to the way God interacts with the world, we are not implying the "world is God's body" nor that God is "a person"—rather that God is more coherently thought of as "at least personal," indeed as "more than personal" (again the "more than" of panentheism). Perhaps we could even say that God is "supra-personal" or "transpersonal," for there are many essential aspects of God's nature which cannot be subsumed under the categories applicable to human persons.

In my view, the panentheistic model allows one to combine a strengthened emphasis on the immanence of God in the world with God's ultimate transcendence over it. It does so in a way that makes the analogy of personal agency both more pertinent and less vulnerable than the Western externalist model to the above distortions of any model of the world-as-God's-body.

The fact of natural (as distinct from human, moral) evil continues to challenge belief in a benevolent God. In the classical perception of God as transcendent and as existing in a space distinct from that of the world, there is an implied detachment from the world in its suffering. This renders the problem of evil particularly acute. For God can only do anything about evil by an intervention from outside, which provokes the classical dilemma of either God can and will not, or he would but cannot: God is either not good or not omnipotent. The God of classical theism witnesses, but is not involved in, the sufferings of the world—even when closely "present to" and "alongside" them.

Hence, when faced with this ubiquity of pain, suffering, and death in the evolution of the living world, one is impelled to infer that God, to be anything like the God who is Love in Christian belief, must be understood to be suffering in the creative processes of the world. Creation is costly *to God*. Now, when the natural world, with all its suffering, is panentheistically conceived of as "in God," it follows that the evils of pain, suffering, and death in the world are internal to God's own self: God must have experience of the natural. This intimate and actual experience of God must also include all those events that constitute the evil intentions of human beings and their implementation—that is, the moral evil of human society.

The panentheistic model of God's relation to the world is therefore much more capable of recognizing this fundamental aspect of God's experience of the world. Moreover, the panentheistic feminine image of the world, as being given existence by God in the very "womb of God," is a particularly apt one for evoking an insight into the suffering of God in the very processes of creation. God is creating the world from within and, the world being "in" God, God experiences its sufferings directly as God's own and not from the outside.

In a more specifically Christian perception, God, in taking the suffering into God's own self, can thereby transform it into what is whole and healthy—that is, be the means of "salvation" when this is given its root etymological meaning. God heals and transforms from within, as a healthy body might be regarded as doing. The redemption and transformation of human beings by God through suffering is, in this perspective, a general manifestation of what is, for Christians, explicitly manifest in the life, death, and resurrection of Jesus the Christ. In brief, this redemptive and transforming action of God is more congruent with the panentheistic model than with the Western classical externalist interpretation of God's relation to the world.

Theological resources for imaging a theistic naturalism and panentheism

In the foregoing I have been referring to this classical kind of theism as "Western" because it has been dominant in Western Christianity (Roman Catholic, Anglican, Protestant), with some notable exceptions, such as Hildegard of Bingen. But it is the Eastern Christian tradition that is most explicitly panentheistic in holding together God's transcendence and immanence. For example, Gregory Palamas (ca.1296–1359 CE) made a distinction-in-unity between God's essence and God's uncreated energies in the world, and Maximus the Confessor (ca. 580–662 CE) regarded the Creator-*Logos* as characteristically present in each created thing as God's intention for it—its inner essence *(logos)* which makes it distinctively itself and draws it towards God.

I confine myself to mentioning some other threads in the Christian inheritance (East and West) pertinent to articulating God's presence in the world as expressed in the more abstract concepts devoted by a "theistic naturalism" and "panentheism."

The Wisdom (Sophia) and the Word (Logos) of God

Biblical scholars have in recent decades come to emphasize the significance of the central themes of the so-called Wisdom literature (Job, Proverbs Ecclesiastes, Ecclesiasticus, and Wisdom). In this broad corpus of writings, the feminine figure of Wisdom *(Sophia)*, according to J. G. Dunn, is a "convenient way of speaking about God acting in creation, revelation, and salvation: Wisdom never becomes more than a personification of God's activity."[20] This "Wisdom" endows some human beings, at least, with a personal wisdom that is rooted in their concrete experiences and in their systematic and ordinary observations of the natural world—what we would call science. But it is not confined to this and represents the distillation of wider human, ethical, and social experiences and even cosmological ones, since knowledge of the heavens figured in the capabilities of the sage. The natural order is valued as a gift and source of wonder, something to be celebrated. All such wisdom, imprinted as a pattern on the natural world and in the mind of the sage, is but a pale image of the divine Wisdom—that activity distinctive of God's relation to the world.

That wisdom is an attribute of God, personified as female, has been of especial significance to feminist theologians, amongst whom Celia Deane-Drummond has argued, on the basis of a wider range of biblical sources, that the feminine in God refers to all persons of the Christian Triune God, and Wisdom *(Sophia)* becomes "the feminine face of God."[21] In the present context, it is pertinent that this important concept of Wisdom *(Sophia)* unites intimately the divine activity of creation, human experience, and the processes of the natural world. It therefore constitutes a biblical resource for imaging the panentheism we have been urging.

So also does the closely related concept of the Word *(Logos)* of God, which is regarded[22] as existing eternally as a mode of God's own being, as active in creation, and as a self-expression of God's own being and becoming imprinted in the very warp and woof of the created order. It seems to be a conflation of the largely Hebraic concept of the "Word of the Lord," as the will of God in creative activity, with the divine *logos* of Stoic thought. This latter is the principle of rationality as both manifest in the cosmos and in human reason (also named by the Stoics as *logos*). Again we have a panentheistic notion that unites, intimately, as three facets of one integrated and interlocked activity: the divine, the human, and (nonhuman) natural. Needless to say, it is significant that for Christians this *logos* was regarded as "made flesh"[23] in the person of Jesus the Christ.

A sacramental universe

The evolutionary perspective recounts in its sweep and continuity over aeons of time how the mental and spiritual potentialities of matter have been actualized above all in the evolved complex of the human-brain-in-the-human-body. The original fluctuating quantum field, quark soup or whatever, has in some 12 or so billion years become a Mozart, a Shakespeare, a Buddha, a Jesus of Nazareth—and you and me!

Every advance of the biological, cognitive, and psychological sciences shows human beings as naturally evolved psychosomatic unities—emergent as persons. Matter has naturally manifest personal qualities—that unique combination of physical, mental, and spiritual capacities. (I use "spiritual" as meaning "relating to God in a personal way.") For the panentheist, who sees God working in, with, and under natural processes, this unique result (to date) of the evolutionary process corroborates that God is using that process as an instrument of God's purposes and as a symbol of the divine nature, that is, as the means of conveying insight into these purposes.

But in the Christian tradition, this is precisely what its sacraments do. They are valued for what God is effecting instrumentally and for what God is conveying symbolically through them. Thus, William Temple[24] came to speak of the "sacramental universe" and we can come to see nature as sacrament, or at least as sacramental. Hence, my continued need to apply the phrase of "in, with, and under," with which Luther referred to the mode of the Real Presence in the Eucharist, to the presence of God in the processes of the world.

Conclusion

With such reflections we begin to touch the hem of the finely spun robe of the Christian claim that the self-expressive, creative Word *(Logos)* that was and is God-in-the-World was incarnate in a historical person, Jesus of Nazareth. The panentheistic framework, upon which I have concentrated as encapsulating my other themes and resources, is very congruent with the affirmation that God-as-Word could be expressed in a human being evolved within the world. For panentheism implies a much tighter coupling between the transcendent God and the created order than does classical theism. The incarnation can thus be more explicitly and overtly understood as the God *in whom the world already exists* becoming manifest in the trajectory of a human being who is naturally in and of that world. In that person, the world now becomes transparent, as it were, to the God in whom it exists: the Word which was before incognito, implicit, and hidden now becomes known, explicit, and revealed. The epic of evolution has reached its apogee and consummation in God-in-a-human-person. Indeed, the preceding could be regarded as a footnote to and paraphrase of the Johannine Prologue—"In the beginning was the Word, and the Word was with God, and the Word was God. . . . All things came into being through him. . . . What has come into being *in him* was life . . . and Word was made flesh."

CHAPTER 6

Natural Being and Becoming

The Chrysalis of the Human

The "new philosophy": science

John Donne, the English divine and poet, writing in 1611, half a
century or so after Copernicus's *De Revolutionibus*, could expound his
Anatomie of the World thus:

> And new Philosophy calls all in doubt,
> The Element of fire is quite put out;
> The Sun is lost, and th'earth, and no mans wit
> Can well direct him where to looke for it.
> And freely men confesse that this world's spent,
> When in the Planets, and the Firmament
> They seeke so many new; then see that this
> Is crumbled out againe to his Atomies.[1]

Here we sense something of that anguish which was experienced
with the breakdown of the medieval perception of a divinely ordered
and hierarchically organized cosmos in which humanity had an intermediate but highly significant location as a bridge between the
earthly and the heavenly. We hear an echo of the desolation that was
felt at the loss of an awareness of organic unity—"'Tis all in pieces"
—of a divine placement for humanity, and indeed of all things living

Lecture at Georgetown University Bicentennial Conference, "Utraque Unum,"
April 1989, in *Individuality and Cooperative Action*, ed. Joseph Earley (Washington,
D.C.: Georgetown University Press, 1991). Reprinted by permission.

and nonliving, in an organic whole. The roots of this organicism, including a distinctive role for humanity, can be traced back to the Greeks and Romans and found expression too in the Christian concept of the church as the "body," the *soma*, of Christ.

But neither Scripture nor the poets could stem the tide of a rising individualism in which the self surveyed the world as subject over against object. This way of viewing the world involved an abstracting in which the entities and processes of the world were broken down into their constituent units, which were conceived as wholes in themselves, whose lawlike relations it was the task of the "new philosophy" (what we call "science") to discover.

The triumphs of this approach in mechanics and astronomy that we associate with Newton and his successors established it as the normative way of questioning the natural world. It may be depicted, somewhat oversuccinctly, as the asking of "What's there?"; then, "What are the relations between what is there?"; and, the ultimate objective, "What are the laws describing these relations?"

Reduction and realism

To implement this aim a *methodologically* reductionist approach was essential, especially when studying the complexities of matter (chemistry) and of living organisms (biology). The natural world studied by an increasingly detached "objective" observer came to be described as a world of entities involved in lawlike relations which determined the course of events in time. The staggering success of these procedures cannot be overestimated. In the course of three hundred years they have altered the whole perspective of Western humanity so that the historian Herbert Butterfield, in his introduction to some Cambridge lectures in 1948, could declare that

> Since that [scientific] revolution overturned the authority in science not only of the middle ages but of the ancient world . . . it outshines everything since the rise of Christianity and reduces the Renaissance and the Reformation to the rank of mere episodes, mere internal displacements, within the system of medieval Chris-

tendom. Since it changed the character of men's habitual mental operations even in the conduct of the nonmaterial sciences, while transforming the whole diagram of the physical universe and the very texture of human life itself, it looms so large as the real origin both of the modern world and of the modern mentality that our customary periodisation of European history has become an anachronism and an encumbrance.[2]

The success of the methodologically reductionist procedures of this natural science has continued to the present day, in spite of the revolution in our epistemology of the physics of the subatomic world that has been necessitated by the advent of quantum theory. For at the macroscopic level that is the focus of most of the sciences from chemistry to population genetics, the unpredictabilities inherent in the Heisenberg Uncertainty Principle are ironed out in the statistical certainties of the behavior of either large populations of small entities or (what often comes to the same thing) simply by the entities under examination themselves being large so that the quantum uncertainties are negligible. Predictability was expected in such macroscopic systems and, by and large, it became possible after due scientific investigation—or so it has seemed until the last few decades. For it has turned out that science, being the art of the soluble (to use Medawar's phrase), has concentrated on those phenomena most amenable to such lawlike and deterministic interpretations. What I intend to point to are some developments from within the sciences themselves that are beginning to change our perspective on the natural world in a manner that promises to allow for a coherent "placement" of human beings, with their distinctive qualities and activities, in the natural order.

Such a taking seriously of developments in the sciences involves both particular assumptions concerning their reliability—that they are not just ephemeral speculations that may pass away tomorrow—and a general conviction concerning the status of scientific affirmations. As regards the former, I can but exercise my judgment, in the confidence that fellow scientists will be quick to point out where the ice is thin! As regards the latter, I shall be adopting a realist view of scientific propositions which is not "naive," but critical and qualified. It is realist in the sense of Jarrett Leplin, namely, that

> What realists . . . share in common are the convictions that scientific change is, on balance, progressive and that science makes possible knowledge of the world beyond its accessible, empirical manifestations.[3]

Science is aiming to depict reality. It is "critical" and "qualified" in the sense that it recognizes that the language of science is necessarily both metaphorical and revisable and is shaped by continuous development in continuing linguistic communities. As Ernan McMullin has put it,

> The basic claim made by [such a critical] scientific realism . . . is that the long-term success of a scientific theory gives reason to believe that something like the entities and structure postulated by the theory actually exists.[4]

During the last two centuries, sciences such as chemistry, cell biology and geology, to name only a typical few, have progressively and continuously discovered hidden structures and processes in the natural world that account causally for observed phenomena. We can with some confidence, therefore, now examine certain general features of the scientific account of the world and assess their general import— with the ironic outcome, as we shall see, that some of these features call into question our ability to ascertain "causes" in and to predict the future of certain kinds of far from uncommon systems. So what do the sciences tell us is there in the world?

By far the greater proportion of the sciences are concerned with that region that lies between the subatomic and the cosmological, and it is in this range that a visitor to Earth from, say, some other inhabited planet would be struck by the enormous diversity of the structures and entities that exist on our planet, both living and nonliving. But, were he/she/it scientifically informed, this visitor would soon realize that this rich complexity can be seen as a diversity-in-unity wherein relatively simple laws, principles, and relationships weave, through their operation over long periods of time, the almost extravagantly rich tapestry of our world on the basis of the givenness of certain fundamental parameters (the speed of light, mass and charge of elementary particles, fundamental force interaction constants, etc.). Furthermore, the sciences of the twentieth century (let us forget our visitor now) show that these diverse organizations of matter constitute a complex hierarchy of levels, in which each successive member in a series is a "whole" constituted by an organization of "parts" preceding it in the series. Think of the sequence: atom—molecule—macromolecule—subcellular organelle—cell—multicellular organ—whole living organism—a population of organisms—an ecosystem. This is not the only kind of "hierarchy"—some exhibit relations between functions, rather than the spatial inclusion, like a set of Russian dolls, of the series just instanced. We have to take seriously this picture of the world from the natural sciences as a complex hierarchy of complexities, with each "level" usually having a corresponding science for which it is the principal focus.

Now it is a natural transition for, say, a molecular biologist who is accustomed to breaking down complex (biological) entities into units small enough to be examined by the techniques of that discipline to transform this practical, *methodological* necessity into a more general philosophical belief that (in this case) biological organisms *are* "nothing but" the bits into which they have been analyzed (in this instance, atoms and molecules). A strong case can in fact be made that there are concepts applicable to the more complex ("higher," for brevity) levels which are not logically reducible to the concepts applicable to and appropriate for the lower levels. For example, in no way can "biological information," the *concept* of conveying a biologically significant message (concepts from communication theory) be articulated in terms of the *concepts* of physics and chemistry, even though the latter can now be shown to explain how the molecular machinery (DNA, RNA, the appropriate enzymes, etc.) operates to convey information. Thus, at the initiating point of the twentieth-century revolution in biology—the discovery in 1953 of a structure of DNA that could convey biological information—we find this latter new concept being required to understand the higher-level system, the DNA operating in the milieu of an evolved, living cell or organism. For such reasons many biologists have argued against "takeover" bids by molecular biologists (such as Francis Crick's "the ultimate aim of the modern movement in biology is in fact to explain *all* biology in terms of physics and chemistry");[5] anthropologists against biologists; psychologists against neurophysiologists, etc.!

Such an *epistemological* antireductionism does have some *ontological* implications for a critical realist. The concepts, if well established as required to refer to the higher-level system in question, are, no doubt qualifiedly and reviseably, nevertheless attempting to depict realities at that higher level. Because of widely pervasive reductionist presuppositions, there has been a tendency to regard the level of atoms and molecules as alone being "real." However, there is no sense in which subatomic particles or atoms are to be graded as "more real" than, say, a bacterial cell or a human person or a social or cultural fact. Each level has to be regarded as a slice, as it were, through the totality of reality—that which we cannot avoid taking account of in our interactions with and reflections on the world. So terms such as "consciousness," "person," "society," and, in general, the languages of the humanities, ethics, the arts, and theology—to name but a few—are not prematurely to be dismissed from the vocabulary used to describe all-that-is in the world, for in these instances a strong case can be made for the distinctiveness and nonreducibility of the concepts employed. This is not, of course, to say that in using such terms we already know all we want to know about them: such a term is used to *refer* to a reality which is only fallibly depicted in metaphor and model, without our ever being able to presume we know what it is "in itself," any more than we do in the case of subatomic particles.

Process, causality, and predictability

So far we have been taking a rather static scientific view of the world, but scientists also address themselves to the question "What's going on?"—a question about the processes of the world. All observable entities in the world are subject to change, albeit on widely disparate timescales, so that all "being" is in fact in process of "becoming." As is well known, time in classical physics may be reversed without changing the applicability of the laws governing motion. But, from the discovery of geological time in the eighteenth century, through the nineteenth century's major discoveries (of biological evolution, and the second law of thermodynamics and irreversibility), to our current recognition of the universe as having a beginning in the "hot big bang," the "time" with which scientists have to deal has been regarded as having a direction. And this direction is one, moreover, that seems to run parallel to that of our own consciousness. So we seek explanations of past changes in order to understand the present and, moreover, hope to be able to predict changes with time in the entities and systems of the world.

The notions of explanation of the present by examination of the past and predictability of the future are closely interlocked with the concept of causality (which, incidentally, is not vitiated by relativity theory, for the succession of events in causal chains is independent of the choice of frame of reference). "Causality" is explicated in terms of lawlike relations, if not in single causal chains, and any system for which these have been ascertained would seem ipso facto to be predictable. This was achieved for a number of relatively simple, dynamic systems which ranged from the movements of the planets round the Sun, to the fall and motion of bodies on the Earth, including the swing of pendula subtending only low angles. It was this ability to predict that so impressed the contemporaries of Newton—and indeed their successors for three centuries, not excluding ourselves who have seen men landed on the moon, with a precision of seconds after immense journeys, by application of this same Newtonian mechanics. In spite of its applicability to only a very restricted subset of natural phenomena, the sheer intellectual power and beauty of the Newtonian scheme led to domination both of the criterion of predictability as that which characterized successful science and of a view of the world of nature as mechanistic and deterministic. As is well known, this determinism was encapsulated in the statement of Laplace in his *Essai philosophique sur les probabilités* (1776) that "an intelligence which at any given instance comprehends all the relations of the entities of this universe, . . . could state the respective positions, motions and general affects of all these entities at any given time in the past or future."

The underlying basis of this schema did, of course, undergo a devastating blow with the advent of quantum theory and the realization that certain pairs of quantities (e.g., position and velocity) characterizing the properties of subatomic particles could never both be determined with complete accuracy (the Heisenberg Uncertainty Principle). Even so, the relative uncertainties were not large for systems greater than the atomic: and the probabilities of such particles evidencing particular values of some variables could be ascertained so that the behavior of assemblies of large numbers of, say, radioactive atoms could be predicted with respect, for example, to the time it would take for half of them to break up radioactively. So in practice the advent of quantum theory did not deter scientists concerned with large numbers of constituent entities or with larger sizes than the subatomic from continuing to make deterministic assumptions and from aiming to ascertain the "laws" controlling the systems with which they were concerned.

For it was in this way that science had apparently successfully reduced the apparent "chaos" (defined, in this context, as "the state of utter confusion and disorder" [*O.E.D.*]) of the natural world to an orderly "cosmos" ("the world or universe as an ordered system; . . . a harmonious system" [*O.E.D.*]) The whole operation, it was widely thought, increasingly allowed predictability, in principle, at the—vastly preponderant—macroscopic levels beyond those where quantum uncertainties operated. Total macroscopic predictability seemed to be attainable: that, at least, was the ostensible aim. We can now see that it was only a very selected subset of natural phenomena that were actually being successfully subsumed in this program. In the last two decades we have increasingly learned to recognize the existence of systems for which it is the case that, although simple deterministic laws control the behavior of their constituents, their macroscopic behavior as systems is, in principle and provably, not predictable—or at least only partially so. And these systems are far from esoteric—they include the weather, the dripping of water from a tap (faucet), and the upward convection of a liquid heated from below! It now turns out that simple, deterministic laws operating at one level in a system can produce apparently random behavior in the system as a whole, so that order breeds its own kind of "chaos," a word that now has a special mathematical connotation, to be distinguished from the ordinary usage of the dictionary definition above. As James Crutchfield et al. have put it,

> . . . simple deterministic systems with only a few elements can generate random behavior. The randomness is fundamental; gathering more information does not make it go away. Randomness generated in this way has come to be called chaos. A seeming paradox is that chaos is deterministic, generated by fixed rules that do not themselves involve any element of chance . . . small uncertainties are amplified, so that even though the behavior is predictable in the short term, it is unpredictable in the long term.[6]

So, paradoxically, we now have to accept *both* that the uncertainties and randomness at a micro-level (e.g., radioactive atom decay, collision of molecules in a gas) can produce predictable order with respect to at least certain macroscopic properties (e.g., half-life of radioactive decay, pressure-volume-temperature relations for a gas); *and* that systems that are deterministic and rule-obeying at one level can nevertheless exhibit a randomness, mathematical "chaos," at a higher level, so that they are unpredictable in the long run. Awareness of the existence of this latter—of the existence of chaotic dynamics in, particularly, dissipative systems—constitutes a major shift in our perception of the natural world ranging over the subject matter of many scientific disciplines, for example, ecology, meteorology, physics, chemistry, biochemistry, engineering, fluid mechanics, etc. Recognition of new fundamental limits to our ability to make predictions cannot but lead to a radical revision of the widely held presumption that we live in a predictable, because deterministic, world—an assumption that has characterized much of our philosophizing (and indeed theologizing) hitherto.

Unpredictability and patterns in complex dynamical systems

Let me briefly—and it cannot but be inadequately both because of the time at my disposal and because I am not a mathematician—give you at least an impression of what these new developments are. They have in fact been a time bomb ticking away under the edifice of the deterministic/predictable paradigm of what constitutes the world-view of science from at least as long ago as 1903. The French mathematician Henri Poincaré then pointed out that, since the ability of the (essentially Newtonian) theory of dynamical systems to make predictions depended on possessing knowledge concerning not only the "dynamic" (the rule[s] for describing how a system will change with time) but also knowledge of the initial conditions of the system, such predictability was extremely sensitive to the accuracy of our knowledge of the parameters characterizing those initial conditions.

Take, for example, the results of collisions between, say, billiard balls, occurring without loss of energy. An error on the thousandth decimal place in our knowledge of the angle of impact of the first collision has the consequence, as the errors accumulate and grow, that all knowledge of the velocities and positions of the individual balls would be lost after a thousand collisions. Or, more strikingly, suppose the colliding objects were gas molecules behaving in this respect like billiard balls. It turns out that the gravitational disturbance created by the movement of one electron at the edge of our galaxy would render the molecular motion unpredictable after only fifty collisions, that is, after about 10^{-10} seconds for such an assembly, or a minute for actual billiard balls. So, *pace* Laplace, detailed predictability is rapidly lost as the uncertainty increases with time. This lack of predictability has been obscured by the fact that it is usually not such detailed knowledge we are seeking. Thus, we do not want to know where each constituent unit has gone and how fast it is moving in the case of the assembly of gas molecules (though not, I would hasten to add, in the case of the billiards player!); all we want to know are macroscopic quantities such as the pressure, volume, and temperature, and these the kinetic theory of gases satisfactorily provides. But this relatively limited success has veiled the magnitude of our actual ignorance and inability to predict in this quite classical situation involving "closed" solutions.

This unpredictability arises from the increasing divergence of errors with time which entails a dependence on initial conditions that is so exquisitely sensitive that, for such systems, we know we can never acquire the accuracy desired for prediction, especially when eventually we have to enter the range of quantum uncertainty of variables. To put it another way, two very close, but not identical, initial states of such a system at first follow a course of development very close to each other but then increasingly diverge—and this happens however close we let the initial conditions be presumed to come. So even a committed classical Newtonian would have to admit that although, for example, we can calculate accurately enough for our purposes the trajectory through space of a ball or a spaceprobe, that of a flying balloon leaking air cannot be predicted. Mathematically, the answer is that although the dynamical relations of some systems can be expressed as differential equations that have "closed" solutions— that is, they will predict future states without going through all the intermediate ones—this is not true in general. For many natural systems, the controlling equations are nonlinear, and one cannot predict the future from the initial conditions. Examples of such chaotic time dependence include turbulent flow in liquids; predator-prey patterns; stirred reactor systems that include autocatalytic relations; yearly variation in insect and other populations in nature; and the weather. The last-mentioned involves what has been called the "butterfly effect" (Edward Lorenz), whereby a butterfly disturbing the air here today could affect what weather occurs on the other side of the world in a month's time through the amplifications of errors and uncertainties cascading through a chain of complex interactions.

It is now realized that the time sequence of complex dynamical systems can take many forms. Those that have "closed" solutions to the relevant differential equations can settle down either to one particular state or oscillate, in a "limit cycle," between a sequence of states that are traversed periodically, like the pendulum of a grandfather clock. Or, consider chemical reaction systems. Normally, these are taken to come to the resting state of chemical equilibrium; but there are chemical systems, including some significant biochemical ones, that involve positive and negative feedback and, under particular initial conditions, settle down to regular oscillations in time and space with respect to the concentrations of key constituents. The same applies to populations of predators and prey. In both cases the mechanism involves particular values for the parameters that control formation/destruction of the units in question and their rate of movement through space. These are very striking phenomena to observe—startling even—and I mention them particularly because all this talk of "chaos" might obscure something that has, I think, been of particular significance for reflection on living systems—namely, the way *patterns* emerge in them.

What has transpired, as I read it, is that the mathematicians find that when they build up piecemeal, usually with the help of modern computers, the kind of solutions that are given by the nonlinear equations governing many natural complex dynamical systems, they find the following. Variation of a key controlling parameter (or parameters, in some cases) can at first lead to a single unique solution and all seems quite "normal" and well behaved from a determinist viewpoint—all is still predictable. (Their orbit in phase space exhibits a nonchaotic "attractor.") But at a certain critical value of this key parameter, the solutions bifurcate into two possible solutions, either of which may occur first as this critical point is passed, but *which* one is not predictable. As time proceeds, the system can "flip" between these two alternative allowed states and, under some circumstances, these interchanges can constitute regular oscillations. As the key parameter increases, all kinds of further complexities can occur—further successive, numerous bifurcations into 4-states, 8-states, *ad infinitum;* periods of entirely erratic behavior, mathematically "chaotic"; and again bifurcations into 3-states, then 6-states, etc. Finer and finer subdivisions numerically of the key parameters keep on repeating such sequences.

So the plots that mathematicians customarily use to depict changes in the state of a system (diagrams in "phase space") keep on revealing complexities and sequences of states at every level of magnification. In other words, they look like the pictures illustrating "fractals" with which Mandelbrot has familiarized us. Indeed, mathematically the regions in the phase space to which the systems gravitate (the states they tend to take up in ordinary language) can be proved to be fractals, having noninteger dimension and revealing more detail as they are progressively magnified. The line depicting the state of the system continuously folds back on itself, going through states close to, but never identical with, previous ones—like dough, containing a drop of dye, that is kneaded by a baker. Such systems possess what is provokingly called a "strange attractor" to distinguish it from the more ordinary "attractors," the points, lines, or regions in phase space to which nonlinear systems may move in time. This "fractal" character of the mathematical representation of these particular nonlinear systems is another way of expressing that special feature of their exquisite sensitivity to the values of their distinctive parameters which makes very close states in time lead to widely different results. In other words, small fluctuations in the system can lead to very large effects (the "butterfly effect" again) with loss of all predictive power.

In the real world most systems do not conserve energy: they are usually "dissipative" systems through which energy and matter flow, and so are also "open" in the thermodynamic sense. Such systems are typically characterized by the presence of "attractors" and they are often "strange attractors," giving rise to the kind of sequence just mentioned. At one set of values of a controlling system parameter there are nonchaotic attracting orbits, at first quite simple, representing an equilibrium or near-to-equilibrium or steady state in which typical characteristics of the system (e.g., reactant concentrations) do not vary with time. At somewhat higher values of this same system parameter, the solutions bifurcate and seemingly stable behavior occurs, patterned in space and/or time (e.g., limit cycles). This may be succeeded at still higher values of the controlling parameter by chaotic behavior. Many examples of this latter kind of system are now known: the formation of vertical hexagonal cells of convecting fluids in liquids heated from below; the transition to both irregular and periodic fluctuations in space and time of the concentrations of reactants in chemical systems that exhibit positive and negative feedback with diffusion; pattern formation in developing tissues through which both activators and inhibitors diffuse; the distribution of predators and prey in a particular territory; and so on.

Let us pause briefly to recognize how startling is this kind of behavior. To take the first example, one of the commonest in our experience: how is it that at a certain point in the heating of a liquid from below, all the molecules "decide" simultaneously to have a common upward component in their velocity and move upwards *together*? Or, how is it, in the famous Belousov-Zhabotinski reaction, that, at a given moment, all the eerie and cerous ions at a particular physical level in a test tube "decide" simultaneously to be eerie, while in the band below they have all now become cerous ions and so alternately in horizontal bands down the tube? In both cases the system properties are causally effective in determining what happens to the components, even though the properties of the system itself depend on the individual properties of the components. An example of "top-down" causation, one would have to say, or, rather, the co-presence of both "top-down" *and* "bottom-up" causation.

In the changeover to these temporal and spatial patterns of system behavior, we have examples of what Ilya Prigogine and his colleagues at Brussels have called "order through fluctuations."[7] For in these systems, at the critical points of bifurcation an arbitrary fluctuation has been amplified to such an extent that its scale becomes comparable in magnitude to that of the whole system and effectively takes it over, as it were, with a consequent transformation of the system's properties. A new regime emerges. In the last two decades, the Brussels school has studied the thermodynamics of such irreversible processes in open, dissipative systems that are a long way from equilibrium and are nonlinear (with respect to the relation between controlling fluxes and forces). Thermodynamics, one of the greatest scientific achievements of the last century and a half, comprises its famous second law to the effect that, in isolated systems undergoing natural irreversible processes, the entropy and "disorder" (appropriately defined) always increase. Ilya Prigogine and his colleagues were able to demonstrate that the emergence of new, more "ordered," or rather "organized" regimes were *required* by the thermodynamics for systems of this kind.

This work has special significance in relation to the quandary of our forbears in the nineteenth century who had to witness the apparent disjunction between, on the one hand, the second law prescribing increasing disorder, with the heat death of equilibrium as the eventual outcome of all natural processes; and, on the other hand, their increasing conviction by Darwin that living organisms had evolved by a purely natural process, with emergence of increasingly complex and organized forms. The results of the Brussels school now show how living organisms might come into existence, swimming, as it were, against the entropic stream that carries all else to disorder. For living organisms are paradigm cases of open, nonlinear dissipative systems far from equilibrium, and they depend for their existence on networks of chemical reactions (notoriously nonlinear in the required respect) which have positive and negative feedbacks and therefore are ripe to exhibit "order through fluctuations." The work of the Brussels school, together with that of Manfred Eigen and his colleagues at Göttingen[8] on the competitive kinetics of self-copying macromolecular systems, has succeeded in bridging the conceptual gulf which opened up in any consideration of the origin of life on the Earth— the gulf between nonliving and living matter. The entropic stream, we could say, flowing under constraints, generates patterned eddies near to its banks, and these have included the proto-patterns of living matter. We cannot go back and observe the first flicker of life in the primeval "soup" on the Earth's surface. But we can now see from the work of Prigogine and Eigen et al. that the probability (Eigen says "inevitability") of its emergence is built in, as it were, into the kind of natural processes we actually have; and we can also see from the recent understanding of complex dynamical systems that such systems are fecund of new unexpected regimes and patterns—unpredictable beforehand, although intelligible *post hoc*.

Our reflections on "What's going on?" in the natural world, on "natural becoming," have given us a new awareness of the significance of time. Much of physics appeared to be time-reversible, which led to much heart searching when the second law appeared to give an arrow to time. The problems this generated concerning the relation of microscopic reversibility to macroscopic irreversibility have even now not been resolved to everyone's satisfaction. Macroscopic irreversible processes now transpire to be the necessary matrix for the emergence of new patterns and regimes in the natural world, and the direction of their formation is that of increasing time (physicist's, clock time). Dissipative systems, with their particular dynamics, can generate new self-organizing, self-copying patterns in matter which then become irreversibly imprinted in the natural world so that a ratchet-like effect ensures their continuance. From the entropic stream there emerges dynamically the living with a new flexibility and open-endedness that the biologists have to learn to cope with. This, combined with our newly won awareness of the flexibility and unpredictability of complex physical systems with nonlinear dynamics, reinforces the judgment expressed in that striking description by the physicist Harold Schilling of time as the "locus of innovative change."

Our seeking of scientific answers to the questions about the world—"What's there?" and "What's going on?"—has opened up for us a new vista on the natural world, very different from that which prevailed in the mid-twentieth century. For we now have to recognize that the lawlike, deterministic dependabilities which the sciences unveil at some levels may so combine that they can, often unpredictably, lead to the emergence at other levels of systems of subtle complexities. In these systems, the behavior of the components depends not only on their well-established individual properties but also on the constraints exercised upon the parts by being incorporated into the whole—and some of these systems behave very surprisingly when viewed in the light only of the properties of the individual components. With respect to such systems, it is proper to speak not only of the already recognized "bottom-up" type of causation whereby the properties of components affect those of the whole, but also of a "top-down" causative influence of the whole system on its components. For the system as a whole has emergent properties not obvious from those of the constituents and in many cases not strictly predictable from them. The irreducible concepts needed to describe the behavior of more complex systems, especially biological ones, frequently refer to and are aimed to depict—however provisionally, reviseably, and metaphorically—new realities that exist at those levels.

All these features acquire a new intensity and significance in living organisms. In biological evolution, the appearance of increasingly complex organisms and structures has become possible, along with the continued existence of many of the forms that precede them in the biological story. Myriad combinations of different kinds of skills and sensitivities are to be found appropriate to the biological niche of each living organism—and not least in the way individuality is combined with social organization. This complexity reaches its apogee in the human-brain-in-the-human-body which is the most complex organization of matter we know. The increasing flexibility and open-endedness of natural processes is manifest in biological development as an increasing sensitivity to changes in the environment, based on complex anatomical and neurological elaboration. This is accompanied by a growth both in exploratory behavior and in the individuality of each organism as one follows the biological tree of evolution.

As nervous systems become more refined in their sensitivities, their information processing becomes more comprehensive as mobile creatures explore their environments. We then find it necessary to attribute a causative agency in their behavior for which we can only draw on analogies from our human experience—so we call it "consciousness," differing degrees of which we have to recognize in different creatures. In using such a word, we are not postulating the existence of any occult entity in the constitution of the higher mammals and primates. But we are recognizing that there is a "top-down" causative role that is played by some holistic state of the organisms, so that we cannot avoid using some such term to refer to aspects of their behavior which have parallels in our own. The understanding of the operation of the brains of the higher mammals and primates in terms of neuronal nets with the associated unpredictabilities that such non-linear dynamic systems tend to display encourages one to think that here we might well have a physical corollary of those signs of decision making such organisms display. Successive states of the system as a whole are not strictly predictable from the states of individual components: the only available "logic" is the language we have available from our knowledge of the relationships we experience in the succession of our own mental states. These living creatures to which we tend to attribute consciousness manifest a significant development of that flexibility in response which is required for survival—in a world in which not only the crossing of unrelated causal chains can cause surprises but also the unpredictabilities which we now recognize to be inherent even in their physical environment.

The *humanum*

So far so good—but there is an Achilles heel to the whole exposition up to this point. For we have failed to include a singular actualization of the potentialities inherent in the natural processes of the world—namely, *ourselves.* We have failed to ask that further question about the natural order, "*Who*'s there?" The most striking feature of the universe is one so obvious that we often overlook it—the fact that we are here to ask questions about it at all! That the regular laws of nature acting upon and in the entities and through the processes we have been considering should, in the course of time, have culminated in an entity, humanity, which can know the route by which it has arrived on the scene, is an astonishing outcome of that highly condensed nodule of matter-energy enfolded in the tight knot of space-time with which this universe began. Attempts to delineate what constitutes the *humanum*, the distinctively human, are legion, and any account attempted by me at this late stage of this paper could only be painfully inadequate. The evolutionary biologist Konrad Lorenz, concerned with evolutionary epistemology, lists[9] as "integrated into systems of a higher order" a number of cognitive functions also to be found in animals, namely: the perception of form

which then constitutes a mechanism of both abstraction and objec-
tivization; the central representation of space, especially through sight;
locomotion, following on from visual orientation; memory, storing of
information, as the learned basis of insight-controlled behavior; voluntary movement in conjunction with the feedback it produces; exploratory behavior; imitation, the basis for the learning of verbal languages; and tradition, the transmission of individually acquired
knowledge from one generation to another. Human beings have a capacity for self-awareness—we use the word "I" of ourselves in semantically peculiar ways—which is the root both of our capacity for intersubjective communication and the integrating activity which gives
each of us our sense of personhood, of being a particular *person*. As
Ian Ramsey put it:

> personality [is] to be analysed in terms of a distinctive activity, dis-
> tinctive in being owned, localized, personalized. The unity of the
> personality . . . is to be found in an integrating activity, an activity
> expressed, embodied and scientifically understood in terms of its
> genetic, biochemical, [etc.] manifestations. What we call human be-
> haviour is an expression of that effective, integrating activity which
> is peculiarly and distinctively ourselves.[10]

This "integrating activity" includes our sense of being agents in the
world, making choices for what appear to be "reasons"—even though
these are often the net sum of complex motivations other than the
rational. In such decisions we have the experience of free choice and
of not being deterministic systems controlled by the laws that the
natural sciences have hitherto supposed to tell us determine pre-
dictably all that goes on in the natural world. We have been surveying
what science is today telling us broadly about the world. It now appears that the world contains entities in a hierarchy of complexity in
which complex systems manifest genuinely new realities and that
these emerge in time by processes which, although resting on deterministic laws at one level, nevertheless can unpredictably produce in-
tricate sequences of events and new entities. Among these, the emergence of human personhood must be reckoned as both the most

unpredictable, *ante hoc,* and the most significant. The integrating activity that constitutes our personhood, both at the individual level of the sense of being an "I" and at the intersubjective level of human society and culture, is distinctive and genuinely emergent. Yet it arises out of an order of natural being and becoming that contains features the extrapolation and development of which make this emergence possible.

The cosmological anthropic principle has already in our generation served to demonstrate, whatever other conclusions might be drawn from it, that the existence of all life, including human, is closely bound up with this universe having particular values of certain, basic physical parameters that control its physical form. Were they to be even minutely different, life, and we, would not have been possible. Now, I am suggesting, our *scientific* perspective no longer, if indeed it ever did, precludes, or makes absurd, or reduces to nullity, both the naturalness *and* distinctiveness of human personhood, freedom, and consciousness. These can be recovered as genuine realities in the world—part of the data awaiting conceptual explication based on experience (and experiments, a scientist would say). For the natural world itself, in its being and becoming, has inbuilt propensities to: complexity; open-endedness; flexibility; and "top-down" causation from higher systemic levels of complexity to lower, as well as the reverse. This renders coherent and plausible the possibility of there emerging a self-consciousness as the holistic self-referring state of a brain-in-a-body that could be a free, self-aware, thinking being—in fact, a person. As Crutchfield et al. conclude:

> Even the process of intellectual progress relies on the injection of new ideas and on new ways of connecting old ideas. Innate creativity may have an underlying chaotic process that selectively amplifies small fluctuations and molds them into macroscopic coherent mental states that are experienced as thoughts. In some cases the thoughts may be decisions, or what are perceived to be the exercise of will. In this light, chaos provides a mechanism that allows for free will within a world governed by deterministic laws.[11]

It is now becoming at least intelligible, *post hoc*, as with all genuine emergents, how natural being and becoming could be the matrix of the personal—the chrysalis of the human. *That* humanity is itself now faced with the awesome recognition that it could be the "butterfly," the cumulative effects of whose unconsidered actions might be amplified, precipitating consequences for nature, its chrysalis, of an unimaginably catastrophic *or* fulfilling magnitude.

Some chrysalis—some butterfly!

A further question

But now a further question presses itself on us as we reflect on this natural world that includes ourselves. There are propensities that are manifest in the processes of natural becoming that reach their fullest expression in ourselves—the dice appear to be loaded in our direction. *Why* are the dice so loaded? Any answer to such a question of such cosmic import, any inference to the best explanation at *this* level, can resort only to concepts that aim to depict a reality which is causative in a "top-down" modality on the total complex of the world system; and operates at a level analogous to, and an extrapolation of, that most complex, open, dissipative, free, flexible level that we know—that of *human* agency.

So, the Enlightenment has run its course and our contemporary scientific perspective presses on our culture an old question in a new form:

Who loaded the dice?

CHAPTER 7

The Nature and Purpose of Man in Science and Christian Theology

It is the height of intellectual perversity to renounce, in the name of scientific objectivity, our position as the highest form of life on earth, and our own advent by a process of evolution as the most important problem of evolution.[1]

Man's chief end is to glorify God and to enjoy Him for ever![2]

Anyone attempting to shape a view of man in accord with scientific knowledge that would provide a foundation for responding to questions about human goals, purpose, and values must first be clear about two questions: (1) whether or not, in principle, any understanding of human goals, purpose, and values can be deduced directly from the scientific account of man and his origins, and (2) what kind of context this scientific account provides for any re-formation, or discovery, of these goals. The position I shall adopt is that, as regards (1), the fundamental philosophical[3] criticisms of evolutionary ethics negate any possibility of deducing values or ethical judgments from the evolutionary sequence; however, with respect to (2), I will urge

From *Zygon* 8 (1973): 373–94. First presented at a symposium on "Science and Human Purpose," organized by the Institute on Religion in an Age of Science at Rensselaerville, New York, October 25–30, 1972. Reprinted by permission.

that the actual history and sequence of development revealed by the sciences do serve to evoke questions about man and his relation to the cosmos which cannot be answered from within the realm of discourse of natural science alone. I shall set alongside this scientific perspective on man and the questions it raises an account of the understanding of man which prevails in the Judeo-Christian development and, in particular, of the implications of the distinctively Christian affirmations which concern the incarnation and the person of Jesus. Only thus can one hope to discern any mutual illumination or complementarity between these two perspectives.

An evolving cosmos

Inevitably, any account of the relevance of the scientific perspective in the assessment of possible human goals, and so forth ([2] above) will itself depend on our interpretation of the interrelationships among the various kinds of natural science. For consideration of the succession of forms of matter, at first nonliving and then living, which constitutes the evolutionary process, leads to the view that, for each particular level, science has developed concepts, methods, and forms of language appropriate to that level in the whole hierarchy of forms.[4] Moreover, the configuration and boundary conditions characteristic of a particular level of organization of matter cannot be subsumed or explained in terms of the language and concepts which have been developed for the simpler units of the level "below."[5] Thus, to regard a biological organism simply as a complicated piece of physics and chemistry would be to ignore those features of it which are characteristic of it as a total living organism interacting with its environment and which could not, in principle, be properties of the individual separated molecules that constitute it.[6] In other words, to ignore the emergent properties characteristic of each level of organization of matter when we are considering the evolutionary sequence renders us insensitive to the really significant feature of that particular emergent entity and of the processes giving rise to it.

Biological organisms, or "levels of organization of matter," as they have just been called, have the character of increasingly subtle and complex interlocking relationships with their environment (which, in the case of man, include his cultural environment ["World 3" of Popper]).[7] These relationships consist of a complex web of positive and negative feedbacks which themselves as systems exhibit new qualities and features.[8] It can therefore be misleading to isolate an admittedly "complex" organism from its even more complex interrelationships in an evolving ecosystem (and cultural system, in the case of man), an idea Emerson[9] develops in his paper with his emphasis on the teleonomy of "dynamic homeostatic systems." Thus, "levels of organization of matter" and "organism" must be taken to include these interrelationships just mentioned, though, for brevity, they will not always be explicitly mentioned in what follows.

If we are to interpret the whole cosmic development accurately, we must look at all the facts, however uncongenial to our presuppositions; and the outstanding fact of biological evolution is that, along many unknown paths, interspersed with long periods of apparent stagnation, and concomitant with many other lines of development, it has given rise to a unique creature, man, who, by purely biological criteria,[10] stands at a unique point of evolution. Whether or not one is prepared to affirm, on the basis of man's complexity of life and behavior and his adaptability, that man stands at the "highest" point is less important than the realization of the fact that new properties of matter have emerged (or its potentialities realized) when it is organized in the form of self-conscious man. In man, the stuff of the universe (we still have to call it "matter") has become conscious and self-conscious, aware of its past evolution and, more to the present point, aware that it has a future. Man is an organism who uses his intelligence and his organizing and communicating abilities to shape and choose his own environment which then reacts back on himself and so alters his future possibilities. Natural selection, in the strictly biological Darwinian sense, has ceased to be the means whereby man's future is shaped in the way it set the course of all his predecessors. Man's evolution is now dependent on man's action on himself and on his environment, and these actions depend on his choices, aims, ethics, inherited culture through education, development of creativity, and so on. Speaking epigrammatically, we could say that in man "evolution" has been superseded by "history."

Man is the first animal who, by self-consciously shaping and choosing his own environment, has stepped outside the process of evolution by natural selection operating on mutations. Huxley[11] calls this form of evolution or selection "psychosocial." The term "history" reminds us that men who are conscious of themselves now participate by means of that consciousness in shaping their own development and future.

Man has emerged from the biological evolutionary process we have delineated and, like other emergent forms, displays new characteristics which can only be described by their appropriate languages and concepts and which necessitate modes of inquiry and elaboration peculiar to themselves. Particularly significant, because they are uniquely human, are those activities for which man has developed modes of discourse which allow his diverse experiences to be mutually shared. The fact that we use such a variety of special modes of discourse about man is itself witness to the special character of the human animal who has emerged from the evolutionary process; and that this is as much an observable fact about the development of the cosmos as the need to use, say, the language of chemistry for molecules, of physiology for the interrelation between organs, of ethology for animal behavior, and so on.

Man has the feature of being conscious of his environment. Higher animals probably also have some form of consciousness but at its best it seems to be only a fragmentary and reduced version of man's, fascinating as are the attempts to determine its content. But man is also self-conscious, he knows that he knows; he uses the word "I" of himself in ways which are, in many respects, semantically peculiar. This affirmation of the reality of conscious and self-conscious activities is not dependent on any particular philosophy of the relation of an entity called "mind" to one called "body." All I am concerned with here is that there are human activities and experiences which demand this special language, and that to which these languages refer is uniquely and characteristically human. These include, *inter alia*, the activities referred to when we say men are capable of rational action, of making moral choices, of choosing among beliefs, of forming personal affections; that men are "persons" in the sense that each is a bearer of rights, is unique, and is someone with whom we can imagine ourselves changing places; that men explore their environment and formulate concepts to organize what they find; that they are unique users of language and of its symbols; that they are creative and worship and pray; and that they have consciously to come to terms with the anticipation of their own individual death (they alone of all living creatures bury their dead with rites of passage). All this, according to the scientific evidence, is the outcome of the continuous evolution of matter according to natural laws. What is the meaning of, what are the appropriate terms in which to describe, such a universe?

The perspective which science has provided of the inorganic and biological worlds, culminating in man, poses us this question but it is not able to answer it within its own terms. For the techniques and languages scientists have fashioned to analyze and make coherent their investigations of the various levels of the organization of matter have not been contrived to answer questions about the scope and direction of the whole process which these investigations unravel. However, the perspective now afforded by the sciences has served to clarify to what sort of universe any question and answer about its meaning is referring. This perspective serves as an arrow, pointing the direction of the road ahead without specifying what we shall find along that unexplored way. The head of the arrow, if we may continue the metaphor, is the fact of the presence of man in the universe and all that he is and does, so briefly and inadequately hinted at above. The shaft is the evolutionary process which has led to him, and the metaphor is meant to suggest that we can only find the direction to which our answers to questions about the meaning of the whole cosmic process should be referred by looking at what his emergence from that process implies about its nature and about the matter, the world-stuff, which is undergoing these successive transformations. The clue to the significance and meaning of the whole cosmic process is more likely to be found in that in which it has culminated, namely, man, than in any of the previous intermediate levels, fascinating and beautiful though many of them are. What "value" these other forms have "in themselves" is a question on which we might be exercised, but, meanwhile, we cannot avoid the fact of man in the universe. It is unscientific and unobjective to ignore and renounce the position of man as the product of the evolutionary process, with all that man is and does, for man alone transcends the process since he alone is aware of the ladder by which he has climbed.

At this point we meet the discontinuity in our thinking which meets us in our experience, the discontinuity between objects, including other people, and the "I" who experiences and knows. To be true to the actual situation, we have no other resources to describe the human experience except to employ modes of discourse which men have fashioned and developed to describe their experiences—the languages which use "I," languages of personal relationship, of art, poetry, literature, philosophy, religion, and theology. In availing ourselves of the experience of the human condition we are not thereby betraying the scientific method in the interest of an unjustifiable mysticism. We are simply doing what science has always done, namely, recognizing that each level within the hierarchy of the organized forms of matter has language and methods of inquiry appropriate to it. There could be nothing more unscientific and unobjective than to refuse to look at all the facts because of mechanistic or "materialist" presuppositions of an old-fashioned kind. I suggest that our consideration of the continuity of the whole cosmic process now sharpens to the point where we can no longer avoid the question of the significance of a cosmic process which has culminated in man. What we can say about the nature of man in view of his evolutionary origin must now be further examined.

Man in the perspective of evolution

Man as a psychosomatic unity: a person

The continuity of the processes of inorganic and biological evolution, their subjection to "natural laws," and their culmination in the emergence of man reveal man as a part of the material structure of the world. A man, like any other observable structure, may be subdivided into brain, organs, cells, macromolecules, small molecules, atoms, and so on. Yet, in evolution, at each new level of organization of matter, there emerge new features, properties, and activities of the new wholes which did not appear in the constituent parts. In a man, new properties and activities of matter emerge which cannot be subsumed or described in terms of the languages and concepts used for the forms preceding him. So, when we view man in his evolutionary context, it is necessary to affirm both his "physical" nature and all that which is specific and unique to him as a man, even if rudimentary forms of, for example, his intelligence are to be discerned in other higher mammals, especially the primates. I have referred to some of the distinctive activities of men, and, for brevity, I will include all of these—his intelligence, curiosity, adaptability, creativity, use of language, ability to form personal relationships, consciousness and self-consciousness, openness to God (his "spirit"), ability to transcend in thought his environment and survey it as subject, his use of "I"—in the adjective "mental." The adjective is applied to activities with the deliberate intention of avoiding any postulate of a distinct entity called the "mind" which performs these activities. These mental activities are activities which emerge distinctively and characteristically in matter organized at the level we call man. They can be attributed only to the whole man who includes the hierarchy of levels of structure of matter which we have referred to above. Thus both the physical and mental activities are activities of the same entity which might properly then be given a special name— "person" seems the most appropriate.

This way of describing man does justice to man's evolutionary origins out of the matter of the world, on which he is still dependent for life, and to the truly emergent mental activities which characterize man specifically. Man has been said to be a psychosomatic unity. Perhaps one would rather say he is one person possessing both physical and mental attributes, each explicated by appropriate sets of predicates. This way of putting it avoids the posing of misleading questions such as "At what point in the evolutionary scale, or in the growth of an embryo, does mind or 'soul' enter the biological world?" and "How can a physical entity possess a nonmaterial 'mind'?" For the activities and attributes described as mental are now regarded as one, albeit the most recent and significant, in a whole series which have emerged at different stages in the cosmic evolution. Indeed, the close relation between mental activities and physical organization of men's bodies and brains has been supported by every advance in psychology, psychiatry, medicine, biology, and physiology.

It is worth emphasizing again that to ascribe both physical and mental attributes to a single entity, a person, or to affirm, as I have tended to do with reference to the evolutionary context, that mental activities are properties of matter organized in the way we call human brains in human bodies, is not to mean that mental processes are *caused* by purely physical, physiological events and that they are "nothing but" such events. The emergent mental attributes are attributes of the new whole (man's-brain-in-man's-body), which requires specific and appropriate concepts and language ("laws" even) to describe the interrelatedness of its activities. These concepts and languages cannot in principle be broken down into those applicable to the component units of structure and activity, in this case anatomical, physiological, and biochemical (cf. the discussion in Polanyi's analysis[12] of the relation of the engineering language appropriate to engines vis-à-vis the physics of an engine's component pistons, etc.).

This way of talking about man has a significant consequence concerning his possible future evolution. Whatever form such evolution might take, it is clear that it must be of such a kind that it transcends, or incorporates into a more comprehensive diversity-in-unity, *both* the physical and mental activities which constitute man as he has emerged from biological evolution.

The introduction of the entity of "person" as that of which both physical and mental attributes may be predicated is consistent with our individual sense of being one person, but it is not, on this account, meant to deny the very real and familiar dichotomy in our experience. The mental event of willing to raise one's arms seems to occur in a quite different milieu from the actual movement of muscle and bone then set in motion after the ionic pulses have passed through brain and nerves. Although it is still *our* consciousness which undergoes this mental experience and *our* arm which rises, nevertheless the dichotomy remains baffling and part of the data of both science and philosophy. The interrelationship of the two sets continues to be vigorously debated. Man remains a diversity-in-unity and neither the diversity nor the unity can be properly denied as being characteristics of man, who, standing at the summit of the evolutionary process, himself reflects on the ladder by which he has climbed out of insentient matter.

Man evolving: an unfulfilled paradox

This dichotomy in the human experience and the resulting tension and sense of incompleteness, tragedy even, to which it gives rise at first appear to be a situation specific to man. The nature of the incompleteness is indeed unique to man, but further reflection on the character of the evolutionary process and the conditions of emergence of new forms suggest that each stage of evolution represents not only a new attainment but also a more acute inadequacy of realization of potentialities. Each level at every temporal stage in evolution expresses a potentiality, until then unrealized, of the preceding forms of organization of matter. *Post hoc*, we can see that each level was, at that point, also an inadequate realization of the potentialities of matter which still had the possibilities of taking on many new forms, and the cosmic development shows that eventually it did so. Thus, each stage had a "value" in so far as it represented a new level of organization of matter and so made new developments possible, but it also represented hitherto undeveloped possibilities whose range had been brought into sharper definition by the fact of that stage having been reached at all. But, as we pointed out above, man is the first organism to be conscious of the possibilities and potentialities which are open to him and aware of his freedom to choose by altering both himself and his environment. The evolution of man now depends on his freely willed conscious response to the challenge of what he might become. In man, the evolutionary process has given rise to a creature conscious of where he has come from and capable of seeing where he might go—and capable of accepting or refusing the challenge. Man is challenged by an immense variety of calls—to creative activity, to loving actions, to duty, to social justice—but in all these respects the best and wisest of men recognize their own failure and that of their societies. Man is the only creature who, aware of the pinnacle on which he stands, is also tragically aware of the possibility of his not fulfilling his own potentialities.

We have the paradox of man as the summit of the cosmic development so far, for his mental activities transcend all, yet at the same time he is tragically aware of his personal and social shortcomings and subject to the tension between the awareness of the finitude of his individual life and the infinity of his longings. He is aware both of that from which he has evolved and of his tendency always to fall short of the full realization of his own individual and corporate potentialities. Thus the nonrealization of the potentialities inherent in the universe has, in man, become the responsibility of that creature himself. This nonrealization, in man, is a result of his own decisions or lack of them and is quite different from the situation of unrealized potentiality in the molecule or cell which is eventually expressed in, *inter alia,* living organisms. Man constitutes a break in the evolutionary process which had hitherto depended on the continuous operation of natural "laws." For man appears to himself to have a free will allowing him to make choices and is free to fail to respond to the challenge presented to him. The Genesis story, which depicts evil as entering the universe with man when he acquires the "knowledge of good and evil," is a shrewder diagnosis of the human condition than is usually allowed.

Man's dilemma is real, for how is he to know which way to go, to which challenge he should respond, what his real potentialities might be? What does it involve to be a man, to be fully a person? What should constitute personalness in its richest manifestation? What should a man—what should men—strive to become? Moreover, given that he knows the answers to these questions, how is a man— how are men—going to overcome their inherent limitations and deficiencies freely to will to move in the sought-after direction? For any such change of direction cannot be imposed if it is to be effective in his "inner," mental life. The evolutionary sequence clearly shows that the answers to these questions are vital for man and his future but, at the same time, provides nothing from within the process itself which will tell us what men *ought to become,* how they should achieve their ends in a way which recognizes their personalness, that psychosomatic unity which differentiates them from the rest of the cosmos.

Man in the perspective of theology

It is appropriate at this point to attempt to summarize some features in the Christian account of man which have significance in the light of the scientific perspective.

The biblical psychosomatic view of man and of his "sin"

The early Christian and especially the New Testament understanding of man is rooted in its Hebraic background, though this was sometimes overlaid by later Hellenistic influences. For the Hellenistic distinctions between flesh and spirit, between body and soul, and indeed those between form and matter, and between the one and the many, were never made by the Israelites.[13] In particular, the concept of an immaterial entity, the soul, imprisoned in a material frame, the body, is entirely contrary to their whole way of thinking. "The Hebrew idea of personality is an animated body, and not an incarnated soul," H. Wheeler Robinson[14] affirmed over forty years ago in a famous epigram, and, more recently, Eichrodt[15] described this view as, "Man does not *have* a body and a soul, he *is* both of them at once."

This is not to say that, within this view of man as a psychosomatic unity, there was no awareness of the distinctive character of his "inner" conscious life as contrasted with physical processes. For there is a word for the living body of a man, namely, *basar,* the "flesh," which has a distinct range of usage from and can occur in a certain opposition to other words, such as *ruach* ("vitality"), *nephesh* ("person" or "living being"), and *leb* ("heart"), which have a closer connection with man's inner, psychic life. For the principal feature of Hebrew anthropology, being the result of the direct experience of the living encounter between man and man, is to see man primarily as a unity with various differentiating organs and functions in any of which the person in his totality can express himself and be apprehended. Man is a unity and does not subdivide into immortal and mortal parts. Indeed, to the Hebrews, personal individuality was constituted not by the boundary of a man's body but by the indivisible responsibility of each man to God and so by the uniqueness of the divine call to him—and certainly not by his "flesh" *(basar)* as such. Thus, J. A. Baker stresses both the "earthiness" and the personal aspects of the Hebrew view of man:

> Man is formed of matter. His every thought, feeling, action, his most transcendental conceptions, have their origin in, and are made possible by, the same basic particles as those from which the whole cosmos is built . . . but the paradox of man's being is that, though he is thus physical through and through, he is also something much more—a nonphysical reality, a person. This truth is bound up with his self-awareness, which is of such a kind that he can address himself as "thou," and speak of his own personhood as if it were another being, someone whom he can judge, exhort, comfort.[16]

Although it is not easy to develop any intellectually precise anthropology from the Hebrew literature, in this tradition of over a thousand years, a common theme—that of man as a psychosomatic unity—clearly emerges through all its variations. This Hebraic background is the key to understanding the New Testament writers, especially Paul's use of *sarx* ("flesh"), *soma* ("body"), *kardia* ("heart"), *nous* ("mind"), *pneuma* ("spirit"), and *psyche* ("soul"). The relationships of these terms both to each other and to the Hebrew terms is a highly complex web which is not rendered less easy by variations of usage and meaning.[17] The consensus of scholarship indicates a view of man in the New Testament very much like that of the Old with respect to its understanding of man as a psychosomatic unity, a personality whose outward expression is his body and whose center is in heart, mind, and spirit. (The contrast in some Pauline passages of *sarx* ["flesh"] and *pneuma* ["spirit"] is not, as is commonly believed, that of matter and body, conceived as evil, as against disembodied and eternal soul, conceived as good.)

This biblical view of man, and the Christian teaching which stemmed from it, is thoroughly realistic in its recognition of man's paradoxical character. It sees the height of his possibilities and his destiny, with their occasional and intermittent realization, conjoined to a degradation and wretchedness which can engender only cynicism and a sense of tragedy: it sees his eternal longings and his individual mortality. Man is, like all other beings, regarded by the biblical writers as existing by the will of God who sustains the cosmos in being. He is furthermore regarded, especially by the "priestly" writer of Genesis, as created in the "image" and "likeness" of God in the sense that: "[On man] personhood is bestowed as the definitive characteristic of his nature. He has a share in the personhood of God; and as a being capable of self-awareness and self-determination he is open to the divine address and capable of responsible conduct."[18] He is, however, regarded as responding only incompletely to, indeed rebelling against, the call of God to his high destiny and potentialities in relation to himself and his dominance of the earth. This failure to become what God intends him to be is freely willed by man and is, in essence, the setting by man of himself in the center of his individual and social life. This constitutes "sin," the breakdown of relationship between God and men or, rather, the nonattainment of that harmonious relation with God, in which God wishes man freely to participate. Only a self-conscious being could freely thwart the divine purposes. Thus "sin" and "evil" became possible, and indeed actual, with man. Within this framework of biblical ideas, how were men to know what they should do and become? Even if they did know, how were they to be enabled freely to choose what God required, that is, to act in accordance with his creative purpose both for men and for their environment? Men need to know which direction they should take and how to take it. The biblical authors thought they themselves had had, over the centuries, sufficient signposts from God himself concerning the direction their lives should take and, speaking from this stance, the early church affirmed that this historical revelation had culminated in a particular person, Jesus of Nazareth. I cannot here indicate why I think the early church was basically right, allowing for all the particular myopia of the times,[19] for we must pass on to summarizing what is of ultimate significance in what they, and their successors in the Christian community, believed had happened in and with the coming of a particular man, Jesus, into history.

The Christian understanding of man in the light of Jesus the Christ

The early Christians, utterly monotheistic Jews though they were, found themselves driven to the conclusion that, in Jesus of Nazareth, God had in some sense revealed himself and had acted in a way which had universal significance for man, a significance which was also a revelation of man in the sense of revealing the full possibilities of human nature, hitherto unrealized and unattained. This conviction was expressed at first in a variety of terminology and titles primarily of Hebraic origin (e.g., Son of Man, Messiah [or Christ], kingdom of God, Son of God), to be followed later by terms of a more Hellenistic origin (e.g., Lord, Word [*Logos*], second "Person" of the triune God). These and other terms in which the early Christians expressed the relation between Jesus and God and the meaning and nature of what Jesus did cannot be understood by twentieth-century man without much exploration of the thought of the first and immediately succeeding centuries AD. Moreover, the significance attributed to Jesus' coming finds its context in the Christian understanding of God's relations to the world. Briefly, this is that the world is dependent upon God for its existence and continues to exist only because of his continuing to will it so. God is not dependent on the world and is other than it, but creation, which is a continuous action of his will, has for God a significance analogous to the personal fulfillment of a human creator. Although other than the world, and thus transcendent, God holds the world in being by his will in a way which is further indicative of the nature of God's being, that is, is indicative of the least imprecise ways of thinking of him. The world is created by God, in the timeless sense of the word "create" which has been used above; but time is created with the world, and, in this dimension, the world is seen to be in process of development, of evolution, in which new forms of its basic stuff emerge continuously, creatively but according to regularities of relationship, which we call the "laws of nature," of the stuff of the world. Through this knowledge of the world, our understanding of God is extended by attributing immanence in the world to him in the sense that it is held in being by his will and that this sustaining involves a continuous process of change. God in his transcendent aspect limits himself by bringing into existence a created order which has derived being and a degree of autonomy under its own law of development. To this extent, creation is an act of love, and this is a true description of God's being since it represents, by analogy, a center of personalness which is self-limiting on behalf of another. This "Love that moves the sun and the other stars"[20] eventually brings into existence, into the world he has created, through the matter he had endowed with this potentiality, a creature, man, who partakes sufficiently of God's own personalness that he may be described as the "image of God." Yet man emerging from, and as a new pattern within, the stuff of the universe is incomplete and as yet unfulfilled, and, although through his emergent personalness he now apprehends something of God's being and is aware both of himself and his environment, he has a propensity to repudiate that cooperation with God wherein his potentialities might be fulfilled and takes courses of his own devising. In all of these, man puts himself at the center of his universe: this constitutes his "sin" in the traditional language. He has not yet fully incarnated all the possibilities which God as Creator intends for his destiny. His relationship with God is thereby ruptured or, rather, never becomes what God wills it should be.

The basic and specifically Christian affirmation is rooted in history. It claims that, in a particular time and place in history, the God who had all along been immanent implicitly in the whole temporal creative process then expressed himself personally in and through a particular man, Jesus of Nazareth, who, humanly speaking, was completely open to God. The effort to describe with least inaccuracy the nature of that one person who was, to the men who understood their experiences of him, God-and-man, God-made-man, the divine-Word-made-flesh, constituted in the long run a major transition in the way men thought of nature, of God, and, in particular, and significantly in the present context, of man.

In Jesus, men came to see what all men might become: the full potentialities of human nature were, it was thought, shown in their essentials in Jesus. The humanity of Jesus stands out starkly in the text of the Gospels without any attempt at reduction alongside those actions, claims, and events which constituted the experience which impelled his monotheistic followers to acknowledge him also as God-in-man. His humanity was seen to represent the ultimate in the fulfillment of human life by virtue of his utter self-offering love to man and obedience to God which was vindicated by his resurrection. It was the survival of no ghost, of no eternal soul released from a corrupt body, that turned upside down the lives of his disciples, but the transformation of a complete human personality, which had been self-offered to the point of a shameful death, into a new mode of existence, able to express himself to the disciples. This act of God was seen first as a vindication of the perfection of Jesus' self-offered humanity and also formed the basis of the earliest preaching: "Jesus is Lord," the victor over all the powers and features of the world apparently hostile to men. It also then formed the basis of the Christian hope of the destiny of all men, who are now enabled to partake and participate in that union with God which is uniquely that of Jesus (the) Christ.[21] Historically, the ascension, the last of the definitive appearances of the risen Christ to his disciples, clearly carried with it a sense that the whole being of Jesus is now at the center of the life of God (whatever external manifestations accompanied that event as a matter of history). This life of Jesus, "ascended" to God, includes his human life and so, especially in the Eastern church, this ultimate event in the history of Jesus was seen as the sign that the destiny of a transformed humanity is to live within the presence of God. Thus, by virtue of what that human life was and what it became, it was clear that a new view of man and of his potentialities was necessitated by the "things about Jesus," and that the realization of these potentialities had been the purpose, in God's sight, of the incarnation itself and of the life of the historical Jesus. "Because of his measureless love," wrote Irenaeus in the second century, "he became what we are in order to enable us to become what he is."[22] For Paul, in the perfected human nature of Jesus the Christ, God achieves his purpose and Jesus is the new beginning of a fulfilled humanity which is, or is at least becoming, what God intends—so Jesus is a "second Adam," a second progenitor of a mankind realizing its potentialities. "If any man is in Christ, there is a new creation."[23] "The defaced image of the Creator is being renewed: the old humanity is being put off and the new humanity is being made, in which the former distinctions of race, religion, culture and class are being done away."[24] The love of God, which was expressed in creation and in his incarnation, acts in the individual man to fulfill his human nature if that individual will identify himself with Christ and follow his way of life. Thus "grace," as this loving action is called, does not destroy but completes human nature.

The person of Jesus

These transformations of the understanding of nature, God, and man, which reflection on the data of Jesus' life, death, resurrection, and ascension engendered, were only elucidated along with a long development of thought in the church which culminated in the Definition of the Council of Chalcedon (AD 451). Chalcedon concentrated on the relation of the human and divine natures and the center of unity of Jesus Christ, and its conclusions may be summarized as "one person in two natures." Expressed so tersely, the words are mere ciphers for many complexes of ideas. As the valuable treatment of D. E. Jenkins puts it:

Jesus Christ is all that is involved in being man including the possibility of analytical reduction to whatever are the units of the stuff of the universe. . . . But the Chalcedonian Definition is a symbol of the discovery and assertion that in the purposes of the transcendent and independent God, and by the power of this God, a union has been achieved between that evolutionary product of cosmic dust which is a human being and that transcendent and wholly other purposeful personalness who is God. Transcendent and independent personalness is at one with derived, dependent and evolved personality whose whole basis can be reduced to that impersonal materiality out of which it has developed and on which it depends. And the result is the personal union of God and man who is himself the person, Jesus Christ. In this there is discovered the personal fulfilment both of God and of man. We have the fulfilment of the personalness of God because God has achieved the expression of his purpose of love.[25]

This understanding of the significance of Jesus Christ which the Christian community arrived at with so much difficulty saw in him the hope of a new transformation of all men. To consider how this transformation can occur in the individual man would take us deep into a discussion[26] of how the apparently past historical fact of Jesus can be made effective here and now in drawing man into a new and fuller relationship with his Creator and so to an undreamt-of realization of his human, and so utterly personal, potentialities. The claim— "I have come that men may have life, and may have it in all its fulness"[27]—has the awkward quality of authenticating itself only as the consequence of a prior act of willing commitment in which a man identifies himself with Jesus Christ at least to the extent of attempting to follow his way. Here, theology merges into the life of religion and existential commitment.

Christ and evolution

The principal features both of the scientific perspective on man in the cosmos and of the Christian understanding of man and of Jesus have been outlined, and they must now be brought into juxtaposition. Evolution takes on a new meaning and dimension if the "things concerning Jesus" have the significance Christians claim, and he and the community he engendered have a new relevance for modern man if the scientific story is taken seriously enough to provide a new factual and conceptual framework for viewing man and the cosmos.

The spectrum of the sciences demonstrates that man is clearly continuous with the material universe out of which he has evolved. It is therefore a fact, and a highly significant one, that the matter of the universe has been evolving into persons, a word designating *all* that it means to be human. We have seen, moreover, that future transitions in human life depend on man's choices in a way which never arose with his biological predecessors so that human evolution is now "psychosocial." But man is an unfulfilled paradox consequent on his being a person rooted in the materiality of the cosmos and tragically unable, and aware of this inability, to effect in any convincing way any transformation of himself which would fulfill his potentialities.

Now, in the light of Jesus Christ and the significance attributed to him on account of the data concerning him, it can be affirmed that the derived and evolved personalness[28] of man was in Jesus Christ united with that transcendent personalness who is the ground of all being and that this union is that consummation of human personality for which man yearns both individually and corporately. It is a consummation in which men are invited to participate by identifying themselves with Jesus the Christ and by committing themselves to that to which *his* life was committed. The scientific enterprise leads one to a perspective of the cosmos in which personalness in man is the summit of the evolutionary processes which the matter of the cosmos has undergone. The "things concerning Jesus" led *their* witnesses and successors inexorably to the conclusion that, in his person, man was transformed so that he was or, rather, became a "new creation" drawn up into the very life of God himself, the originator and sustainer of the creative processes of the cosmos. The results of the scientific and theological enterprises here complement and mutually fulfill each other so that some hybrid terminology which has reference to both almost seems called for. Thus one might affirm that in

Christ a "trans-mutation" (rather than the "mutation" of biology) of human life was effected at a new depth of the personality and that men who participate in, or acquire, this new depth of life in Christ are becoming a new sort of human being (dare we say "species"?). Such terms, although having the virtue of emphasizing the analogy with the earlier biological transitions, could be misleading if they led one to ignore the special character of the "trans-mutation" effected in Jesus Christ. For this new realization of human potentialities occurs not in man's DNA but within his total personality. It is a function of the *whole* organism of the person, including his self-conscious and mental life. The Christian transformation, once accepted as a reality through reflection on the historical evidence, can properly be viewed as a new phase of that cosmic development which is disclosed by science and which had hitherto culminated in man, the unfulfilled person and paradox. The results of the two enterprises do, it seems to me, fit together with immense mutual illumination of each.

Just as the "psychosocial" transformation of man which biology now points to as the only possible one must inevitably be that of a population of individuals to be effective, so the Christian faith has always viewed the response of the individual man to the divine challenge in Christ as the response of a man-in-relation-to-man. For the fact and form of the challenge are regarded as mediated to the individual by a historical community which was initiated by Jesus Christ and is the primary witness to him. The New Testament employs a number of metaphors to describe what this human community, the Church, might effectively come to be, for example, the "body of Christ," the "people of God." Like the individual, the community of Christians has not reached its perfection *in via,* it is not yet the "kingdom of God" or the "new Jerusalem," any more than any individual Christian has attained any perfection that he can be aware of. It is, in the Christian belief, a community moving, like the individual, in the direction God intends and cooperating with his creative purposes. So the response to the challenge which is Jesus the Christ heightens the awareness of the individual, and of the Christian community into which he is incorporated, of his and their lack of fulfillment of God's purpose; and it restores that lost experience of hope, to which I have already referred. For if Jesus Christ has the significance which I have tersely summarized in the preceding section, namely, that in him there was a union of the two natures of God and of man in one "Person" and that God continues to effect, in those open to this initiative, a reconciliation between God and man, thereby transforming man, then men may know that the cosmic process has a direction which is concordant with the realization of their own personal and corporate potentialities—and so of their own aspirations. The historical fact which is Jesus Christ is, when assessed fully, the ground for hope that the cosmic development has not, after all, come to an impasse in man, the unfulfilled paradox; that it is not after all "played out." For if Jesus Christ is both truly God-made-man and the only proper Man, then, in him, God opened to men the possibility of a new kind of existence. This new kind of life is both exemplified in him and made available to us through him and his continued action through the community he founded.

The understanding of Jesus as God Incarnate also acquires a new relevance when he is seen as the consummation of a process of cosmic evolution which occurred as an expression of God's creative will. The meaning of the incarnation of God in the man Jesus and the realization of all that men might be, all that God intended men should be, in the person of Jesus of Nazareth are illuminated in various ways by the scientific account of man's origins. For God-becoming-man, the incarnation, as an event in human history, can now be seen as the consummation of that evolutionary process in which the rise of man succeeded the general biological sequence. The sequence observed and inferred scientifically implies for Christians that both the processes of cosmic evolution and the incarnation are alike expressions of the creative, self-limiting love of God. The expression of the being of God in Christ was particular, and explicit, whereas in the processes of creation it was general, and implicit, but it was the same God who was operative in both. Both involved self-limitation on behalf of an end in which, if judgment is based on its culmination in the risen and ascended Christ and God's dwelling in man as "Holy Spirit," derived and transcendent personalness enter into a new diversity-in-unity. Since God willed it so, we must presume that, in some sense, this consummation intensifies and enhances the inner life of God whose only name is Love.

These reflections have led us to a point at which we are now impelled to take seriously "God the Holy Spirit" as the vital, processive mode of God's being who links God acting personally in Christ, there and then in history, with God acting personally in us here and now, and, indeed, throughout created time and space. For God as Holy Spirit represents that mode of God's being who is immanent in creation and who re-creates the inner life of man according to the pattern of Christ. In Christian thinking, it is he who directs men to Christ and nurtures in men, through prayer, sacrament, and obedience, the "new creation" of man in Christ. He was also, according to the New Testament,[29] operative in the crucial events of Jesus' life, and Paul describes the Holy Spirit as the agent of the resurrection and the source of Christian love.[30] In the light of the scientific perspective, a wider significance can now be discerned in the distinctive activity of God as Holy Spirit. For his action and presence in the incarnate life, just described, cannot be discontinuous with this activity in the earlier stages of evolution culminating in man.

Cannot we therefore now think of God the Holy Spirit as the personal mode of God's being who is immanent in the created world in an action which culminates in Christ and in what he can effect through Christ in Christian man, but who is also active at all the preceding levels? God the Holy Spirit would then be conceived of as the power and presence of God as he fulfills the potentialities of the world-stuff ("matter") at each level and stage of the cosmic process through the laws it obeys. At every level the created order reflects in its own measure something of the quality of deity: "From atom and molecule to mammal and man, each by its appropriate order and function expressed the design inherent in it, and contributes, so far as it can by failure or success, to the fulfillment of the common purpose."[31]

God as Holy Spirit can therefore be regarded as God dynamically active in eliciting the realization of the potentialities of the created order: in particular, in life; more particularly, in the human "spirit" (which I take to mean all that is distinctive of the human person, both individual and corporate, especially in man's openness to the address of God);[32] and, supremely, in the person of Jesus the Christ. This approach is very much in accord with that of Philip Hefner.[33] There are parallels between our two lines of thought, in spite of different terminologies. All I would wish to add, in the light of his presentation, is the following.

Here the incarnation has been expounded as the culmination and chief exemplification of the creative, dynamic activity of God in the cosmic development of the "world-stuff," and the "things about Jesus" have been regarded as showing him as the expressed, intelligible answer (or "Word," to evoke the right nuances) by God to the question "What should man become?" This exposition is very close to that of Hefner who, at first following other twentieth-century theologians, speaks of God as Holy Spirit as manifest as the ecstatic self-transcendence of life in its total "environment" (Worlds 1, 2, and 3 of Popper),[34] but who then goes on very interestingly to develop this understanding in terms of the category of the self-definition of life. The "self" in this term is demonstrably self-conscious man, both individual and corporate, and "self-definition" Hefner describes as a process both of understanding who man is and for what end he exists, and of acting upon this understanding so as to actualize it concretely. I would like to suggest that the self which man seeks to define for himself, and so to become, both in understanding and in action, *is* that perfected humanity of Jesus the Christ which God as Holy Spirit called into being in Jesus in history and now re-creates dynamically in those who are prepared to follow the way of self-offering which Jesus supremely exemplified. One recalls Paul's yearning[35] that the Galatians should "take the shape of Christ," which seems to me to be an excellent Christian expression of Hefner's idea of self-definition, which he so carefully, and rightly, tries to root in our contemporary personal, group, and human realities. Clearly, there is a fruitful convergence between our respective lines of thought on the classical Christian doctrines of the Holy Spirit, in his case, and, in mine, that of the incarnation.

The exposition elaborated in this paper has, I think, important implications, developed elsewhere, for the resuscitation of a humanism which is genuinely Christian[36] and for the meaning men might see in the ordinary, everyday work of the modern technological world.[37] However, space allows only one implication to be developed—and that in the context of hope.

Man's hope

One of the cardinal lost virtues of our age is that of hope, and this loss infects every aspect of our cultural and social life. The angst and despair, or the wild search for substitute ends which dominates the affluent West, are sometimes attributed by Christians to a loss of hope of personal "salvation," conceived as the restoration of the eternal "soul" of a man to the presence of God. But "salvation" has always meant the "making whole" of the whole man, and we have already seen that the Hebraic-Christian view of man allowed no Manichaean dichotomy of an evil body from a spiritual, potentially good, soul. Thus, even on a Christian basis, men must center their hope on this world in the sense that the arena of their hoping and surviving must be the world they know. Any end to be achieved in a sacramental universe must be in and through the medium of the world we are actually in.

In spite of the optimism of scientific and technological endeavor in the short run, in the long term the predictions of science afford no grounds of hope or optimism for man. For example, Hoyle states that "5,000 million years hence the oceans will boil because the sun will then have become too hot. No life as we understand it will then survive on the Earth."[38] There is only a finite amount of hydrogen in the Sun to change into helium and so to be a radiant energy source for the Earth, and so the days of all life, including human, on the Earth are numbered.

This judgment of the actual future of life on the Earth as a planet is more soundly based than the extrapolations based on the second law of thermodynamics. This law, which in one of its forms affirms that entropy in an *isolated* system always increases with time, has been applied by some to the universe as a whole. There is no knowing if this application is justified, and any conclusions on this basis about the universe as a whole are unwarranted. The above prediction of the ultimate extinction of all life, including man's, on the planet Earth is based on observations of changes which occur in observable planetary systems in galaxies and can be taken as almost certain on this basis, without asserting what will happen to the whole universe.

Given this scientific background, the questions which are the concern of that aspect of Christian thinking called "eschatology" (the doctrine of the "last things") may seem less preposterous than hitherto. "What is the final destiny of mankind in general?" is the question to which Christian teaching on the "last things" has directed itself, prompted by the attempts made in the official Hebraic-Christian literature and in the less reputable apocalyptic writings.

I would stress not the content of these various traditional Christian speculations concerning the "last things," the "eschaton" or "end" of the Earth, but the pertinence of the question to that discussion of "human goals, purpose, and values" to which we have been directing our attention at this symposium. Five thousand million years is too long for our limited imaginations to encompass, but it is the principle which is important. No sacrifices on behalf of a terrestrial utopia have much point if the significance and destiny of man is described only in terms entirely limited to man's existence as a biological species on the planet Earth. Some transcendent and cosmic role and significance for man is an essential precondition of any shorter term "goals, purpose, and values" he may wish, indeed need, to set before himself. I argue that it is this cosmic and transcendent role for man which, *per impossibile,* God has made known in Jesus the Christ. We experience as immanent the God who is transcendent because we have encountered him as incarnate in Jesus the Christ. In and through this self-revealing of God we can see man's origin and destiny in the following terms, now enlarged and extended and deepened by the scientific perspective on man and nature, and through this perception see our possible more immediate "human goals, purpose, and values" in Christian and scientific terms mutually illuminating each other.

The cosmos depends for its being on God who is at least personal and has created personalness in man out of nonpersonal materiality. Man as a person in time can come into relation with the God who is the ground of all being and the Creator of time itself. In coming into such a relation, both the individual and the community of such reformed humanity enter into a mode of existence which, while fully expressible in the temporal, has its origin and being in God's nontemporal mode of existence. The basis of hope is therefore our trust that God will continue this relation and bring his purposes to fruition not only beyond the limits of our finite lives but beyond even the disappearance of that part of the material cosmos, the Earth, in which he has been at work to achieve his ends. The Christian believes that God has and does act in this world to achieve his purposes, and it is for man to cooperate with him. On this view, our destiny is in God's hands but our lives here and now are ours to direct, in his way, if we so choose.

The working out of this existential demand placed upon us is the perennial, but immediate, the general, but individual, challenge to all men first manifested in the life of Jesus—"Jesus came into Galilee proclaiming the Gospel of God: 'The time has come; the kingdom of God is upon you; repent, and believe the Gospel.'"[39]

PART 3

THEOLOGICAL EVOLUTION– THE RESHAPING OF BELIEF

CHAPTER 8

Science and the Future of Theology

Critical Issues

The intellectual reputations of science and theology

Seventy or so years ago the mathematician–philosopher Alfred North Whitehead (quoted by Brooke[1]) considered that the future course of history would depend on the decision of his generation as to the proper relations between science and religion—so powerful were the religious symbols through which men and women conferred meaning on their lives and so powerful the scientific models through which they could manipulate their environment. We, in a later generation, certainly still have the same *pragmatic* task with religious fundamentalisms still inflaming the political and international scene. Furthermore, the technological applications of science are generating environmental effects, such as global warming, that are already threatening biological and human life. Even more basic is the intellectual task of integrating the search for *intelligibility*, epitomized by the natural sciences, and that for *meaning*, enshrined in the world religions. These hard-thinking tasks in our societies are, or should be, undertaken supremely in our universities—and paramount will be the relating at the intellectual level of the distinctive explorations of science and of theology, the intellectual articulation and justification of religious beliefs. However, too often the science and theology dia-

From *Zygon* 35 (2000): 119–40. Reprinted by permission.

logue has been dominated by what I might call the "bridge" model. Just as a bridge can throw an apparently frail but actually immensely strong bond between the solid rock of the lands on either side of a stretch of water, so the interaction of science and theology has been conceived of as building such a bridge between two solid established disciplines. Across the bridge, dialogue is conceived to occur with the hope of achieving at least consonance and, maximally, integration. However, that picture represents only the Christian medieval enterprise of relating a natural philosophy to a revealed theology, much as it might appeal to any neo-Barthians still around.

Be it noted too that, in those medieval times, one had to change vehicles halfway across the bridge as reason was left behind and the deliverances of a revealed faith took over in going from science to religion. The reverse route from theology to science was soon rendered impassable, from the point of view of the scientists at least, by certain notorious interventions of the church in purely scientific matters. Since the Enlightenment, this bridge building has proved to be hazardous, and the attempt has often been abandoned altogether. For although the foundation on the science side of the gulf seemed solid rock enough to the modern mind, that on the side of theology was regarded as but shifting sand, having little solid rational basis.

For many decades now—and certainly during my adult life in academe—the Western intellectual world has not been convinced that theology is a pursuit that can be engaged in with intellectual honesty and integrity. Our unbelieving contemporaries have been and still are often the "cultured despisers" with whom Friedrich Schleiermacher felt impelled to deal in the early years of the nineteenth century. There are also many wistful agnostics who respect Christian ethics and the person of Jesus but also believe that the ontological baggage of Christian affirmations can be discarded as not referring to any realities.

This deep alienation from religious belief of the key formers of Western culture of recent times has been almost lethal to a Christianity which has nearly always based its beliefs on authorities of the form "The Bible says," "The Church says," "The Magisterium says," even, at least in the past, "Theologians say"! Educated people know that such authoritarian claims are circular and cannot be justified, because they cannot meet the demand for validation of their claims from any external universally accepted stance. No one expressed it better than John Locke:

> For our simple ideas, then, which are the foundation, and sole matter of all our notions and knowledge, we must depend wholly on our reason; I mean our natural faculties; and can by no means receive them, or any of them, from traditional revelation. I say, *traditional revelation*, in distinction to *original revelation*. By the one [original revelation], I mean that first impression which is made immediately by God on the mind of any man, to which we cannot set any bounds; and by the other [traditional revelation], those impressions delivered over to others in words, and the ordinary ways of conveying our conceptions one to another.[2]

Traditional revelation is, for him, revelation from God that is handed down from its original recipient through others by means of already-designating words and signs. His subsequent percipient comments on the relation of faith and reason could not be more relevant:[3]

> Whatever God hath revealed is certainly true; no doubt can be made of it. This is the proper object of faith: but whether it be a *divine* revelation or no, reason must judge; which can never permit the mind to reject a greater evidence to embrace what is less evident, nor allow it to entertain probability in opposition to knowledge and certainty. There can be no evidence that any traditional revelation is of divine original, in the words we receive it, and in the sense we understand it, so clear and so certain as that of the principles of reason; and therefore *Nothing that is contrary to, and inconsistent with, the clear and self-evident dictates of reason, has a right to be urged or assented to as a matter of faith, wherein reason hath nothing to do.*

I find myself warming to such passages as one for whom the inheritance of the Enlightenment is regarded as irreversible in its effects on theology—not in the exaltation of "Reason" alone to Olympus but in the pursuit of reasonableness, of reason based on experience, of probability as being the "very guide of life," as the redoubtable

Bishop Joseph Butler asserted: "For surely a man is as really bound in prudence to do what *upon the whole* appears, according to the best of his judgement to be for his happiness, as what he *certainly* knows to be so."[4]

Science withstands the postmodernist critique

In my view, the "modern," Enlightenment situation, one almost may say plight, of theology—as not meeting the epistemological standards of rational inquiry—continues. However, more recently, for causes obscure and (to me) themselves irrational, the very word *rationality* has come under a cloud of suspicion. The gale of postmodernism blows in from who knows what alien strand and not only removes, it would claim, any need for a bridge between science and theology at all, but pulverizes the foundations on each side into shifting quicksands.

Or so it is said.

"Relativism rules" is all the cry, so that some theologians are seduced into retreating into spelling out the "grammar" of their received, confessional, indeed parochial (even when called "catholic") traditions and are thereby self-exonerated from justifying their beliefs in the arena of public discourse. So the supporting base for structures on the theological side are deemed to have quailed before the onslaught of postmodernist relativism. We shall return to this state of theology later.

But, now, what about the other side of the water? Scientists still go on their way believing that they are exploring a reality other than themselves; that, even after the demise of positivism, their researches still aim to enable them to depict reality, namely, the entities and processes of the natural world; that they do so fallibly, making use of metaphors and models that are revisable; and that, because their procedures make it possible to predict and sometimes even to control natural processes, their efforts are getting them nearer to depicting nature with such increasing verisimilitude as is vouchsafable to finite human minds.

They would point out that even the postmodernist literary critic or sociologist relies on solid-state physics being true enough for his PC to function as a word processor! I well remember, at a 1979 meeting convened by the Church and Society section of the World Council of Churches at M.I.T. on "Faith, Science, and the Future," the indignant reply of an Australian astronomer to delegates from the "South" who, based on their unhappy experience of multinational corporations using technology to exploit their countries, criticized the content and integrity of science. He affirmed—with some passion, it must be said—that "quantum theory does *not* change as you go south across the equator."

The philosophical debate concerning scientific realism that raged some ten years ago has quieted down considerably. Some kind of real reference of scientific terms involving entities and processes, and often theories, seems to be widely accepted, with "realism" preceded by adjectives such as *qualified, critical, skeptical, dialectical critical, convergent,* even *metaphysical.* All of them are characterized by not being naive— that is, not regarding terms in scientific theories as *literal* descriptions of the entities and processes to which they refer, not believing that there are facts to which all scientific propositions correspond if they are true, and not thinking scientific language can exhaustively describe an external world. I said "some kind" of realism. Jarrett Leplin, who in 1984 edited a comprehensive volume on the question, in his "Introduction" expressed the judgment that "like the Equal Rights Movement, scientific realism is a majority position whose advocates are so divided as to appear a minority."[5] I judge that, as against (say) instrumentalism, realism is still the majority view of philosophically informed practicing scientists who would not pursue their exacting profession if they did not think they were uncovering real aspects of the underlying mechanisms and relationships in the natural world. (Those most at risk would be the cosmologists, whose theories are and always will be grossly underdetermined by the facts. Theologians need to remember this in dialogue with them!)

This firm, yet appropriately circumspect, character of scientific realism (that is, realism as a proposal about science as such, not because it is "scientific" in any other sense) is accurately captured in an exposition of Ernan McMullin:[6]

> The basic claim made by scientific realism . . . is that the long-term success of scientific theory gives reason to believe that something like the entities and structure postulated in the theory actually exists. There are four important qualifications built into this: (1) the theory must be a successful one over a significant period of time; (2) the explanatory success of the theory gives some reason, though not a conclusive warrant, to believe it; (3) what is believed is that the theoretical structures are *something like* the structures of the real world; (4) no claim is made for a special, more basic, privileged, form of existence for the postulated entities.

Basically, scientific realism is "a quite limited claim which purports to explain why certain ways of proceeding in science have worked out as well as they [contingently] have."[7] As McMullin admits, the qualifications ("significant period," "some reason," "something like"), although vague, seem to be essential to a defensible scientific realism. Their vagueness is, in fact, largely dispelled by consideration of the use of metaphors and models in science. In any case, he was able to mount a formidable case for scientific realism based on the historical fact that in many parts of natural science (e.g., geology, cell biology, chemistry) there has been over the last two centuries a progressive and continuous discovery of hidden structures in the entities of the natural world, structures that account causally for the observed phenomena.

Leplin[8] has developed a sustained argument for a realist interpretation of science based on the concept of predictive novelty. The successful prediction of novel empirical results can be explained only by attributing some measure of truth to the theories that yield it (and to the referential character of the theory's terms). Moreover he contends, I think convincingly, that science proceeds by a combination of induction and inference to the best explanation (IBE). His understanding of scientific realism is, too, worth noting:

> To interpret a theory realistically is only to suppose that its explanatory mechanisms capture some of the features of natural processes well-enough not to be misleading as to how the effects

these mechanisms explain are actually produced. A realist interpretation claims that the theory reveals some significant truth about real processes, where "significance" is relevance to explanatory ends, and "some" is a measure proportionate to those ends.[9]

My only major caveat about his convincing contribution arises from his concentration on physics, whereas if he had given more weight to the historical sciences—such as geology and biology, which are trying to work out what has happened in the past to the Earth and to living organisms—he would have had to recognize that inference to the best explanation of a wide range of data dominated such sciences but without being able to rely on novel predictions. For example, Lyell's geological uniformitarianism and Darwin's key proposal of natural selection as the mechanism of biological evolution were both arrived at and substantiated by such inference long before more direct, confirmatory experimental observations were available. Leplin, in fact, recognizes this in relation to the attempts to construct a Grand Unified Theory of the forces that are now the focus of fundamental physics. In this context, he reckons that "we are witnessing changes of evaluative standards that elevate explanationist desiderata over novel predictive success."[10] By "explanationist" he means not just inference to the *best* explanation among competing ones, but inference to a *good* explanation that is self-recommending (by precluding rivals) and coherent (in this case) with the rest of physics. It will be useful to bear these considerations and criteria in mind when we come back to theology.

But how has all this broad consensus among philosophers of science, and even more among scientists, withstood the gales of postmodernism? I would judge—very well indeed. In concord with that Australian astronomer at the WCC meeting, it is still the experience of scientists in all fields that in global congresses the criteria for good science transcend all ethnic, religious, political, and social backgrounds. Clearly, these latter affect the provision of grants, the scientific questions selected for study, and the imaginative and intellectual resources available to scientists—but not the accepted *content* of science.

Academics, especially in America, need no reminding of how the postmodernist critique of science was false-footed by the famous hoax in which Alan Sokal published, in the American cultural-studies journal *Social Text*, a parody article crammed with nonsensical, but unfortunately authentic, quotations about physics and mathematics by prominent French and American intellectuals of the postmodernist school. In their significantly entitled *Intellectual Impostures*, Sokal and Jean Bricmont[11] recount the full story, give critiques of the writings of many of these same intellectuals, and provide valuable essays on "Epistemic Relativism in the Philosophy of Science" and on "Chaos Theory and 'Post-Modern Science,'" showing particularly that the last named is a vacuous concept. To be sure, the role of the social context in the historical development of science cannot be controverted. Individuals and groups of scientists depend and feed on social resources of funds, institutions, symbols, and concepts and the general *Zeitgeist* of society, like everyone else. But the justification of scientific theories and of the putative existence of the entities and processes to which they refer is subject to a subsequent rigorous sifting in the scientific community that eventually makes their enterprises an exploration of reality.

A medical scientist, Henry Harris,[12] could stress that, although it is true in physics that Einstein's equations superseded those of Newton, yet this

> is no argument at all for the notion that all scientific conclusions are similarly bound eventually to be displaced. I do not believe that it will ever be shown that the blood of animals does not circulate; that anthrax is not caused by a bacterium; that proteins are not chains of amino acids. Human beings may indeed make mistakes, but I see no merit in the idea that they can make nothing but mistakes.

The "Legend," as Philip Kitcher[13] calls it, that science delivers *the* true story of the world in some ahistorical way by using *the* scientific method, has to be recognized as just that; but it also has to be accepted as a more accurate view of the scientific process that

Flawed people, working in complex social environments, moved by all kinds of interest, have collectively achieved a vision of parts of nature that is broadly progressive and that rests on arguments meeting standards that have been refined and improved over centuries. [The] Legend does not require burial but metamorphosis.[14]

Let us return to that bridge hopefully spanning the gulf between science and theology. It now seems that the science side is certainly not quicksand but much more like the lava flow from a volcano, which inexorably moves forward in a fluid manner (often fierily destructive of preconceptions) but leaves behind an increasingly solid base of established knowledge about the natural world. My conclusion, so far, is that science has proved a bastion against the gales of postmodernism and serves to preserve, and even restore if we strayed so far, a conviction that the processes of human rational inquiry, fallible though they are, are not always fated to be engulfed in relativism, social contextualization, and even nihilism. By its very success in withstanding the weasel words that lead to abandoning any search for *justified* belief about what really is the case, science challenges humanist disciplines, including theology, to live up to its epistemological standards in relation to the data and intellectual histories specifically relevant to those disciplines.

Evolution and human rationality

There has, of course, been much debate about whether or not any basis for a common rationality is now possible in these nonscientific disciplines. None of us wants to be a foundationalist, which in theology involves fideism and fundamentalism.[15] So which way do we go from here? Curiously, certain perspectives in modern biology indicate that the exercise of human rationality is not likely to be fruitless and end up in an unreliable, relativistic circularity of affirmation. For, as I have earlier put it:[16]

Evolutionary biology can trace the steps in which a succession of organisms have acquired nervous systems and brains whereby they

obtain, store, retrieve and utilize information about their environments in a way that furthers their survival. That this information so
successfully utilized must be accurate enough for their survival has
led to the notion of "evolutionary epistemology."[17] This finds a
warrant for the reality of reference of the content of such awareness of living organisms, especially human beings, in their actual
successful survival of the naturally selective processes. Awareness
and exploration of the external world reach a peak in *Homo sapiens*
who, through the use of language, primarily, visual imagery and,
later, mathematics, is able to formulate concepts interpreting the
environment. . . .

The natural environment, both physical and social, is experienced and becomes a possible object of what we then call "knowledge"—that which is reliable enough to facilitate prediction and
control of the environment, and so survival. Our sense impressions
must be broadly trustworthy, and *so must the cognitive structures
whereby* we know the world—otherwise we would not have survived. . . . In human beings a number of cognitive functions, that
are also to be found in animals and that individually make their
own contribution to survival, are "integrated into a system of
higher order," to use a phrase of Konrad Lorenz.[18]

In a nutshell, our cognitive faculties *qua* biological organisms must
be accurate enough in their representations of reality to enable us to
survive. In the case of human beings, these cognitive faculties include
the representations of external reality we individually and socially
make to ourselves. Hence, these representations have at least the degree of verisimilitude to facilitate survival in the external realities of
our environments. The extent to which evolutionary biology will actually help us understand the cognitive processes whereby this reliable
knowledge about the environment was acquired is still an open, indeed confused, question. However, there can be little doubt that there
is a continuity in the evolution of *Homo sapiens* between (a) the cognitive processes that allow a physically relatively poorly endowed
creature to survive against fiercer predation and in a variety of environments; (b) the processes of ordinary "common sense" ratiocination
applied in everyday life; and (c) the ability to think abstractly and to

manipulate symbols in mathematics, art, science, music, and the multitudinous facets of human culture. As Sokal and Bricmont say in their defense of science as a practice yielding reliable knowledge:[19]

> [T]he scientific method is not radically different from the rational attitude in everyday life or other domains of human knowledge. Historians, detectives and plumbers—indeed, all human beings—use the same basic methods of induction, deduction and assessment of evidence as do physicists or biochemists. Modern science tries to carry on these operations in a more careful and systematic way. . . . Scientific measurements are often much more precise than everyday observations; they allow us to discover hitherto unknown phenomena; and they often conflict with "common sense." But the conflict is at the level of conclusions, not the basic approach.

The central consequence for this inquiry is an enhancement of our confidence in the reality-referring capacity of our cognitive processes that evolution has provided. It warrants the postulating of the existence of a general rationality in *Homo sapiens* which yields, for the purpose of living, reliable knowledge and justified belief. This encourages an examination of the nature of the selfsame perceived cognitive processes. This warrant for such an examination has recently also been strongly emphasized by Wentzel van Huyssteen, who writes that "our mental capacities have their roots in organic evolution and it is important to study these roots to learn something about the genesis and development of our ability to know and interrelate with our world."[20]

This approach goes back much earlier to Karl Popper,[21] Konrad Lorenz, and especially Donald Campbell, who first named the approach as "evolutionary epistemology." However, biology as such gives few clues about the evolution of human cognition. Moreover, this enhancement by evolutionary considerations of confidence in the possibility of human ratiocination providing reliable knowledge does not in itself exonerate us from inquiring into the validity of the actual content of the deliverances of human ratiocination and also from asking about the criteria that should operate. To this we must now attend.

Reasonableness through inference
to the best explanation

We are obtaining from evolutionary epistemology the stimulus to take again seriously the results of the processes of human cognition and rationality. Can we discern any features of these processes that are common to biological survival, everyday experience, *and* the explanatory accounts we give of the activities that constitute human culture in *inter alia* the sciences, the humanities, and theology? It is hardly necessary to remind the reader of books entitled *Higher Superstition*[22] and *Intellectual Impostures*[23] about the present postmodernist *Zeitgeist* and academic political correctness of the controversies that rage around such a seemingly innocent question. I have given grounds why I think science has been able to resist the siren calls of postmodernism. The continuity of its procedures with those of reasonable decision making in ordinary life, which can now be attributed to their common biological origin, is significant for our estimate of human rationality in general. When these two kinds of exercise of human rationality are analyzed, I think a strong case can be made for asserting that such deliberations are not purely deductive, nor purely inductive, but a composite of a particular kind, namely, inference to the best explanation (IBE—sometimes called abduction). This latter is described thus in Peter Upton's key work:[24]

> According to Inference to the Best Explanation, our inferential practices are governed by explanatory considerations. Given our data and background beliefs, we infer what would, if true, provide the best of the competing explanations we generate of those data (so long as the best is good enough for us to make any inference at all). . . . One of the main attractions of the model [of IBE] is that it accounts in a natural and unified way both for the inferences to unobservable entities and processes that characterize much scientific research and for many of the mundane inferences about middle-sized dry goods that we make everyday.[25]

It is pertinent to recall the conclusion of Paul Thagard[26] to his article, important in the general recognition of the significance of IBE, that a "final merit" of IBE is that

> it makes possible a reunification of scientific and philosophical method, since inference to the best explanation has many applications in philosophy, especially in metaphysics. Arguments concerning the best explanation are relevant to problems concerning scientific realism, other minds, the external world, and the existence of God. Metaphysical theories can be evaluated as to whether they provide the best explanation of philosophical and scientific facts, according to the criteria of consilience, simplicity and analogy.

Decisions have, of course, to be made about which is the best of competing, plausible explanations, but note that strict falsifiability à la Popper is not emphasized nor is any absolute requirement for novel predictions. This allows theology to adopt more readily this model of explanation, which is so adequate to science and everyday life. What are the criteria for deciding which is the "best" explanation among any set of plausible proposals—that is, the one "which would, if true, provide the most understanding"[27] of the field in question? In this context, Philip Clayton speaks of the "explanatory virtues"[28] rather than direct talk about "truth criteria."[29] Clayton's and Lipton's list of general *desiderata* for helping to decide between scientific explanations include theoretical elegance (beloved of theoretical physicists but making biologists wary!), simplicity, coherence, precision, provision of causal mechanisms, fitting a given phenomenon into the broadest possible theoretical structure (a "unified explanatory scheme"[30] and, it is assumed, fit with the data).[31]

Bearing in mind the intention to use IBE in theology, I prefer to distinguish the following as the criteria for deciding on a "best" explanation:

1. *Comprehensiveness*—the best explanation accounts for more of the known observations by giving a unified explanation of a diverse range of facts not previously connected. There are converging lines of argument based on different kinds of data with which the best expla-

nation fits. Such data will, for theology, comprise human experience, including (though not exclusively) those designated as "religious."

2. *Fruitfulness*—the best explanation can often, but (note) not always, suggest new and corroborating observations. The best explanation is not ad hoc, just to one specific purpose.

3. *General cogency and plausibility*—because the best explanation fits with established, background knowledge (compare Lipton's "unified explanatory scheme").

4. *Internal coherence and consistency*—no self-contradiction.

5. *Simplicity or elegance*—avoiding undue complexity.

In IBE, as John Wisdom[32] had put it in 1953, "The process of argument is not a *chain* of demonstrative reasoning. It is a presenting and representing of those features of a case which severally co-operate in favour of the conclusion."

It would be naive to think that these criteria depicted with such a broad brush do not need thorough analysis, justification, and development. Often they have to be held in mutual tension with each other. Their discussion has been grist to the mill in the last few decades of the philosophy of science and, more widely, of epistemology. I cannot pretend to do justice to that complex discussion—though I do note that the term "inference to the best explanation" seems to be broadly acceptable to the practitioners of a wide range of disciplines in the sciences and the humanities. I also observe that the emphases on internal coherence (4) and on fit with established, background knowledge (3) agree well with the contextual, pragmaticist coherence theory of M. Rescher, expounded and deployed recently by Niels Henrik Gregersen[33] in relation to the current dialogue between theology and science. Such considerations seem to me to be part of the necessary amplification of those criteria. As Philip Clayton has rightly said:[34]

> This theory of explanation reflects a more general paradigm shift regarding the rationality of both scientific and meta-physical debates . . . in place of foundationalist understandings of knowledge it presupposes a coherentialist framework. This brings inference to

the best explanation into close contact with the "holistic view"[35] of scientific explanation.

The direction in which such proposals are leading appears to me to be entirely in accord with the critical realist view I have myself espoused[36] and, I think, with the postfoundationalist stance of J. Wentzel van Huyssteen[37] with the gravamen he lays on all epistemologies to create what he calls "interdisciplinary spaces"—especially between theology and science.

Theology today and tomorrow

Earlier I drew attention to the parlous state of the reputation of theology as an intellectual discipline. A large proportion of educated people do not find Christian (or any) theology reasonable—it is not seen by them as realizing the standards of modern intellectual life, not least in its relation to science. It is thought to have been tried in the balance and found wanting.

So I would describe the first key critical issue for theology, exemplified supremely in its relation to the natural and human sciences, as the following:

1. Dare theology proceed in its search for even provisional "truth" by employing the criteria of reasonableness that characterize the rest of human inquiries, in particular the sciences? In the natural and human sciences, a strong case has been made that they achieve their aims of depicting, reviseably and metaphorically, the realities of the natural and human worlds by inference to the best explanation (IBE). Because of the epistemological revolutions of our time, it is now essential that the theological pier of the bridge to science be subject to the same demands for epistemological warrant and intellectual integrity as other disciplines, especially science—and to relinquish the unestablished confidence of, for example, neo-orthodoxy, that it is divinely authorized.

Theology needs to be, as Hans Küng[38] has put it, "truthful," "free," "critical," and "ecumenical"—a theology that deals with and interprets the realities of all that constitutes the world, especially human beings and their inner lives. Dare theology, by using IBE, enter the fray of contemporary, intellectual exchange and stand up and survive in its own right? To do so, it has to become an open exploration in which nothing is unrevisable.

The bridge model for the science-and-theology enterprise must be replaced by the sense of a *joint* exploration into a common reality, some aspects of which will prove, in the end, to be ultimate—and pointers to the divine. Let us now look at how theology is actually practiced.

Theology as it is

What do we find?—a variety of theological procedures that do *not* meet these criteria:

1. *Reliance on an authoritative book.* "The Bible says." Even those not given to biblical literalism and fundamentalism still have a habit of treating the contents of the Bible (now mostly two thousand or more years old) as a kind of oracle, as if quotations from past authorities could settle questions in our times. Although it is unlikely that many readers of this journal hold this view, it is the one that, whatever they themselves believe, ordinary Christians think clergy and ministers *ought* to believe (and are paid to do so!). Yet, the library of books we call the Bible itself is constituted by a self-critical dialogic process of constantly revising, repudiating, and extending the work and experience of earlier generations; we see this even within the period of authorship of the New Testament itself.

2. *Reliance on an authoritative community.* "The Church says," "The Fathers said," "The Creeds say," "The Magisterium says." Here the religious community listens and talks only to itself, following the "cultural-linguistic" (or "regulative") pattern espoused by George Lindbeck.[39] According to this interpretation, the doctrines of the Christian Church function to establish the framework for that community's conversation which elucidates the grammar of its own internal discourse without ever exposing itself to any external judgment of reasonableness. At its best it can be faith seeking understanding

(fides quaerens intellectum), but even this prescinds from rational justification of the faith. I would urge that the only defensible theology is one that consists of "understanding seeking faith" *(intellectus quaerens fidem)*, in which "understanding" must include that of the natural and human worlds which the sciences have *inter alia* unveiled. (I am, of course, not meaning to exclude the aesthetic and other experiences of humanity from this "understanding.") There can be within communities of faith a kind of submission to what is regarded as a revelatory dogmatism or doctrinal fundamentalism. It is often taken for granted that what "the gospel" was was precisely understood and universally agreed upon—when in fact it wasn't. The "Word," it is often said, has been given by God to the community of Christians and has had to be expounded—but its authenticity as the Word *of God* was never established. So, however much the faith *(fides)* is explicated and enriched within the community, it fails to equip itself with the means whereby it can convince those outside it to take seriously its affirmations. For it has foregone and repudiated what I would regard as the God-given lingua franca of human discourse—the use of criteria of reasonableness, as in IBE. If we follow Lindbeck's recipe, how can Christian communities ever convince the outside world that they proclaim any kind of "truth" comparable in cogency to that which that world recognizes and, in their application of science, also utilizes?

3. *Reliance on a priori truth.* In some forms of philosophical theology, the internal "basic truths" held by the Christian community are regarded almost as a priori truths arrived at by pure ratiocination. This kind of foundationalism is rare today because of the wider recognition of the cultural conditioning of what can seem to be a priori. Clearly, such a theology would find it very difficult to come to terms with the world whose realities are discovered by the sciences.

Theology as it might be

If theology is to meet the intellectual standards of our times by, for example, utilizing IBE, and not by relying on authorities or claimed a priori notions, it will have to take account of:

S—the realities of the world and humanity discovered by *Science;*

CRE—the Jewish and Christian communal inheritance of claimed, *Classical Revelatory Experiences* (in the Scriptures, liturgies, aesthetic expression, music, and so forth); and

WR—the perceptions and traditions of other *World Religions.*

Hence the "data" of theology are:

S+CRE+WR

II. Here we have, regretfully, to put on one side *WR*, but let it be noted at this point that a second critical issue for Christian theology in relation to the sciences is the perception of how other religions have related and are relating to the scientific worldview and what can be learned from that. But for our present purposes let our data be taken to be

S+CRE

III. If we put these together, I think we are faced with our third critical issue, namely, that a very radical revision of past notions concerning what Christians can in future hold as credible, defensible, and reasonable becomes imperative. We have had, as it were,

CRE→*T*, where *T* is orthodox Christian *Theology.*

But now, we need to have

S + *CRE*→*RT*, a radically *Revised Theology,*

which, I am suggesting, will not live at all comfortably with the *T* as promulgated by church bodies and in most pulpits. Eventually, of course, we need

S+CRE+WR→*GT*, a *Global Theology.*

What are we aiming for, in the nearer future, in that *RT*? What will its truth deliver for the person of the twenty-first century?

It is useful to remind ourselves what religion in general is about, and I am attracted to a recent definition made by Gerd Theissen[40] of religion as "a cultural sign language which promises a gain in life by corresponding to an ultimate reality." I am also attracted to what could be regarded as an elucidation of this definition by David Pailin, who suggested that we should want to give people

> the conviction that the basic structure of reality is such that it is appropriate for people to feel "at home" in it because it is basically a purposive process that, in a significant way, respects human values, both treasuring what has been achieved and fostering further achievements. And, theists maintain, this conviction is based on, and can only be based on, the reality and activity of God.[41]

If this is broadly what theology should be explicating and for which it should be providing the warrant, how should the dialogue and interaction of the sciences with theological formulations of the content of religious experience and traditions of community be conducted?

IV. It is here that we encounter a fourth set of critical issues concerning the methodology of this process. Those of us engaged in the science-and-theology interaction must be committed to certain norms:[42]

1. To avoid importing spurious spiritualizations into our discourse. This is *one* multileveled world; there is no evidence for any other ontologies than those emerging from the natural world. Hence, no magic, no "science fiction," and no fudging to avoid offending notions held simplistically in ignorance of this picture.

2. To be explicit when our language is metaphorical and not be afraid to be agnostic when the evidence does not warrant positive assertions.

3. To avoid fallacies—genetic, naturalistic, and that of "misplaced concreteness" (not all words refer to real entities; they often refer to relations and properties).

4. Not to use marginal and speculative science (an example would be the cascades of paper discussing Hawkins's speculations).

5. Not to be selective of our science by choosing the parts favorable to our theologies.

6. Not to over-socially contextualize science; most people see that science works.

7. To keep a historical perspective but not be bound to the idea that past issues have simply reappeared today. The boundaries of "science" and "religion" are shifting all the time.

8. To distinguish theology, the study of the intellectual content of religious beliefs, from religion, which is about individual and communal experiences. (Is the theology/religion relation paralleled by that of science/technology?)

9. Not to claim for theology credibility based on its long history; it has to meet today's challenges.

10. Not to be tempted to discern prematurely coherences and consonances between science and theology, since the latter may be explicating a prophetic dimension in religion which refers to the as-yet-unknown future.

11. To recognize that much of religious language is functional in society rather than referential, as it should be in theology (it is hoped).

I cannot help wondering if, in spite of the honest efforts of many of us, we have really always maintained such standards.

Further critical issues for theology

There are other tough issues that Christian theology has to consider in the light of the sciences.

v. This is *one world*. A monistic naturalism is overwhelmingly indicated by the sciences. Everything is constituted of "parts," of whatever current physics discovers underlies all matter/energy. This need not be epistemologically reductionist about the many levels in the world, including human beings—who are seen as psychosomatic units, not ontologically distinct bodies and minds and souls (according to both the cognitive sciences and the Bible). With respect to the mind/brain relation, "dual-aspect monism" and, even more so, "emergentist monism" are defensible positions congenial to Christian understandings of human nature. But no "ghosts in the machine." The only dualism now defensible appears to be the distinction between the Being of God and everything else (all-that-is, all that is created). Talk of the "spirit" or of the "soul" of human beings as distinct entities appears to be precluded, as is talk of the "supernatural," and holistic language is generally more appropriate.

VI. This one world is an interconnected web of processes that are increasingly intelligible to the sciences. These processes are more subtle and rational than we could ever have conceived. Their creativity is inbuilt, for theists, by *God*, and it is becoming increasingly incoherent to have a view of God as intervening in these processes to fulfill God's purposes. This is the now notorious problem of God's action in the world and how to conceive of it.

VII. Because of VI, the historical evidence for miracles (disruption of the regularities of nature by God) is usually inadequate to testify to them. Can our theology continue to depend at all on the assertion of the occurrence of miracles in that sense? This will call for rethinking our traditional ways of regarding the virginal conception (the "virgin birth") and the bodily resurrection of Jesus.

1. Does the affirmation of the incarnation have to be closely related to the virginal conception in view of the weakness of the historical evidence for it, its biological implausibility, and its derogating from the full genetic humanity of Jesus?

2. Does the affirmation of the resurrection have to depend on the "empty tomb"—especially as it is clear our bodies are, in principle, not resurrectable (our constituent molecules are soon dispersed and enter those of other living organisms and other people), so the transformation of Jesus' body leaving an empty tomb could never give us any particular hope for our own resurrection if that, too, were to be a transformation of our actual individual bodies?

VIII. Human nature is under the leash of our biologically conditioned and biologically created genes. What is the relation of this to "original sin"? After all, God created us with those biologically derived genes.

IX. Human beings seem to be "rising beasts" rather than "fallen angels." There is no evidence for a past paradisal, fully integrated, harmonious, virtuous existence of *Homo sapiens*, so how should this shape our understanding of the "work of Christ" as "redemption"?

Should we not now be regarding the "work of Christ" less as the restoration of a past state of perfection than as the transformation into a new as-yet-unrealized state? How did and does the life, death, and claimed resurrection of Jesus make any difference?

x. If God is all the time creating in and through the processes of the world, so they are in themselves God's action, then the understanding of God's immanence in the world has to be held in a much stronger sense than ever before. God is closer to natural reality than previously conceived. God is indeed the one in whom "we live and move and have our being."[43] God's relation to the world is through and through sacramental, both instrumentally and symbolically in revelation of God's self. So is not a "sacramental panentheism" called for as representing the closeness of God in creation and yet God's basic "otherness"? We certainly need more dynamic metaphors for that relation than have usually been propounded in the past.

xi. The role of chance and its interplay with necessity (law, regularity) is a real feature of the processes now uncovered by science, whereby new entities have appeared in the world. This needs to be incorporated positively into our account of how God creates. Does God explore or experiment creatively?

xii. Human death. Death of the individual is now seen as part of God's created processes whereby the living creatures preceding humanity and humanity itself have come into existence. So how can the "wages of sin" be "death"[44]?—and what does this imply for many classical understandings of redemption/atonement as the "work of Christ"?

xiii. If there is life on other planets, as is at least possible, what does this imply for the uniqueness of Jesus as Redeemer, Lord, Savior, and *Logos* incarnate?

xiv. The relation of God to time is an issue that has greatly exercised many of us as we relate the perceptions of modern relativistic physics to classical notions of eternity and of God's supposed "timelessness." Suffice it to say there is no agreement—some accept a Boethian view in which God perceives past, present, and future with an eternal immediacy, while many of us believe that the future does not have any kind of existence the content of which an omniscient God could logically know. On this latter view, God alone will certainly be present to all future events, but what they will be is open and not determined and not known to God. The discussions of eschatology have to be set in the context of this unresolved dichotomy of views. Furthermore, we have to ask, on what is much Christian theological talk of eschatology and the future based? Cosmology predicts with very great certainty the demise of this planet and all life on it, including ours. What then is the cash value of talk about "a new heaven and a new earth"? The only propounded bases for this seem to me to be the imaginings of one late-first-century writer (in Revelation) and the belief that the material of Jesus' physical body was transformed to leave an empty tomb. I have already indicated that the latter is at least debatable and the former can scarcely be evidence. So what is left is belief in the character of God as Love and that God has taken at least one human being who was fully open to the divine presence into the divine life—the resurrection and ascension of Jesus. Is not all the rest of Christian eschatology but empty speculation?

Verdict

The foregoing critical issues (I to XIV) consist of both methodological and substantive challenges to Christian theology as it reflects on the nature and character of the cosmos that the sciences have unveiled. Intellectually educated, thinking people, if they are still attached in any way to the Christian churches, are, as it were, hanging on by their fingertips as they increasingly bracket off large sections of the liturgies in which they participate as either unintelligible, or, if intelligible, unbelievable in their classical form. There is an increasingly alarming dissonance between the language of devotion, liturgies, and doctrine and what people perceive themselves to be, and to be becoming, in the world. For they now see themselves increasingly in the light of the cognitive sciences and of the historical sciences (cosmology, geology, biology), those that create the "epic of evolution."

Hitherto apologetic based on science by Christian thinkers has been a well-expressed reinventing of the wheel that strengthens

Christians who are wobbling in their faith, but it is not convincing the general, educated public. It is still too entangled in worn-out metaphors and images. I myself have argued for a more dynamic view of God's continuous action in the processes of the natural, including human, world—the action of a God who is indeed transcendent, incarnate, and immanent, in whom the world exists and who is its circumambient Reality. Be that as it may, what we all have to do in this interaction of theology with the sciences is, by argument and imagination, develop a notion of God, belief in the reality of whom, with all that this entails, can coherently embrace what we now know from science about the cosmos, this planet, and our own and other species. Theology—which I still take to be wisdom and words about God—has to develop concepts, images, notions, and metaphors that represent God's purposes and implanted meanings for the world as we actually now find it to be through the sciences.

We require an open, revisable, exploratory, radical, (dare I say it?) liberal theology. This may well be unfashionable among Christians who seem everywhere to be retreating into their fortresses of classical Protestant Evangelicalism, traditional (Anglo-) Catholicism, and/or so-called biblical theology. Nevertheless, transition to such a theology is, in my view, actually unavoidable if Christians in the West, and I suspect eventually elsewhere, are not to degenerate in the next millennium into an esoteric society internally communing with itself and thereby failing to be the transmitter of its "good news" (the *evangel*) to the universal *(catholicos)* world.

Hence, a paradox: To be truly evangelical and catholic in its impact and function, the church of the new millennium will need a theology that, in its relation to a worldview everywhere shaped by the sciences, will have to be genuinely liberal and even radical. For such a Christian theology to have any viability, it may well have to be stripped down to newly conceived essentials and so be minimalist in its asseverations. Only then will Christian theology attain that degree of verisimilitude with respect to ultimate realities which science has to natural ones—and command respect as a vehicle of *public truth*.

A hopeful afterword

To conclude, I want to indicate why I am full of hope, in spite of the gargantuan task facing Christian theology as it enters its third millennium—a hope based on the perennial character of God's creative engagement with the world. Some years ago, after referring to evolutionary epistemology and how (a) in culture, human beings have developed artifacts helping them to transmit knowledge; (b) in the processes of cultural change, the new has emerged in humanity ("biology" has become "history"); and (c) human intersubjectivity develops in culture with a naturally evolved capacity for self-awareness, I observed that, natural as all this process is, oddly enough there are signs of a kind of misfit between human beings as persons and their environment that is not apparent in other creatures.[45] We alone in the biological world, it seems, individually commit suicide; we alone by our burial rituals evidence the sense of another dimension to existence; we alone go through our biological lives with that sense of incomplete fulfillment evidenced by the contemporary quests for "self-realization" and "personal growth." We have aspirations and what appear to us as needs that go far beyond basic biological requirements for food, rest, shelter, sex, and an environment in which procreation and care of the young is possible. Human beings seek to come to terms with death, pain, and suffering, and they need to realize their own potentialities and learn how to steer their paths through life. The natural environment is not capable of satisfying such aspirations, and the natural sciences cannot describe, accurately discern, or satisfy them. So our presence in the biological world raises questions outside the scope of the natural sciences to answer. For we are capable of happiness and miseries quite unknown to other creatures, thereby evidencing a disease with our evolved state, a lack of fit which calls for explanation and, if possible, cure.

Subsequently[46] I noted that the biological endowment of human beings does not appear to be able to guarantee their contented adaptation to an environment which is, for them, inherently dynamic. For they have ever-changing and expanding horizons within which they live individually and socially, physically and culturally, emotionally and intellectually. In particular, when one reflects on the balanced adaptation of other living organisms to their biological niches, the alienation of human beings from nonhuman nature and from each other appears as a kind of anomaly within the organic world. As human beings widen their environmental horizons, they experience this "great gulf fixed" between their biological past environment out of which they have evolved and that in which they conceive of themselves as existing or, rather, that in which they wish they existed. We may well ask: Why has, how has, the process whereby there have so successfully evolved living organisms finely tuned to and adapted to their environments failed in the case of *Homo sapiens* to ensure this fit between lived experience and the environing conditions of their lives? It appears that the human brain has capacities which originally evolved in response to an earlier environmental challenge but the exercise of which now engenders a whole range of needs, desires, ambitions, and aspirations that cannot all be harmoniously fulfilled.

Such considerations raise the further question of whether or not human beings have really identified what their *true* environment really is—that environment in which human flourishing is possible. Such is the depth of human angst and tragedy that it would clearly be unwise to expect to be able to answer such questions from within the scope of biology—even though modern biology is digging deeply into our origins and has uncovered genetic foundations for more of our personal and social behavior than had been anticipated earlier.

We know only too well that these needs are not satisfied within our grapplings with our biological and even our social environments, and we experience a kind of gap between our yearnings and the actualities of our situations. There seems to be an endemic failure of human beings to be adapted to what they sense as the totality of their environment—an incongruity eloquently expressed by that great nineteenth-century Presbyterian preacher, Thomas Chalmers, in his 1833 Bridgewater Treatise: "There is in man, a restlessness of ambition; . . . a dissatisfaction with the present, which never is appeased by all the world has to offer . . . an unsated appetency for something larger and better, which he fancies in the perspective before him—to all which there is nothing like among any of the inferior animals."[47] Does not the human condition therefore raise the profound question of what humanity's true environment really is? Thus it was that St. Augustine, after years of travail and even despair, addressed his Maker: "You have made us for yourself and our heart is restless till it rests in you."[48] Augustine's Maker is ours, too, and no one who has asked has not received, and no one who has sought has not found.[49] So let us knock, and it *will* be opened to us.

CHAPTER 9

Public Truth in Religion

The challenge of the natural sciences
to those who will create
the culture and inner life of humankind
through the beginning of the third millennium
since the birth of the One
who uniquely shaped the first two.

—*Arthur Peacocke*

I know there is truth opposite to falsehood that it may be found if
people will and is worth seeking.

—*John Locke (1632–1704)*[1]

John Locke, one of the jewels in the crown of the Enlightenment, was the foremost defender of freedom of inquiry and toleration in religion in late seventeenth-century England when political pressure from Charles II and his brother (later James II) was attempting to constrict and confine it. His stance that the only secure basis for

This article appeared in *Currents in Theology and Mission* 28 (2001): 195–201, which was addressed primarily to students and devoted to an appreciation, on his retirement from his professorship at the Lutheran School of Theology at Chicago, of the stimulating influence on the scientific and ecclesial communities of Philip Hefner. Reprinted by permission.

Christianity is its reasonableness (one of his major works is *The Reasonableness of Christianity as delivered in the Scriptures*, 1695) and that the grounds for Christian belief are to be pursued in the spirit on enlightened inquiry is what I particularly associate with Phil Hefner. For him, as for Locke, there is truth opposite to falsehood, it may be found, and it is worth the seeking.

It is this marked feature of his trajectory over the twenty-seven or so years in which I have known and cooperated with him that characterizes his career as a professor of systematic theology. In the circles where church and academe overlap this cannot be taken for granted, for reasons I will come to later. Phil Hefner has, almost uniquely among systematic theologians, absorbed the best knowledge of the world and of humanity from the natural sciences into the very fabric of his professional reflection on God, nature, and humanity. He has sought today's truth in the spirit of Leonard Hodgson's dictum:[2] "if that is how the truth—about God, nature, and humanity—appeared to past Christian believers who wrote and thought like that, what today must be the truth for us?" Though not himself a scientist, the spirit of his theological inquiries has been essentially that of the scientist in examining nature. The basis of inquiry conducted in this spirit is that there is indeed a *public* truth of the matter—whether in religion or science—that is worth the seeking. By "public" truth I mean references to and concepts explicating the realities of God, nature, and humanity that can be intelligibly communicated and shared and assented to. Such assent depends on the justification of such beliefs and this implies their inherent reasonableness—otherwise assent could only be impelled and not voluntary. Only a theology that can be *public* truth, in this sense, is likely to be respected in the intellectual world of the modern university. Phil Hefner by practicing the discipline of systematic theology and *at the same time* opening it up to the scientific understanding of nature and of humanity has enabled that discipline to be perceived, even by skeptical scientists, as at least aiming at a public truth which is accessible to, and worthy of consideration by, all. In that pursuit, he has been open especially to the "epic of evolution" which cosmology and evolutionary biology have evoked, and this has stimulated him to many new insights into the nature of God as Creator and of human beings as co-creators with God.

However, there is a movement which dominates the intellectual scene today, especially that of the humanities, in which I include theology, which is inimical to such an enterprise—namely the cluster of attitudes loosely labeled as "postmodernist." Insofar as these stances stress that we are all captives of our social contexts with regard not only to the issues which generate public interest and which are influenced by political and financial pressures, but also with regard to the conceptual resources of language and images that our reflective imagination can bring to bear on any issues, then they constitute a helpful corrective to narrow-mindedness and bigotry. For we all tend to exchange ideas most readily with the communities that share our preconceptions, presuppositions, and, we must admit, our prejudices. However the most insidious forms of postmodernism go much further than this in affirming that we are forever captives of our intellectual and spiritual communities, that the only appropriate exercise is to learn the "grammar" of exchange within those communities, and that indeed there is *no* public truth ascertainable across and between them. It is urged that the only achievable "truth" is relative, internal to communities, possibly expressible as narrative—and certainly not of universal, human import.

Many students may well already have drunk from this cup, but I consider it a poisoned chalice. For it lulls the recipient into a coma abandoning altogether the search for that public truth which alone can guide us all individually *and corporately* into a fruitful human existence engaging with the best-discerned realties of nature and humanity—and indeed of God too. My confidence in affirming this has been reinforced by the general recognition that science, at least, has been able successfully to withstand the postmodernist critique. I am not so much thinking of that *cause célèbre* in which the two physicists[3] exploded the vacuousness of postmodernist jargon when it tried to enlist the concepts of physics. I am thinking rather of the general conviction of scientists that their methods and the rigorous sifting of its results and interpretations which occur in the scientific community (sometimes over more than one generation of scientists) leads increasingly to more accurate and fruitful ways of depicting the realities of the natural world and of those aspects of humanity amenable to its studies. Scientists generally espouse a realism concerning nature (after all, *applied* science actually works!) while recognizing the provisionality of the metaphors and models they use to depict it. They *aim* to depict reality in the least misleading way possible. The justification for such a qualified, critical realism concerning nature on the part of scientists stems not only from their subsequent ability to predict and control, but also from their ability to render coherent large bodies of otherwise disparate observations—as, for example, in the way Darwin arrived at his proposal of biological evolution, only substantially confirmed and confirmable many decades later.

For these kinds of reasons, I would argue[4] that the natural sciences have proved a bastion against the fashionable gales of postmodernism that are sweeping so chaotically and disruptively through other intellectual pursuits. This success of the sciences in withstanding postmodernist skepticism concerning the deliverances of human reasoning should serve to encourage its revival in the wider intellectual pursuits of the humanities, including theology. For the processes by which scientists arrive at their conclusions, sophisticated as it is in detail and abstract as it often is in its mathematical concepts, nevertheless utilize a widespread intellectual procedure that has been denoted as "inference to the best explanation." There are also grounds (in evolutionary epistemology) for urging that such a manner of proceeding has enabled human beings to survive and evolve by giving them an adequate apprisal of the realities that can threaten or nurture them. More generally, in relation to the "commonsense" nature of scientific inquiry, the two physicists who exposed the postmodernist misuse of science rightly affirm:

> [T]he scientific method is not radically different from the rational attitude in everyday life or other domains of human knowledge. Historians, detectives and plumbers—indeed, all human beings— use the same basic methods of induction, deduction and assessment of evidence, as do physicists or biochemists. Modern science tries

to carry on these operations in a more careful and systematic way. Scientific measurements are often much more precise than everyday observations; they allow us to discover hitherto unknown phenomena; and they often conflict with "common sense." But the conflict is at the level of conclusions, not the basic approach.[5]

This basically "commonsense" approach to problems, namely how best to inquire what really is the case, has been philosophically characterized as "inference to the best explanation." The criteria for the best explanation turn out to be, unsurprisingly: comprehensiveness, fruitfulness, general cogency and plausibility, internal coherence and consistency, and avoiding undue complexity (if possible). In the light of these epistemological standards it cannot be said that the modern world (generally in Europe and in the universities and intelligentsia of the USA) regards theology as actually to be operating in accordance with them. So I can now summarize my challenge to the reader as follows:

Dare theology, the intellectual articulation and justification of religious beliefs, proceed in its search for public truth(s), by employing the criteria of reasonableness through inference to the best explanation, which characterize the rest of human inquiries, in particular the sciences?

Philip Hefner has been one of the few systematic theologians who has so dared, and it is worth recalling the wider situation regarding religion to understand why his approach, which I share, is so urgently required—not least in the relation of religion to the new vistas on the world, including humanity, with which the sciences have enriched the consciousness of our times. This challenge may well be heard differently by the students (to whom it is particularly directed) according to their own particular concerns, life patterns and presuppositions, fluid and revisable as they often still are, fortunately, in that phase of life. For simplicity, I will divide the potential student readers of this challenge into the "seekers" and "theists" (mainly, but not exclusively, Christian ones).

1. By the "seekers," I mean those who have not been able to come to any conclusion, so far, on the existence of any kind of Ultimate Reality which is the source of their being and becoming—even in

the all-pervasive form that the beauty of nature evokes, as famously expressed in Wordsworth's *Tintern Abbey:*

> And I have felt
> A presence that disturbs me with the joy
> Of elevated thoughts: a sense sublime
> Of something far more deeply interfused,
> Whose dwelling is the light of setting suns,
> And the round ocean and the living air,
> And the blue sky, and in the mind of man.[6]

Such seekers, no doubt deterred by the history and/or current manifestations of institutional religions, might call themselves agnostics, nontheists, or even atheists, affirming there is no Ultimate Reality to be named as "God." Nevertheless, seekers they are for they are often still open-minded and know that life beckons with its need for guiding principles by which to live—some identifiable guiding "star." They will need to infer to the best explanation of all-that-is to satisfy this demand. For them, science, with its global validity across all culture, belief systems, nations and races, inevitably shapes the context of the thought world in which they live and move and have their being. For it is the nature of science that it has, in many areas, acquired the justified accolade of being *public* truth for all people, everywhere. However, they cannot avoid asking such questions as: "Why is there anything at all?" "Why should there be a universe at all?" Leading to further questions such as "Why should the universe be of this particular kind, with its embedded rationality accessible to science and with the inbuilt capacity of its very stuff to self-organize into thinking, self-conscious persons with values?"

This might well challenge such seekers to ask further, "What is the best explanation than can be inferred for the existence and character of *such* a universe?" Any positive response to such questions, even if it does not lead seekers to any explicitly religious adherence, could justifiably point them to some Ultimate Reality that is the source of all existence and of the emergence of persons with values. Coming as they do with few preconceptions and responding to the global and holistic vistas of the sciences, the concepts such seekers might form as public truth concerning any Ultimate Reality would inevitably be characterized by having a global and holistic validity for all people, everywhere, regardless of their specific cultural and religious traditions. So that Ultimate Reality is not likely to be conceived by them in anything other than inclusive terms transcending culture, race, religion, and gender—everything that differentiates and divides humanity.

Furthermore, they might then be stimulated to seek this Ultimate Reality as a *communicating* one, in the light of the scientific perspective with which this third millennium begins—namely, nature as a self-organizing, complexifying entity generating through evolution new levels of existence which culminate in human beings who have self-consciousness and are persons with values in relation to each other and to their surroundings. Response to the challenge is then likely also to involve the recognition that how that Ultimate Reality might make itself known will vary and be shaped according to the variegated kinds of humanity open to discerning it. So their response could properly take the form of discerning how in one's own time and place and that of others, in very different contexts, this Ultimate Reality has significantly manifested itself in the past, and might be doing so in the present. For the existence or otherwise of such an Ultimate Reality is clearly the most vital question to which such seekers can direct themselves.

It is now some two and a half millennia since that axial period around 800 to 200 BCE when, in three distinct and culturally disconnected areas of China, India, and the West, there occurred a genuine expansion of human consciousness. Human beings became conscious of Being as a whole, of themselves, and of their limitations. They asked radical questions, and consciousness became conscious of itself. "In this age were born the fundamental categories within which we still think today, and the beginnings of the world religions, by which human beings still live, were created. The step into universality was taken in every sense."[7] Now, early in this third millennium, science is providing across all the global village we now inhabit a common public truth which shapes human horizons. Thereby it provides the challenge and stimulus to discern within and beneath the diversity of human traditions and current experiences the subtle forms of expression of an Ultimate Reality in, with, and under the flux of natural and human history. The seeking students who have no preconceived commitments might well become particularly sensitive to and apt for such a comprehensive, inclusive discernment of the Ultimate Reality and so help thereby to widen the horizons of their contemporaries whose convictions have already been, at least partly, formed.

Note that those with Christian convictions already have a way into this inclusive, global aspect of the communication to humanity of the Ultimate Reality. For the central affirmation in Christian belief and experience, distinctive from that of their monotheistic cousins of Islam and Judaism, is that "God," the Ultimate Reality, who expressed God's inner self in and through creation (as God's "Word"), was explicitly and particularly manifest ("incarnate") in a human person in history, Jesus the Christ. Yet, by its very nature this "Word" of God so expressed particularly is also conceived of as universal, if hidden, in its expression, and so can legitimately and hopefully be sought outside of the confines of the historical tradition in which Jesus was immersed. So an open, inclusive extension of Christian theology is legitimated, if not as yet widespread.

It is now time to assess what our original challenge might mean for Christian belief and the theology that analyzes and attempts to justify it.

11. We can formulate that challenge to Christian theists in the following terms:

Dare Christian *theology, as the intellectual articulation and justification of Christian beliefs, proceed in its search for public truth(s), by employing the criteria of reasonableness through that inference to the best explanation which characterizes the rest of human inquiries, in particular the sciences?*

Briefly, I am of the view that if Christian theology does not so "dare," then its demise and diminishing influence in the serious thinking of Western society will continue and it will never recover from the present parlous state of its intellectual reputation. For even the most sophisticated of current *Christian* theology—and I suspect this would be true *a fortiori* of Islamic (and Jewish?) theology, less clearly of Hindu and Buddhist thought—tends to rely on an authoritative book or authorizing community or on supposed self-evident a priori truths. Unfortunately such claims are circular and cannot meet the demands for validation from any external universally accepted stance and so cannot qualify as *public* truth.

If Christian theology is to meet the intellectual standards of our times by utilizing inference to the best explanation, it will have to take account of the realities of the world and humanity discovered by the sciences and the perceptions and traditions of other world religions—as well as, of course, its own inheritance from the Judeo-Christian traditions of claimed, classical revelatory experiences in its Scriptures, liturgies, aesthetic expressions, music and so forth. The sciences raise many critical issues for any traditional theology based on these last. One could instance: the overwhelming evidence for a monistic naturalism, *one* world without any dualisms or any supernaturalism; evidence for the interconnectedness of the web of natural processes so that the threshold standard for historical evidence for law-breaking "miracles" cannot be met by the traditional Scriptures; the greatly enhanced understanding of the role of genes in human nature; that human beings evolutionarily are "rising beasts" rather than "fallen angels," so that much talk of "redemption" needs radical revision; the problematic relation of God to a time now regarded as created and in which the future does not exist *for* God to know; the role of chance in the creative processes of the world; the function of biological death in evolution and so the qualification of its traditional interpretation as the "wages of sin"; and much else.

In the present context of my urging this kind of challenge to Christian theologians, and *pari passu* to Christian students, I would like also to emphasize more strongly than I have done elsewhere the radical reappraisal of the traditional understanding of the "Christ of faith" that must be undertaken in the light of our often confused and ambiguous evidence concerning the "Jesus of history." This, I realise, is an old theme raised as long ago as the first half of the nineteenth century, but it is one to which systematic theology and popular preaching have alike failed to address honestly and with integrity, in my view. It is not often realized that such is the intensity of literary, paleographical, archaeological, sociological, historical, and other studies and discoveries concerning the first century of the Christian era in Palestine and its contiguous communities that it is true to say that we probably know more (and also how little we know) concerning the historical Jesus than even those who actually lived in the period following the destruction of the Jewish temple at Jerusalem in 70 CE. We know enough to make it clear that it is legitimate to question the basis for the exalted designations and titles attached to Jesus by the writers and editors of both canonical and noncanonical writings of Christian provenance. Such questioning need not inevitably lead to skepticism about these ascriptions, but it may well qualify any absoluteness in the way we hold our beliefs about Jesus concerning his brief life, self-offering death, and transforming resurrection.

I would argue,[8] for example, that, in the light of the historical evidence and of our hard-won knowledge of biological reproduction, the affirmation that in Jesus we encounter an incarnation of the transcendent God does not depend on his being born only of Mary without a human father; and that the affirmation of Jesus' resurrection does not depend on there having been an empty tomb, so that "resurrection," if it is to be a possibility for all human beings, cannot involve a transformation of our actual bodily, physical constituents.

Others responding to the challenge I have elaborated may (and do) come to different conclusions, but clearly the future Christian community will have to accommodate much more openly and willingly than in the past those who respond to the challenge in the way I am proposing. Moreover, responsiveness to this challenge can be creative and constructive, leading to a genuine rebirth of images and a revitalization of a more global, inclusive but still Christ-oriented faith. The paths from science towards God lead us toward what I have called[9] a theistic naturalism and a sacramental pan*en*theism. In following those paths, ancient images in the Judeo-Christian tradition turn out to be reenergized—namely, those of the "Wisdom of God," the "uncreated Energies of God" and, one I have already referred to above for its inclusive significance, "the Word/*Logos* of God."

These are only my own reflections and I hope that the challenge, as I have depicted it, to "seekers" and to Christian theists among college and seminary students, might serve to provide a launching pad for that exploration into new concepts and images with which I associate the work of Phil Hefner. For the hope is that they will provide both a believable theistic framework and the guiding principles required by humanity to dwell fruitfully and creatively within the rapidly expanding horizons of humanity which are being opened up to us by the sciences in this new millennium.

The Incarnation of the Informing Self-Expressive Word of God

The conveying and receiving of information is so common an experience that we scarcely attend to it in ordinary life.[1] Yet a closer analysis can offer a helpful way of penetrating the significance of familiar theological terms peculiar to Christianity. For example, the contemporary concept of "information" can shed important light on the possibility of a "natural" perspective on the traditional notion of revelation, thereby softening the distinction between revealed and natural theology and making the notion of God's "informing" more coherent.[2]

In biblical studies and systematic theology alike, "revelation" has, of course, been the focus of much attention in the twentieth century. Yet the discussions of Christology, especially key concepts such as "incarnation," have rarely been integrated into a contemporary scientific worldview. The consequence has been an artificial division between revealed and natural knowledge. This kind of disjunction between the "revealed" and the "natural" is not only increasingly suspect for theological reasons, it is a distraction from a more lively and compelling view of revelation that coheres with significant aspects of contemporary science. In particular, I believe that the concept of exchange of

From *Religion and Science: History, Method, Dialogue*, ed. W. Mark Richardson and Wesley J. Wildman (London: Routledge, 1996), 321–39. Reprinted by permission.

information offers a fresh perspective on and new ways of thinking about the intelligibility of the affirmation that Christ is the self-disclosure of God, the "Word made flesh." In my view it is capable of accommodating an interpretation of Chalcedonian insights, without compromising its core affirmations, by presenting Christology along lines that regard the self-communication of God to humanity as an "informing" process.

First, we must recapitulate briefly the contemporary context for discussion of Christology as well as some of its historical roots. There has been a continuous, and in recent years an increasingly intensive, study of the historical process whereby the "Jesus" who is uncovered by historical scholarship developed, during the first few centuries of the Christian Church, into the "Christ of faith." This is expressed in terms of that doctrine of the union of God with humanity which is known as that of the "Incarnation." This doctrine found its classical expression in the Definition of Chalcedon of 451 AD.[3] These studies have generated keen debate both about the extent to which this classical christological formulation and its later developments and extensions can be properly inferred and extracted from the New Testament (by virtue both of its historical status and its own theological interpretations of Jesus), and about their validity today for expressing the significance of Jesus and his relation to God in a framework of thought totally different from the cultural milieu within which the Definition was propounded.[4]

The Jesus of history and the Christ of faith

The Word of God, our Lord Jesus Christ who,
of his boundless love, became what we are . . .[5]

In relation to the role of the New Testament in the emergence of the "Christ of faith," there has been growing recognition that the understanding of Jesus in the New Testament is pluriform and diverse, and that the use of the concept of "incarnation" to interpret the significance of the life, teaching, death, and resurrection of Jesus emerges only towards the end of its period (roughly that of the first century

AD) in the Johannine writings, that is, the Fourth Gospel and the three epistles of John. Thus, in a widely respected study, J. D. G. Dunn asks, "How did the doctrine of the Incarnation originate?" and he concludes:

> It did *not* emerge through the identification of Jesus with a divine individual or intermediary being whose presence in heaven was already assumed. . . . It did *not* emerge from an identification of Jesus as Elijah or Enoch returned from heaven—exaltation to heaven was not taken necessarily to presuppose or imply a previous existence in heaven. . . . It did *not* emerge as an inevitable corollary to the conviction that Jesus had been raised from the dead or as part of the logic of calling Jesus the Son of God. . . . It did *not* emerge as a corollary to the conviction that Jesus had been divinely inspired by the eschatological Spirit, a concept of inspiration giving way imperceptibly to one of incarnation. . . . *The doctrine of the incarnation began to emerge when the exalted Christ was spoken of in terms drawn from the Wisdom[6] imagery of pre-Christian Judaism* . . . only in the post–Pauline period did a clear understanding of Christ as having preexisted with God before his ministry on earth emerge, and *only in the Fourth Gospel can we speak of a doctrine of the incarnation.*

Dunn further points out that:[7]

> Initially at least Christ was not thought of as a divine being who had preexisted with God but as *the climactic embodiment of God's power and purpose*—his life, death and resurrection understood in terms of *God himself reaching out to men.* Christ was identified . . . with *God's* creative wisdom, God's redemptive purpose, *God's* revelatory word . . . God's clearest self-expression, *God's* last word.[8]

He argues that the use of "wisdom" and "word" imagery meant that these early formulations of the significance of Jesus were affirmations that

> *Christ showed them what God is like, the Christ-event defined God more clearly than anything else had ever done. . . . Jesus had revealed God,* not the Son of God, not the "divine intermediary" Wisdom, but God. *As the Son of God he revealed God as Father. . . . As the Wisdom of God he revealed God as Creator-Redeemer. . . .* "Incarnation" means

initially that God's love and power had been experienced in fullest measure in, through and as this man Jesus, that Christ had been experienced as God's self-expression, the Christ-event as the effective, re-creative power of God.[9]

A. E. Harvey stresses the constraint of their monotheism on the New Testament writers (and, I would add, also on us):

> The New Testament writers appear to have submitted to this constraint, and to have avoided using the word "god" or "divine" of Jesus. . . . [They] are similarly insistent about the absolute oneness of God, and show no tendency to describe Jesus in terms of divinity.[10]

Harvey agrees with Dunn that the early application of Wisdom language to Jesus precedes the doctrine of the Incarnation, and makes the further point that, although the language of "preexistence" is applied to Jesus in the Fourth Gospel,[11] this does not in any case imply divinity. For "Wisdom's presence at the creation was a way of saying that no part of creation is an afterthought: it was all there from the beginning. So with Jesus."[12] Neither of these authors is especially radical in his handling of the New Testament data. The more conservative R. E. Brown also recognizes a development *into* the usage of calling Jesus God, even if he charts it differently from Dunn and Harvey.[13]

The widely acknowledged diversity of ideas, words, and images in first-century Christian writings concerning the nature of Jesus and his relation to God has been broadly interpreted in two ways, with many gradations in between.[14] It has been seen either as a "development," meaning "growth, from immaturity to maturity, of a single specimen from within itself"; or as an "evolution," meaning "the genesis of successive new species by mutations and natural selection along the way."[15] But we may well question if a sharp contrast between "development" and "evolution" can be maintained in the light of contemporary understandings of doctrinal history which take account of general philosophies of historical existence and interpretation ("hermeneutics").[16]

Clearly, the christological formulations in the New Testament impel us to acknowledge a diversity of interpretations, none of which should be suppressed even if, strictly speaking, they are not all compatible with each other.[17] New Testament scholars have uncovered a rich treasury of interpretations of Jesus' impact on His first disciples and their followers, and have clarified enormously both their relative independence as well as their interrelations. The New Testament vouchsafes not an intellectual synthesis, but a kaleidoscopic variety of poetic insights.

The synthesizing and systematizing activity of the Christian intellect was fully exercised in the following centuries, leading to the Chalcedonian Definition and subsequent elaborations. These ramifications cannot be entered into here, except to recognize that the interpretation of God and Jesus emerging from the Patristic era gained classical, even normative, status as it was enshrined in the church councils of the first five centuries. The "fathers" undertook a task which is still incumbent upon us now in our own historical and cultural milieu.[18]

The problem today is to discern whether and how much the development or evolution of doctrine, especially that of the first five centuries AD concerning the relation of God and Jesus, can help us interpret and understand the same relation as we find it in the New Testament.[19] Inevitably those classical doctrinal formulations were closely integrated with the philosophy and theology of the prevailing Hellenistic culture (mainly neo-Platonic), and were expressed in terms such as "nature," "substance," and "person" in an ontological framework quite unlike our own—and certainly not that of a culture dominated by modern science. This is widely recognized and at least in Britain it has led to an intensive debate with the publication of *The Myth of God Incarnate* (1977)—about how to formulate Jesus' relation to God and to the rest of humanity today.[20]

However, much of this intensive debate about how to formulate Jesus' relation to God and to the rest of humanity has been confused, in my view, by the absence of an intelligible and believable account of God's being and becoming, God's interaction with the world, God's communication with humanity, and the constitution of human beings. These must be considered in the light of what the sciences now tell us of the being and becoming of the natural, created world, including humanity.

This is the contemporary theological framework from which we must consider Jesus' significance for us today. J. D. G. Dunn summed up John's contribution in the New Testament to the beginnings of Christology thus:

> John is wrestling with the problem of how to think of God and how to think of Christ in relation to God in the light of the clarification of the nature and character of God which the Christ-event afforded.[21]

Dunn urges *us* to follow John's model of conveying "the divine, revelatory, and saving significance of Christ" in language and conceptualities contemporary to us.

To do this, we shall have to employ a theological framework that is viable, intelligible, and defensible in the light of the sciences. Is the concept of the "incarnation" still credible in *this* framework? It may be the case finally that we shall find ourselves asking the question which D. Nineham poses in the penultimate paragraph of *The Myth of God Incarnate:*

> Is it necessary to "believe in Jesus" in any sense beyond that which sees him as the main figure through whom God launched men into a relationship with himself so full and rich that, under the various understandings and formulations of it, it has been, and continues to be the salvation of a large proportion of the human race?[22]

Even if it transpires that more can be said than Nineham suggests, we shall have to accept that there is a certain indivisibility about the "Christ-event," as the New Testament scholars tend to denote the "things about Jesus." We have no option, in view of the once-for-all givenness of our historical sources, but to take as *our* starting point the whole complex of the life, teaching, death, and resurrection-exaltation[23] of Jesus, *together with* its impact on his first-century followers that led to the formation of the first Christian community. This is indeed what is meant by the "Christ-event."

Generations of Christians have shared in the experiences of the early witnesses through the continuous life of the ensuing Christian community, as expressed in its liturgy, literature, visual arts, music, and architecture; in a nexus of transformed personal relationships; and through their direct apprehension of God through Christ, revered as the universalized human Jesus "raised" to the presence of God.[24] Thus, that arrow which was shot into history in the Christ-event lands squarely here today, and we ourselves are challenged to interpret it. Of course, "revelation" is relative to circumstances—that is, the meanings which God can express in creation and in human history are relative to the receptiveness and outlook, the hermeneutical horizons, of those to whom God is communicating. So, however strong a case may be made for a "high" ontological Christology having its roots in the Christ-event, we cannot avoid asking whether we too can see what they saw in Him. Even if we were to accept that the New Testament represents a "development" of seeds of judgment and reflection on Jesus, rather than an "evolution" with mutations, we would still be bound to ask about Jesus: "What must the truth have been and be if that is how it looked to people who thought and wrote like that?"[25]

How could God communicate through Jesus?

As we think of the Christ-event from the perspective of the present scientific culture, one potentially valuable resource is the insight gained from information theory. At this point we must say a word more about "information." J. C. Puddefoot has carefully clarified the relation between the different usages of this term.[26] First, physicists, communication engineers, and neuroscientists use "information" which is related to the probability of one outcome among possible outcomes of a situation ("counting-information"). In this sense, it is connected with the notion of entropy. Second, there is the meaning, coming from the Latin root, which is "to give shape or form to" ("shaping-information"). Finally, there is the ordinary meaning of information as knowledge, or the imparting of knowledge ("meaning-information").

Puddefoot points out that information in the first sense must shape or give form to our minds, so "informing" us in the second sense, and thereby conveying information to us in the third sense. In the context of this essay, we will use "information" to represent this whole process, involving transition from the first to the third sense. More-over, the end of the process can be not merely the acquisition of knowledge, for the possibility arises (though not the certainty) that when *persons* acquire knowledge, "meaning" is also disclosed. Pudde-foot suggests that information is meaningless without minds, and he is correct to stress that, even with minds, information can remain meaningless.

The usage of information by physicists, communication engineers, and neuroscientists can be regarded as explicating the underlying processes which "inform" our mental experiences, giving us "knowl-edge." Hence, the language pertinent to information in the technical, scientific sense is one possible, but basic, description of the kind of conscious information we acquire, and such knowledge has the fur-ther potentiality of generating discernment of meaning.

We may characterize God's interaction with the world[27] as a holis-tic, top-down, continuing process of input of "information," con-ceived of broadly, whereby God's intentions and purposes are imple-mented in the shaping of particular events, or patterns of events, without any abrogation of the regularities discerned by the sciences in the natural order. Amongst the constituents of that world are hu-man beings who are persons. These too can be "informed" by God through the nexus of events, which includes events in human-brains-in-human-bodies. When the receipt of such an "input" from God is conscious, it is properly called "religious experience." I have argued elsewhere that such an understanding of God's interaction with hu-man beings can be regarded as revelatory, and as fully personal as that between human beings, in spite of the apparently abstract limitations of the terminology of "information input" and of computer science.[28]

How, in the light of this, might we then interpret the experience of God that was mediated to his disciples and to the New Testament church through Jesus? That is, how can we understand the Christ-event as God's self-communication and interaction with the world such that it is intelligible in the light of today's natural and human sciences? We need to explicate in these terms the conclusions of scholars about the understanding in New Testament times of Jesus the Christ. Note, for example, Dunn's conclusion that:

> Initially Christ was thought of . . . as the climactic embodiment of God's power and purpose . . . God himself reaching out to men . . . God's creative wisdom . . . God's revelatory word . . . God's clearest self-expression, God's last word.[29]

These descriptions of what Jesus the Christ was to those who encountered him and to the early church are all, in their various ways, about God *communicating* to humanity. In the broad sense in which we have been using the terms, they are about an "input of information." This process of "input of information" from God conforms with the actual content of human experience, as the conveying of "meaning" from God to humanity. I have argued that God can convey his meanings through events and patterns of events in the created world—those in question here are the life, teaching, death, and resurrection of the human person, Jesus of Nazareth, as reported by these early witnesses. As the investigations of the New Testament show, they experienced in Jesus, in his very person and personal history, a communication *from God*, a revelation of God's meanings for humanity. So it is no wonder that, in the later stages of reflection in the New Testament period, the evangelist John conflated the concept of divine Wisdom with that of the *Logos*, the "Word" of God, in order to say what he intended about the meaning of Jesus the Christ for the early witnesses and their immediate successors. The *locus classicus* of this exposition is, of course, the prologue to his gospel. John Macquarrie notes that the expression, "Word" or *Logos*, when applied to Jesus, not only carries undertones of the image of "Wisdom," it also conflates two other concepts: the Hebrew idea of the "word of the Lord" for the will of God expressed in utterance, especially to the prophets, and in creative activity; and that of "*logos*" in Hellenistic Judaism, especially in Philo—the Divine *Logos*, the creative principle of rationality operative in the universe, especially manifest in human reason, formed within the mind of God and projected into objectivity.[30]

Macquarrie has in fact attempted to interpret for our times the import of Word-*Logos* in the prologue to John's gospel by substituting "Meaning" for it. His paraphrase, now published in full, is worth quoting, for it succeeds in conveying in today's terms something of what it meant for its first readers (numbers refer to the paraphrased verses of John 1):

> (1) Fundamental to everything is Meaning. It is closely connected with what we call "God," and indeed Meaning and God are virtually identical. (2) To say that God was in the beginning is to say that Meaning was in the beginning. (3) All things were made meaningful, and there was nothing made that was meaningless. (4) Life is the drive toward Meaning, and life has emerged into self-conscious humanity, as the (finite) bearer and recipient of Meaning. (5) And meaning shines out through the threat of absurdity, for absurdity has not overwhelmed it. (9) Every human being has a share in Meaning, whose true light was coming into the world. (10) Meaning was there in the world and embodying itself in the world, yet the world has not recognized the Meaning, (11) and even humanity, the bearer of Meaning, has rejected it. (12) But those who have received it and believed in it have been enabled to become the children of God. (13) And this has happened not in the natural course of evolution or through human striving, but through a gracious act of God. (14) For the Meaning has been incarnated in a human existent, in whom was grace and truth; and we have seen in him the glory toward which everything moves—the glory of God. (16) From him, whom we can acknowledge in personal terms as the Son of the Father, we have received abundance of grace. (17) Through Moses came the command of the law, through Jesus Christ grace and truth. (18) God is a mystery, but the Son who has shared the Father's life has revealed him.[31]

The substitution of "Meaning" for Word-*Logos* helps to convey better the gospel's affirmation of what happened in creation and in Jesus the Christ. For, as we have seen, conveying of meaning, in the ordinary sense, is implemented initially by an input of "information"—the constrained and selected elements among all possibilities that sufficiently delimit signals (that is, language and other means of human communication) so that they can convey meaning. As John Bowker has put it:

> How do we arrive at the sense of anything? How do we construct meaning on the basis of information which arrives at our receptor centres in the form of sensation, or which occurs in the internal process? The biological and neurological answer lies in the (initially latent) structured ability of the brain to code, store, and decode signals and represent them as information. This implies that "meaning" is constituted not by the quantitative amount of information, but by a qualitative selection (control into restriction), which enables meaning . . . to transcend the mathematical base of its constituent elements; the way [in which "meaning" does this] . . . does not mean that there is an automatic, radical disjunction between quantitative (in a semiotic sense) and qualitative information.[32]

The use of the concept of "information input" to refer to the way God induces effects in the world was, to the best of my knowledge, pioneered by Bowker. It also has been used by him to render intelligible the idea of God expressing himself in and through the human being of Jesus:

> . . . it is credibly and conceptually possible to regard Jesus as a wholly God-informed person, who retrieved the theistic inputs coded in the chemistry and electricity of brain-processes for the scan of every situation, and for every utterance, verbal and nonverbal . . . [T]he result would have been the incarnating (the embodying) of God in the only way in which it could possibly have occurred. No matter what God may be in himself, the realization of that potential resource of effect would have to be mediated into the process and continuity of life-construction through the brain-process interpreted through the codes available at any particular moment of acculturation. . . . There is no other way of being human, or indeed of being alive, because otherwise consciousness ceases. . . . That is as true of Jesus *de humanitate* as of any one else.

But what seems to have shifted Jesus into a different degree of significance . . . was the stability and the consistency with which his
own life-construction was God-informed. . . .

It is possible on this basis to talk about a wholly human figure,
without loss or compromise, and to talk also, at exactly the same
moment, of a wholly real presence of God so far as that nature
(whatever it is in itself) can be mediated to and through the
process of the life-construction in the human case, through the
process of brain behavior by which any human being becomes an
informed subject—but in this case, perhaps even uniquely, a wholly
God-informed subject.[33]

This illustrates how the notion of God communicating himself
through the complete person of Jesus the Christ is consistent with all
that we have been saying concerning the nature of God's interaction
with and self-communication to the world. It renders such interaction intelligible in a way that seemed to be impossible for its critics in
The Myth of God Incarnate.

At this juncture in our enterprise, recognition that God has, in
fact, communicated God's own self to humanity in this way—that is,
acceptance of the belief that God was "incarnate" in Jesus—must be
left to the judgment of the reader. That judgment has to rest on the
reader's assessment not only of its intrinsic intelligibility but also of its
moral and religious significance, of the Christ-event in the light of
the New Testament evidence, of whether or not the church teaching
down the ages is to be regarded as providentially guided, and of the
experience of Christ as a living and active presence of God in the
church and in the world.

The present writer judges that these considerations are compelling, so—hoping the reader is prepared to continue with him, at
least provisionally, in this belief—we shall proceed by exploring its
implications and its relation to a more general theology for a scientific age we have been developing. This belief in the incarnation was
founded on the whole complex of what we have called the Christ-
event, which I will now refer to as "Jesus the Christ" to convey the
personal and historical aspects intended. Those who were actually in-

volved historically in the interpretation of Jesus the Christ came to believe that in the completely human person of Jesus, it was *God* whose self-expression they experienced. In the following section, we pursue the question of what (according to this Christian belief) God may actually be said to have communicated to humanity about God's Self in and through Jesus the Christ.

God's self-expression in Jesus the Christ

Any communication of the nature of God's Self believed to have been transmitted in and through Jesus the Christ will have to be related to those insights into what we are able to discern of divine Being and Becoming from more general reflections on natural being and becoming. Of course, we look not for proof, but for a consonance which might consolidate the insights of such a "natural" theology. However, if Jesus the Christ really is a self-communication *from* God and the self-expression of God in a human person, as the church, in concord with the early witnesses, has affirmed, then we can hope for much more. What were glimmers of light on a distant horizon might become shafts of the Uncreated Light of the Creator's own Self. Hints and faint echoes of the divine in nature might become, in Jesus Christ, a resonating word to humanity from God's own Self, a manifest revelation of God. Jesus the Christ would then, indeed, be the very Word of God made human flesh, as the early church came to assert. What is only implicit and partially and imperfectly discerned of God in the created world would then be explicit and manifest in his person. We shall therefore need to reflect on what the early Christian community affirmed as their experience of God in Jesus the Christ, in the light of what we are able to discern[34] of divine Being and Becoming from natural being and becoming.

God as continuous and immanent Creator

From the continuity of the natural processes, we infer that God is continuously creating, as the immanent Creator, in and through the natural order. For the processes of the world exhibit an intelligible continuity, in which the potentialities of its constituents are unfolded in forms of an ever-increasing complexity and organization. These forms are properly described as "emergent," in that they manifest new features that are irreducible to the sciences which describe the simpler levels of organization out of which they have developed. One of the most striking aspects of natural becoming is that qualitatively new kinds of existence come into being. We witness in nature the seeming paradox of discontinuity generated by continuity. Hence belief in God as Creator involves the recognition that this is the character of the processes whereby God actually creates new forms, new entities, structures, and processes that emerge with new capabilities, requiring distinctive language on our part to distinguish them. God is present in and to this whole process.

This has important consequences for our understanding and expression of God's self-manifestation in the human person of Jesus. One might say that God "informs" the human personhood of Jesus such that God's self-expression occurs in and through Jesus' humanity. For when we reflect on the significance of what the early witnesses reported as their experience of Jesus the Christ, we find ourselves implicitly emphasizing both the *continuity* of Jesus with the rest of humanity, and so with the rest of nature within which *Homo sapiens* evolved, and, at the same time, the *discontinuity* constituted by what is distinctive in his relation to God and what, through him (his teaching, life, death, and resurrection), the early witnesses experienced of God.

This paradox is already present in that peak of christological reflection in the New Testament period that comes to expression in the Prologue to the Gospel of John. For in that seminal text, the Word-*Logos*, which both is God and was with God in creating (vv. 1–3), and which becomes human "flesh" (v. 14), is the same "Word" that is all the time "in the world" (v. 10) and giving "light" (vv. 4–6) to humanity, even though unrecognized (v. 10). God had been and was already in the world, expressing God's meaning in and through God's creating, to use Macquarrie's interpretation. But this meaning was hidden and suppressed, and only in Jesus the Christ has it become manifest and explicit, so that its true "glory" (v. 14) has become apparent.

This encourages us to understand the "incarnation" which occurred in Jesus as exemplifying that emergence-from-continuity which characterizes the whole process of God's creating. There both is continuity with all that preceded him, yet in him there has appeared a new mode of human existence which, by virtue of its openness to God, is a new revelation of both God and of humanity. Taking the clue from the Johannine Prologue, we could say that the manifestation of God which Jesus' contemporaries encountered in him must have been an emanation from within creation, from deep within those events and processes which led to his life, teaching, death, and resurrection. According to this understanding of God's creation and presence in the world, "incarnation" is not God's "descent" into the world, wherein God is conceived as "above" (and so outside) it, as so many Christmas hymns would have us believe. Rather, it is the manifestation of the One who is already in the world, but not recognized or known. Thus, by virtue of his response and openness to God, the human person Jesus is to be seen as the locus, the icon, through whom God's nature and character are made open and explicit. Yet it must be kept in mind that God has never ceased to be continuously creating and bringing God's purpose to fruition in the order of energy-matter-space-time.

Because of this continuity between God's continuous creativity and the inherent creativity of the universe, it seems to me that we must see Jesus the Christ not as a unique invasion of the personhood of an individual human being by an utterly transcendent God, but rather as the distinctive manifestation of a possibility always inherently there for human beings by virtue of what God had created them to be and to become. Such a joint emphasis on continuity (corresponding to "immanence") as well as on emergence (corresponding to "incarnation") is vital to any understanding of Jesus the Christ which is going to make what he *was* relevant to what we *might* be. For this interpretation of the "incarnation" entails that what we have affirmed about Jesus is not, in principle, impossible for all humanity. Even if, as a matter of contingent historical fact, we think the "incarnation" is only fully to be seen in him, it is not excluded as a possibility for all humanity.

In proposing a strong sense of God's immanence in the world (largely suppressed in the West for the last three hundred years) as the context for thinking about the incarnation, we must nevertheless recognize the transcendence of God. Admittedly, the sense of transcendence often has been so dominant that the very idea of incarnation has seemed inconsistent, even nonsensical, in relation to talk about God. However, the fact is that the Jewish followers encountered in Jesus the Christ (especially in his resurrection) a dimension of divine transcendence which, as devout monotheists, they had attributed to God alone.

But they also encountered him as a complete human being, and so experienced an intensity of God's immanence in the world different from anything else in their experience or tradition. Thus it was that the fusion of these two aspects of their awareness—that it was God acting in and through Jesus the Christ—gave rise to the conviction that in him something new of immense significance for humanity had appeared in the world. As *we* might say, a new emergent had appeared within created humanity. And thus it was, too, that they ransacked their cultural stock of available images and models (for example, "Christ," "Son of God," "Lord," "Wisdom," *"Logos"*), at first Hebraic and later Hellenistic, to give expression to this new, nonreducible, distinctive mode of being and becoming, instantiated in Jesus the Christ.

God as personal, or "suprapersonal," and purposive

The operation of natural selection in biological organisms has an inbuilt tendency to favor increasing complexity, information processing, and storageability, because of their survival value.[35] These are the foundations for sensitivity to pain, consciousness, and even self-consciousness, which also must be reckoned to have survival value. This process—albeit by the zigzag, random path carved out by the interplay of chance and law—reaches its maximum development so far in the emergence of the human-brain-in-the-human-body, which has that distinctive and emergent feature we call being a "person." One must also consider the "anthropic" features of the universe which allowed the emergence through evolution of human persons and so the appearance of *personal* agency.[36] This would seem to tentatively justify the description of the universe as a "personalizing universe," in the sense that "the whole is to be understood as a process making for personality and beyond."[37] Reflecting on what could constitute the "best explanation" of such a universe, I have concluded that God is (at least) personal or "suprapersonal." The awkward term "suprapersonal" signifies here that any extension of the language of human personhood inevitably, like all analogies based on created realities, must remain inadequate as a *description* of the nature of that ineffable, ultimate Reality which is God.

However tentative any use of personal language must be when applied to God, it remains the most consistent and the least misleading of any that might be inferred from our reflections on natural being and becoming. Furthermore, consideration of the emergence of the experience of transcendence-in-immanence that characterizes evolved human personhood leads us to conjecture that

> in humanity immanence might be able to display a transcendent dimension to a degree which would unveil, without distortion, the transcendent-Creator-who-is-immanent in a uniquely new emergent manner—that is, that in humanity (in a human being, or in human beings), the presence of God the Creator might be unveiled with a clarity, in a glory, not hitherto perceived.[38]

This leads one to ask: Might it not be possible for a human being so to reflect God, to be so wholly open to God, that God's presence was clearly unveiled to the rest of humanity in a new, emergent, and unexpected manner?

It was the affirmation of the early church, and continues to be the church's affirmation today, that in Jesus the Christ this has actually happened. That is, in Jesus the Christ, God's self-expression is such that it validates personal attributions to God, even though we recognize the inherent limitations of these attributions. For in Jesus the

Christ, God has apparently taken the initiative to reveal his presence to humanity in and through a completely human *person*. The early disciples and subsequent members of the Christian Church have no doubt that they encounter God in Jesus the Christ, and that his personhood conveys God's meanings to and for humanity.

Meanings that persons wish to communicate are conveyed through words. Thus, the concept of the Word-*Logos* of God, appropriated to understand the significance of Jesus the Christ, is essentially a personal one.[39] We have already had our understanding of the Prologue to St. John's gospel enriched by Macquarrie's substitution of "Meaning" for Word-*Logos*. The "Meaning" so communicated within the pages of the New Testament is principally about the significance of the personal relation to God as "Love," and of loving interpersonal relationships. Hence John Robinson's paraphrase of the Prologue, in which he substitutes the concept of the "personal" for Word-*Logos*, is particularly illuminating:

(1) The clue to the universe as personal was present from the beginning. It was found at the level of reality which we call God. Indeed, it was no other than God nor God than it. (2) At that depth of reality the element of the personal was there from the start. (3) Everything was drawn into existence through it, and there is nothing in the process that has come into being without it. (4) Life owes its emergence to it, and life lights the path to man. (5) It is that light which illumines the darkness of the sub-personal creation, and the darkness never succeeded in quenching it. . . .

(9) That light was the clue to reality—the light which comes to clarity in man. Even before that it was making its way in the universe. (10) It was already in the universe, and the whole process depended upon it, although it was not conscious of it. (11) It came to its own in the evolution of the personal; yet persons failed to grasp it. (12) But to those who did, who believed what it represented, it gave the potential of a fully personal relationship to God. (13) For these the meaning of life was seen to rest, not simply on its biological basis, nor on the impulses of nature or the drives of history, but on the reality of God. (14) And this divine personal principle found embodiment in a man and took habitation in our midst. We saw its

full glory, in all its utterly gracious reality—the wonderful sight of a person living in uniquely normal relationship to God, as son to father.

(16) From this fullness of life we have all received, in gifts without measure. (17) It was law that governed the less than fully personal relationships even of man; the true gracious reality came to expression in Jesus Christ. (18) The ultimate reality of God no one has ever seen. But the one who has lived closest to it, in the unique relationship of son to father, he has laid it bare.[40]

In this perspective, the self-disclosure that God communicated to humanity in Jesus the Christ was an explicit revelation of the significance of personhood in the divine purposes. The Creator God in whom the world exists has all along been instantiating God's own personalness, and this has been expressed supremely in Jesus the Christ. Again we must note that this is being affirmed as the contingent historical reality, but this affirmation does not confine the incarnating of God the Word to Jesus alone, nor does it preclude the possibility of such language being the appropriate description of at least some other human beings—and perhaps, potentially at least, of all.

The distinctive feature of human beings *qua* persons is that they are potential carriers of values which they seek by purposive behavior to embody in their individual and social life. It was one of the well-attested features of the experience of Jesus the Christ that he not only inculcated values in his disciples through his teaching, but he also exemplified them in his life. Afterward they saw that this was especially the case in view of the circumstance of and reasons for the suffering and death inflicted on him.

We leave the content of these values for another essay.[41] Here we simply note that it is not just any kind of personhood, or personal life, that we see as the purpose of God to bring into existence. The acceptance of Jesus the Christ as the self-expression of God compels the recognition that it is the eliciting of persons embodying values which is the underlying purpose of the divine creative process. Persons can only be carriers of values if they are self-conscious and free, so that the "propensities" of the biological, evolutionary process have their ultimate limiting form in *this* person, Jesus the Christ. The "incarnation" in Jesus the Christ may, then, properly be said to be the consummation of the creative and creating evolutionary process. It would follow that, if Jesus the Christ is the self-expression of God's meaning, then the evoking in the world of *this* kind of person, with *these* values, just is the purpose of God in creation.

God as exploring in creation through its open-endedness

Recognizing that God as Creator acts through chance operating under the constraints of law, and that many of the processes of the world are open-ended (they are irreducibly unpredictable), combined with emphasis on the immanence of God in the creative and creating processes of the world, leads us to suggest that God the Creator is *exploring* in creation. The assertion that "God the Creator explores in creation" means that God improvisingly responds to and creates on the basis of eventualities which are irreducibly unpredictable in advance. The operation of human free will is, of course, a particularly notable and "unpredictable" feature of the world which demonstrates God's willingness to let it have this open-ended character. It is concomitantly a world in which God exercises providential guidance and influence.

Jesus exercises free will in such complete openness to God that his disciples come to designate him as the "Christ" and their successors to develop an understanding of what was happening in him as the "incarnation" of God. That same Jesus risked everything on the faithfulness of God in the hazardous events of his times, and thereby united Himself with God in that painful process, in hope of bringing into existence God's reign, the "kingdom of God." This means that, in the willing act of Jesus the Christ, the open-endedness of what is going on in the world fully and self-consciously united itself with the purposes of God for the still open future. In Jesus' oneness with God we see the openness of the creative process operative in a human person, fully united with the immanent activity of God. God is the source of the open future, and this openness is the medium of expressing God's intentions for humanity and the world. But is not this just that very close linkage between the advent of Jesus and the initiation of the kingdom of God ("God's reign") which is distinctive of Jesus' own teaching?

The historical evidence is indeed that Jesus was so open to God that he entrusted his whole future to God unequivocally to the point of abandoning, at his death, even his sense of God's presence to himself.[42] The evidence attests that the historical Jesus staked all on God's future, and thereby made possible the resurrection. In this manner, God further revealed Jesus as the Christ who would draw all humanity after him into a full relation with God. This is why we may now see Jesus the Christ as a new departure point in the creative process, the beginning of a new possibility for human existence in which new potentialities of human life are actualized in those who are willing to share in Jesus' *human* and *open* response to God.

God as "self-limited" and as vulnerable, self-emptying, self-giving, and suffering love

Elsewhere, I have attributed "self-limitation" to God with respect to God's power over all events and over knowledge of the future.[43] I arrived at this conclusion because of certain inherent yet created unpredictabilities in some systems of the natural world. These included, *inter alia*, the operations of the human-brain-in-the-human-body, and so of the deliberations of human free will. This led to the notion that God had allowed himself not to have power over and knowledge of the future states of such systems, because God wanted them to possess a degree of autonomy that could develop into self-conscious, free human beings.

Now, if Jesus the Christ is the self-expression of God, this inevitably involves a self-limitation of God. For only some aspects of God's own nature are expressible in a human life. In particular, God's omnipotence and omniscience could not be expressed in the limits of the human person of Jesus, whose complete humanity certainly restricted his power and knowledge.

This "self-emptying" *(kenosis)* of God in Jesus the Christ has been

much discussed since its revival in the nineteenth century to reinter-
pret the classical doctrine of the incarnation.[44] It was predicated on a
somewhat overcautious acceptance of the full humanity of Jesus, and
was heavily dependent on the interpretation of certain key passages in
St. Paul's writings as indicating the preexistence of "Jesus Christ"
himself, regarded as the God-Man.[45] There are many difficulties with
this view, including exegetical ones, and there is considerable confusion about what and to whom the notion of "preexistence" refers.
Suffice it to say, for our present purposes, that God (or the Word-
Logos of God as a mode of God's being) and hence God's intentions
and purposes, can be coherently conceived as preexistent in relation
to the human Jesus.[46]

Furthermore, on the interpretation of created natural being and
becoming I have advanced elsewhere, God is all the time self-limiting
in his immanent, creating presence in the world. Indeed, we must
speak of the self-emptying *(kenosis)* and self-giving of God in creation. So the eventual self-expression of God in the restricted human
personhood of Jesus can be seen as an explicit manifestation and revelation of that perennial (self-limiting, -emptying, -giving) relation of
God to the created world, which was up until then only implicit and
hidden. The only temporal *pre*existence implicit in this insight, relative to the Jesus who was in history, is that of *God*, whose transcendent Being is of such a kind that God creatively expresses God's Self
in immanent Becoming in the world throughout created time. In any
case, God always has ontological priority.

Because of the interplay of chance and law in the processes of creation, one can also infer that God may be regarded as "taking a risk"
in creating, and therein making himself and his purposes vulnerable
to the inherent open-endedness of those processes. This vulnerability
of God is accentuated also by the effects of human free will, an outcome of that inbuilt open-endedness. Such a suggestion can be only a
conjecture, an attempt to make sense of certain features of natural
processes that are also seen as created by God. But this suggestion is
reinforced, indeed overtly revealed—that is, communicated by God—
if God truly expressed God's Self in Jesus the Christ. For his path

through life was preeminently one of vulnerability to the forces that swirled around him, to which he eventually innocently succumbed in acute suffering and, from his human perception, in a tragic, abandoned death.

Because sacrificial, self-limiting, self-giving action on behalf of the good of others is, in human life, the hallmark of love, those who believe in Jesus the Christ as the self-expression of God have come to see his life as their ultimate warrant for asserting that God is essentially "Love," insofar as any one word can accurately refer to God's nature. Jesus' own teaching concerning God as "Abba," Father, and of the conditions for entering the "kingdom of God," pointed to this too. But it was the person of Jesus, and what happened to him, that early established this perception of God in the Christian community.

We see, therefore, that belief in Jesus the Christ as the self-expression of God is entirely consonant with the conception of God as self-limiting, vulnerable, self-emptying, and self-giving—that is, as supreme Love in creative action. On this understanding, Jesus the Christ is the definitive communication from God to humanity of the deep meaning of what God has been effecting in creation. And that is precisely what the Prologue to the Fourth Gospel says.

Furthermore, we have inferred even more tentatively from the character of the natural processes of creation that God has to be seen as suffering in, with, and under these self processes, with their costly, open-ended unfolding in time. If God was present in and one with Jesus the Christ, then we have to conclude that *God* also suffered in and with him in his passion and death. The God whom Jesus therefore obeyed and expressed in his life and death is indeed a "crucified God," to use Jürgen Moltmann's phrase, and the cry of dereliction can be seen as an expression of the anguish also of God in creation. If Jesus is indeed the self-expression of God in a human person, then the tragedy of his actual human life can be seen as a drawing back of the curtain to unveil a God suffering in and with the sufferings of created humanity. Moreover, this extends to all of creation, since humanity is an evolved part of it. The suffering of God, which we could glimpse only tentatively in the processes of creation, is in Jesus the Christ concentrated into a point of intensity and transparency which reveals it to all who focus on him.

In this contribution, for the most part I have been thinking about Jesus the Christ in relation to how and what God was communicating through him—in particular, what God was expressing about God's own Self in and through his person and personal history. In this perspective, Jesus the Christ, by virtue of his openness to God as his "Father" and Creator, was able to express in a distinctive way the transcendence of the Creator who is immanent in the world process. Thus his disciples and their followers encountered in him a presence of God which fused God's transcendence and immanence in a way that engendered the language of "incarnation." However, when such incarnational language becomes confined to assertions about Jesus' "nature" and about what kind of "substance(s)" do or do not constitute him, then it loses its force to convey significant meaning to many today who are concerned not so much with what Jesus was "in himself," but rather with the dynamic nature of the relation between God's immanent creative *activity* focused and unveiled in him and the *processes* of nature and of human history and experience, which are all "in God," and from which God is never absent.

What the disciples and their followers experienced in Jesus the Christ and the more general notions of God's continuing relation to the world which were inferred from natural being and becoming clearly render each other more intelligible, and mutually enrich and enhance each other. In him, we can say, general and special revelation of God converge, coincide, and mutually reinforce each other.

CHAPTER 11

DNA of Our DNA

The birth narratives in the early chapters of the Gospels of
Matthew and Luke (Matt. 1:18–2:12; Luke 1:26–56; 2:1–20) have provided the principal basis for the belief that Jesus was born of his
mother Mary without the agency of a human father—that is, by the
direct action of God (as "the Holy Spirit"); and that she was later
married to Joseph. It has also been inferred as congruent with, and a
deduction from, the affirmation of Jesus as being both "God and
man," that is the doctrine of the Incarnation in its most explicitly ontological form. However, according to the Roman Catholic scholar
Raymond E. Brown, "Both Protestant and Catholic theologians have
stated clearly that the bodily fatherhood of Joseph would not have
excluded the fatherhood of God"[1] and quotes the "relatively conservative" Catholic theologian, J. Ratzinger: "According to the faith of
the Church the Sonship of Jesus does not rest on the fact that Jesus
had no human father: the doctrine of Jesus' divinity would not be
affected if Jesus had been the product of a normal marriage. For the
Sonship of which faith speaks is not a biological but an ontological
fact, an event not in time but in God's eternity."[2] The two gospel narratives have been intensively studied in relation to their historicity
and to this we shall have to revert. Before doing so, it is pertinent to
stress the issues raised by so-called "miracles" in general and, in partic-

From *The Birth of Jesus: Biblical and Theological Reflections*, ed. George J. Brooke (Edinburgh: T & T Clark, 2000), 59–67. Reprinted by permission.

ular, by our scientific knowledge in relation to the very notion of a "virginal conception" of Jesus—commonly called the virgin birth, although it is really the nature of Jesus' beginning as a living being that is involved. It is with respect to this that modern biological science poses some hard questions.

Miracle and the scientific view of the world

We are, of course, free to use the word "miracle" in whatever way suits us in the present intellectual climate, and it has, in fact, undergone much redefinition in the course of time. In a *biblical* concordance it will often be pointed out that the English word "miracle" etymologically translates words standing for "wonder," "an act of power," or "a sign." Nevertheless, since the general establishment of the nonbiblical idea of an "order" of nature, ordinary usage of the word implies "some contrast with the natural order" and an event "not fully explicable by naturalistic means."[3] Indeed the *Shorter Oxford English Dictionary* gives as its principal meaning, "A marvellous event exceeding the known powers of nature, and therefore supposed to be due to the special intervention of the Deity or of some supernatural agency." It is in this sense that the virginal conception of Jesus is usually taken to be a miracle that initiates his human life.

Clearly there are general considerations which weigh heavily against the occurrence of such events at all:

• our increasing ability in the last 300 years to account for the general sequence of regular events in terms of a closed causal nexus;

• the recognition that one of the principal grounds for affirming the existence of God as Creator, who is other than the observed world (including the human one) and is both the source of the very existence of that world and of its inbuilt rationality, is the scientific account of the causal nexus;

• and the requirement that historical evidence for such events to be convincing has to be proportionally greater the more unusual the event, the more it is said to rupture known regularities—especially in the form of well-established scientific "laws of nature."

In the case of the alleged virginal conception of Jesus, there are further particular considerations that are relevant:

• it scarcely needs the warrant of science, ancient or modern, to affirm that the birth of a human baby normally requires intercourse between a man and a woman (even when, as the errant servant girl said to her mistress, on the birth of her unannounced baby, "It's only a very little one"!);

• the ancient belief that the female human being is a mere receptacle for the new life which comes entirely from the male is false, for in the last 150 years or so biological science has firmly established that the human embryo begins with the entry into a female ovum of a male sperm;

• hence, the historical evidence that a woman has, after the usual nine months' gestation, had a baby without having been the recipient of a male sperm would have to be exceedingly strong—and it is notoriously very weak indeed in the case of Jesus' mother.

For even the cautious Raymond Brown has concluded that "the *scientifically controllable* biblical evidence leaves the question of the historicity of the virginal conception unresolved."[4] By "scientifically controllable biblical evidence" he quite properly means "evidence constituted by tradition from identifiable witnesses of the events involved, when that tradition is traceably preserved and not in conflict with other traditions."[5] Brown's verdict of "unresolved" would be regarded as overcautious by other scholars less restrained by traditional dogma. Thus John Macquarrie, an Anglican, affirms that ". . . our historical information is negligible . . . apart from . . . scraps of doubtful information, the birth narratives [of Matthew and Luke] are manifestly legendary in character."[6] And C. J. Cadoux, a Congregationalist, concluded his discussion of the matter thus: "Nor indeed is it enough for scholars to leave the issue [of the virginal conception] open, on the sole ground that the evidence for the miraculous birth is insufficient. If a miracle is asserted to have occurred, and cogent evidence for its occurrence cannot be adduced, and belief in it can be readily accounted for along other lines, the duty of scholars is not to leave the reality of it an open question, but to reject it, not as inconceivable, but as in all probability not true."[7]

There are, moreover, further developments in our knowledge of human nature which cannot but affect our judgment in this matter:

• that, in accordance actually with the prevailing biblical understanding, human beings are psychosomatic unities—not made up of two or three distinct entities (body/mind/soul) but constituted of whatever the physicists find basic (atoms, or, below them, quarks or whatever) with real emergent mental and (I would add) spiritual capacities;

• human beings are now realized to be much more under the leash of their genetic endowment than previously thought—not controlled or directed but constrained by it.

The virginal conception and biology

This is the background to considering other hard questions concerning the virginal conception which biology poses for us today. The relevant facts, determined by the biology of the last 150 years, are as follows. Any complete human being begins life by the union of an ovum from a female human being and a spermatozoan from a male one. The sex of the fertilized ovum, and so of the baby that is born, is determined by a particular pair of chromosomes present in all the ordinary (somatic) cells of human beings—those in females being both of the same type denoted as X (so XX), and those in males being different, one X and the other of type Y (so XY). These pairs of chromosomes carry in their DNA genes various characteristics, as do the other twenty-two pairs of chromosomes in somatic cells that do not differ in kind from male to female. In the formation of ova and spermatozoa these ordinary, somatic cells split so that the members of the various pairs of chromosomes separate out into new half-cells (an ovum or a sperm cell) containing one chromosome only of each of those pairs. Human conception begins with the union of two such "half-cells," one from each parent. The ovum from the mother *always* contributes an X-type chromosome to this new line of cells while

the father contributes *either* an X *or* a Y: if the former, a female combined cell (XX) results; if the latter, a male one (XY)—with a 50:50
chance. This is how all human beings begin, and this is how the sex of
the resulting child is determined from its beginning. Furthermore, if
no male is involved, as in insect parthenogenesis, the offspring are female, because no Y chromosomes are available. It is no use calling
upon cases of *natural* parthenogenesis to support the virginal conception of a *male* Jesus!

For Mary to have been pregnant with the fetus that became Jesus
without the involvement of a human father—that is, without a Y
chromosome coming from (say) Joseph—there are, biologically, only
two possibilities. Either (1) Mary provided the ovum which was then
transformed by an act of God (impregnation by the Holy Spirit?) into
a viable, reproducing cell, as if a sperm had entered the ovum; or (2)
there was created such an impregnated ovum within her uterus with
no contribution from Mary's own genetic heritage at all. As Canon
Derek Stanesby has put it, in a trenchant analysis of what the virginal
conception really implies: "Biologically, either Mary provided the
ovum for impregnation by the Holy Ghost and so contributed to her
son's genetic inheritance, or she was simply a vessel containing and
nourishing the divinely implanted seed, that is, a surrogate mother."[8]

According to the first possibility for a virginal conception (1),
Mary would have contributed an X chromosome to the cells of Jesus
but, for Jesus to be male, the Y chromosome (not coming from a human father) would have had to have been created *de novo* by God.
The X (and other) chromosomes in Jesus' cells would have had,
through Mary's genetic predecessors, a particular inheritance as a
member of the evolved species *Homo sapiens*. But, we cannot avoid
asking, what genetic characteristics would be created in Jesus' Y (and
other) chromosomes, normally derived from the sperm of a human
father? The genetic constitution of a human being is foundational to
their humanity and so of their personhood. So, in case (1), really to
have been human, Jesus would have had to have been provided with
an intact created set of human genes, on the Y and other chromosomes. What genetic information was encoded in these miraculously

created genes? Did God give him a set to make his characteristics (shape of nose, color of hair, blood group, etc.) mimic what Joseph *would* have provided had he been involved, or what? Implausible though this all sounds, this possibility at least has the merit of retaining a link of Jesus with humanity through the genetic contribution of Mary.

But even that is precluded by the possibility (2), mooted above, in which Mary is simply a vessel in which is implanted an already fertilized ovum—indeed a kind of surrogate mother. In this case (2), Jesus' entire genetic constitution (carried on the X and Y and all the other chromosomes) would have had to have been created *de novo*. So the question arises *a fortiori*, what genes did God choose to put in the cells from which the embryo of Jesus developed during what is implied, in the two gospel accounts, to be the normal gestation period? *Could* Jesus then be said to be genuinely human at all if this was his miraculous origin? Or was he just a *copy* of a human being but with all his genetic endowment, and so bodily features, not actually continuous with our evolved nature at all?

To pile Ossia on Pelion, one improbability on another, one has further to recognize what is actually being proposed in either form of the virginal conception in the light of the knowledge we now have of the processes of life. This belief means that God must suddenly have brought into existence either (1) a complete spermatazoan, which then entered an ovum of Mary, or (2) a completely fertilized ovum, since all the reports assume the usual nine-month gestation period needed for the multicellular embryo to develop to be ready for birth Each of these biological entities, especially the second, is an enormously complex system of thousands of atoms in actual molecules, some very large such as DNA, engaged in dynamic biological activity in an organization more complex than that of any modern factory! This really would be a wonder-working magical kind of act—a "special creation" *de novo* of exactly the type the so-called "creationists" argue for—an act producing an entity resembling a human being but not actually sharing in our evolved humanity.

Thus the present understanding of the biology of reproduction and of heredity reveals the doctrine of the virginal conception to be postulating an extraordinary, almost magical, divine act of suddenly bringing into existence a complex biological entity. All the evidence is that is *not* how God has created and is creating—certainly not the God whose mode of being and becoming it is possible to believe in today.

Biology and doctrine

In the light of our biological knowledge it is then impossible to see how Jesus could be said to share our human nature, if he came into existence by a virginal conception of the kind traditionally proposed. This means that the doctrine of the virginal conception is also *theologically* inadequate if Jesus is to be relevant to our human destiny. As Stanesby says, "In summary, a divine set of genes nurtured by a surrogate mother would hardly result in the Incarnate Lord of the Christian faith. If the world, including man, has an evolutionary history, then incarnation (for salvation) must involve identification with, not dissociation from, that history."[9]

Macquarrie has expressed the point thus:

> . . . if we suppose Christ to have been conceived and born in an altogether unique way, then it seems that we have separated him from the rest of the human race and thereby made him irrelevant to the human quest for salvation or for the true life. We would be saying not that he is the revelation of God shedding light on our darkness, but that he is an altogether unintelligible anomaly, thrust into the middle of history.[10]

Indeed it is now, in the light of the science I have been indicating, actually inconsistent with the doctrine of the Incarnation which insists that it is a *complete* human nature that is united with God (as *Logos*, or as "God the Son"). Jesus must be bone of our bone, flesh of our flesh, and DNA of our DNA, DNA from a human father, in order to have any salvific role for humanity. For, as Gregory of Nazianzus has said, "what he has not assumed he has not healed."[11]

Furthermore, these scientifically based considerations also now show, in a way which was less obvious before they could be brought to bear on the question, that theologically speaking the doctrine of the virginal conception is actually "docetic"[12] in its implications.[13] For if Jesus' humanity *was* only apparent, in the biological sense described above, and so not real (indeed artificial, not natural) and if Jesus was, in some way, also divine, then he would indeed have been "a divine being . . . dressed up as a man in order to communicate revelations," which is the core of the definition of the heresy of docetism.

Conclusion

Briefly, for Jesus to be fully human he had, for both biological and theological reasons, to have a human father as well as a human mother and the weight of the historical evidence strongly indicates that this was so—and that it was probably Joseph. Any theology for a scientific age which is concerned with the significance of Jesus of Nazareth now has to start at this point.

CHAPTER 12

The Challenges and Possibilities for Western Monotheism–Christianity

The advent of a third millennium of the presence of Christianity in the world evokes variegated emotions in its followers. Looking back one could ask, with the apocryphal and somewhat seedy heckler of the Christian evangelist at London's open-air forum in Hyde Park: "Christianity has been in the world for nearly two thousand years, and look at the state of the world!" To which the prompt reply was, "Soap has been in the world for four thousand years, and look at the state of your neck!" Minimally, like all religions, Christianity has been both the focus of idealistic aspirations and the milieu within which human fallibilities, and even wickedness, have been exercised. The proximity of the year AD ("Of the Lord") 2000 cannot but provoke reflection on the whole sweep of Christian history and of the situation of that faith as we enter its third millennium.

Insofar as we focus on "Western" societies, the most prominent counterculture to Christian faith has transpired to be not Marxism, which has risen and fallen, but a materialist-secularism engendered, it is widely believed, by the dominance both of scientific ideas and of

Paper delivered at a conference at Berkeley, California, June 7–10, 1998, and published in *Science and the Spiritual Quest: New Essays by Leading Scientists,* ed. W. M. Richardson, R. J. Russell, P. Clayton, and K. Wegter-McNelly (London: Routledge, 2002), 233–42. Reprinted by permission.

science-based technologies in our lives. The all-pervading effect of this last I must leave to the social historians and social psychologists, but the former—the effect of scientific ideas—is certainly within the scope of the Science and the Spiritual Quest Project. Early on, in the first quarter of this last century of the second millennium of Christianity, the philosopher-mathematician A. N. Whitehead could aver with prescience that

> the future course of history would depend on the decision of his generation as to the proper relations between science and religion—so powerful were the religious symbols through which men and women conferred meaning on their lives, and so powerful the scientific models through which they could manipulate their environment.[1]

Now, as we approach the end of this century, we can see that the task he gave that earlier generation is still incomplete; only now is the study of the interaction of science with religious perceptions in general, and Christian ones in particular, being undertaken with any rigor and sophistication in our universities and becoming the concern of thinking believers. To what extent this interaction is proving challenging and fruitful, or merely destructive, I will advert to later. But first let us recall the various cultural milieux in which what we have known as the natural sciences have emerged and developed.

Science

One of the most significant periods in all human history, but perhaps the least widely recognized, was that around 500 BC (800–200 BC) when, in the three distinct and culturally disconnected areas of China, India, and the West, there was a genuine expansion of human consciousness: in China, Confucius and Lao-tse and the rise of all the main schools of Chinese philosophy; in India, the Upanishads and Buddha, Zarathrustra in Iran; in Palestine, the Hebrew prophets; and, in Greece, we witness at this turning point of human history the appearance of the literature of Homer, the pre-Socratic philosophers, followed by the whole of that great legacy of Greece to human culture.

In Ionia, the Greek colonists established a vigorous and hardworking culture, flexible and open to many influences. It was a time of travel, movement of populations, breakdown of the old, and rising of the new. It was in this milieu of fluidity and change that science was born. The earliest scientific documents that we possess that are in any degree complete are in the Greek language and were composed about 500 BC. The Ionian Greeks brought to bear in their questions about the natural world a systematic and rational reflection that was distinctive and has remained the central characteristic of science ever since.

We find Thales (b. 625 BC) asking the question "What is everything made of?"—the first person, as far as we know, to look behind the infinite variety of nature for some single principle to which it could be reduced and be made intelligible. It is significant that in this search for unity behind the diversity of things the Ionians refrained from evoking any of the deities and mythologies of nature that were to be found in Homer and Hesiod.

Later, having moved westwards, the Pythagoreans discovered the significance of numbers, but they were handicapped by the want of adequate instruments of research and they thought it vulgar to employ science for practical purposes, though we have brilliant anticipations of modern discoveries. Yet, as Sir Richard Livingstone said,

> [Their] real achievement . . . was in fact they wanted to discover and that by some instinct they knew the way to set about it . . . they started science on the right lines . . . the desire to know . . . the determination to find a rational explanation for phenomena . . . [with] open-mindedness and candour . . . industry and observation.[2]

So science was born among the Greeks. But with the coming of Roman dominance, although science continued, somehow its flame flickers to only a dim glow. From here the torch is, as it were, handed on to the Muslim culture. We in the West often forget that Muslim science lasted for nearly six centuries—longer than modern science itself has existed! When one becomes aware of the full extent of Muslim experimenting, thinking, and writing (in Arabic), one sees that without the Muslims, European science could not have developed when it did. They were no mere transmitters of Greek thought, for they both kept alive the disciplines they had been taught and extended their range. When Europeans become seriously interested in the science and philosophy of their Saracen enemies about AD 1100, these disciplines were at their zenith; and the Europeans had to learn all they could from the Muslims before they could make further advances. Hence Islam was really the midwife to the Greek mother of our modern, Western scientific outlook.

The reception in the West of Muslim science and philosophy and that of the Greeks laid the foundation both of medieval natural philosophy and of that remarkable awakening in the sixteenth and seventeenth centuries to the power of human reason, especially in the form of mathematics when combined with experiment, to interpret natural phenomena. It is well-authenticated that those involved in this development saw their activities as an outward expression of their Christian belief both in the orderliness of a world given existence by a God who transcended and instantiated human rationality; and a belief that the world, as the free act of the Creator, was contingent, so that how rationality was embedded in it had to be discovered by experiment. Kepler and Newton regarded the enterprise as "thinking God's thoughts after him." So a monotheistic culture was an intellectually appropriate matrix within which the natural sciences could flourish, even though it involves certain famous misunderstandings and adjustments in the relations between this new knowledge and that assumed by the traditions of the church and in the interpretations of Scripture. Historians have shown that the boundary between "religion" and "science" was always a very fluid one and differently located in different individuals, different societies, and at different times.

From that origin in the West some four centuries ago has arisen the modern world in which science dominates our intellectual culture and, I believe, will continue to do so in spite of postmodernist misgivings. For the claim of the sciences to refer to and to depict a natural reality other than ourselves is continuously and pragmatically vindicated by the successful technological applications of those same sciences. This is enough for most people to maintain its eminent position in any hierarchy of reliable knowledge. As an intellectual enterprise science is characterized by vigor, openness, flexibility, innovativeness, a welcoming of new insights and ideas, and a genuinely international, global community. In all of these respects, it stands in marked and usually unfavorable contrast to the public image of religious communities, including Christian ones. *They* tend to be seen as, if not lethargic and supine, yet as closed, inflexible, unenterprising, and immune to new insights, continually appealing to the past, to the "faith once delivered to the saints," and socially divisive as different Christian and other religious communities clash. So the Christian churches certainly have an uphill job to commend themselves globally to a humanity aware of the vastness of the new vistas and opportunities now opened up to it.

More particularly, there is, in the West at least, a collapse in the credibility of *all* religious beliefs as they are perceived as failing to meet the normal criteria of reasonableness: fit with the data, internal coherence, comprehensiveness, fruitfulness, and general cogency. Yet spiritual hunger is endemic in our times—and attempted satisfaction of it leads to many aberrations in the so-called "new religions." Our society is, to my observation at least, full of wistful agnostics who would like to be convinced that there *is* indeed an Ultimate Reality to which they can relate.

Cultural transitions in Christianity

Religion in general has been defined as "a cultural sign language which promises a gain in life by corresponding to an ultimate reality" (Gerd Theissen).[3] Through its language, symbols, rituals, scriptures, music, and architectural "sign language," the Christian faith has promised the fruition of human existence in profound and eternal relation to the Ultimate Reality of God as manifested and made effectual in and by the life, death, and resurrection of a particular person, Jesus of Nazareth.

More than almost any other religion, Christianity has elaborated a complex conceptual system of beliefs to give intellectual coherence to its intuitions and practices. What is affirmed, how it is affirmed, and what sort of metaphors are utilized to elaborate its system of beliefs have, much more than most Christians would admit, continually changed—and sometimes with an abruptness comparable with that of the paradigm shifts said to characterize the history of science.

In the two millennia of Christian history one can identify many such transitions induced by the facing of threatening challenges that generated a new vitality and relevance. In the very earliest days, recorded within the pages of the New Testament, one witnesses the challenge to Paul of taking the insights of the first Jewish followers of Jesus—claimed to be the hoped-for Messiah, the "Anointed One" in their terms—into the wider Jewish diaspora (hence his struggles with and analyses of "law" and "grace"). Even more daringly, Paul deliberately, as the "Apostle to the Gentiles," entered the wider Hellenistic culture. His journeys from Jerusalem to Athens and then to Rome symbolize a profound transition in and challenge to the faith and experience of the early Jewish witnesses which was magnificently surmounted, enabling Christianity to qualify to become the conduit, some two-and-a-half centuries later, of the religious impulses of the whole Roman Empire.

It then had to come to terms publicly with the intellectual life of that empire expressed as it was in the sophisticated and philosophical terms of a modulated Hellenism. It was to this challenge that the Cappadocian Fathers (Gregory of Nyssa, Gregory Nazianzen, and Basil of Caesarea) rose when they were able to articulate a system of Christian beliefs consistent with and in terms of the most convincing philosophy of their day. They out-thought their opponents both inside and outside the Christian Church.

The arrival in the West during the eleventh and twelfth centuries, through the mediation of the Muslims, of great swaths of Greek literature, and notably the intellectually comprehensive works of Aristotle, constituted a potentially traumatic challenge to the received beliefs of Christendom. To this Albert the Great and his pupil Thomas Aquinas responded so effectively that the intensive and intellectually powerful synthesis of faith and reason of the latter dominated the church for more than six centuries. It is still today an intellectual construct that Christian philosophers ignore at their peril.

Apart from certain famous *contretemps*, the emergence of what is identifiably modern natural science in the seventeenth century was nurtured by its advocates and practitioners in a way that was seen by them both as consistent with and a natural consequence of their general understanding of nature as "creation"—that is, as being given existence by a transcendent, Ultimate Reality, named as "God" in English.

However, the following eighteenth century too readily interpreted the astonishingly successful Newtonian science to imply a natural order that was so mechanistic and clocklike that God was often relegated to the role of the original Clock-winder. This concept of the inevitably absentee god of deism undermined the belief of Christians (and indeed of many adherents to the Hebrew Scriptures) in God as "living" and immanent in the processes of the world. Yet, in the nineteenth century, Darwin's discovery of the evolving nature of the biological world and of the role in it of natural selection, which entailed for some the final demise of a God no longer needed to account for biological design, actually reinstated the idea of God as *creating all the time* through natural evolution. So, as one Anglican theologian said in 1889, "Darwinism appeared, and, under the disguise of a foe, did the work of a friend." Nevertheless, the supposed "warfare" between science and religion imprinted itself on the popular mind in the English-speaking world, not least after the 1880s because purely legendary accounts of the 1860 Oxford encounter between the Bishop of Oxford, Samuel Wilberforce, and Thomas Henry Huxley were propagated.

An uneasy truce between science and the Christian religion prevailed, each thereafter preserving a demarcated field for itself. It took over a hundred years, until the middle of the twentieth century, for it to become apparent, with some notable exceptions, to a number of thoughtful scientists who were also Christian thinkers that the situation was not that simple and that the whole relation of science to religious belief, in particular to Christian belief, was ripe for reappraisal. The existence, for example, of the Center for Theology and the Natural Sciences in Berkeley, which has made such a distinguished contribution to this reassessment, is—if, I may so put it—but the "tip of the iceberg" of a burgeoning plethora of activities in the field of science-and-religion. This has, up till now, taken place mainly in the academic world but, because of the prominence of ethical issues, is now spilling out into the life of the churches and that of the wider society. Present academic activities include: the development of an increasingly sophisticated literature; the establishing of academic centers in North America and Europe and of societies devoted to these issues; the publishing of international journals in the field; the organizing of public lectures and a swarm of conferences and symposia; the funding of academic courses (greatly assisted by the Templeton Foundation); and—at long last—the beginning of funding of permanent academic posts in this field. All of which has led to

The challenge to and reinvigoration of Christian thinking today by science

What characterizes science, as we saw, is a method which has been manifestly capable of producing reliable knowledge about the natural world, enough for prediction and control and for producing coherent, comprehensive conceptual interpretations of it. Such authority as the scientific community has can always be called in question, even though no individual scientist can ever repeat all past experiments, which have to be taken on trust. Yet, the scientific community has a limited and never absolute authority. The mere existence of such a method and of such a corpus of reliable knowledge resulting from it is in itself a challenge to traditional religious attitudes. I believe the time has come when mere assertion of authority by religious leaders and communities of the kind "The Church says," "The Bible says,"

"The Magisterium affirms," will no longer carry conviction—for all such pronouncements are fundamentally flawed because they are circular and unable to justify themselves except by quoting themselves, or each other! Pronouncements of authority cannot be at the same time both self-warranting *and* convincing. Truths asserted in the promulgations of the ecclesiastical, scriptural, or other authority cannot avoid running the gauntlet of those criteria of reasonableness we have already mentioned: fit with the data, internal coherence, comprehensiveness, fruitfulness, and general cogency. Theology, like science, can claim to depict reality only if it is subject to these criteria and accepts that its formulations, couched inevitably (like those of science) in metaphorical language, are revisable in the light of new knowledge and perceptions.

To convince our contemporaries, the theology of all religions requires now that theology must operate by inference to the best explanation, applying the above criteria. We need—as Hans Küng has argued—a theology that is "truthful," "free," "critical," and "ecumenical"—that is, a theology that deals with and integrates the realities of all that is discovered to constitute the world, and notably human beings. This reality has been largely unveiled by the natural sciences in forms never dreamt of by the founders of Christianity and those of other religions—forms that have a splendor and scope that no previous generation of human beings has witnessed. For we are now aware of what has been called the great "epic of evolution"—of the cosmos evolving and expanding by natural processes some 12 billion years ago from the "hot, big bang" to the formation of the galaxies, stars, and planets; to the emergence of sentient life on planet Earth; to the arrival of persons, to the advent of a Mozart, a Shakespeare, a Buddha, a Jesus of Nazareth—and you and me. The fragility of the individual human life is now set within this cosmic context and humanity sees itself both as a part of nature—we are stardust—and yet *apart* from nature, as we survey it from our subjectivity looking outwards.

Such a vista cannot but change how we view the physically based nature of humanity and the destiny of humanity in the divine purposes. At the same time, it invigorates and enhances many strands of the received tradition, giving them a new significance in this wider vista. Certainly Christian hope, for example, acquires a new pertinence but also a new context. Let us examine some instances.

God

How we are to regard God's relation to the world is challenged and enriched by this vista. God's immanence in the creative processes of the world now reemerges with renewed cogency as an aspect of the divine nature, along with that transcendent otherness which all the Abrahamic religions must continue to affirm. God is all-the-time Creator, and creation is continuous for God is crea*ting* in and through the processes of the world—God is indeed the "living God" of the Hebrew Scriptures.

This new emphasis on God working creatively in and through the very processes of the world, together with the recognition of the comprehensive explanatory power of the sciences in relation to those same natural processes, makes increasingly implausible any talk of God "intervening" in the world to change the course of events. God, as is said to be the case in the Christian sacraments, must now be regarded as operating "in, with, and under" the world processes of which God is the circumambient Reality. For God is "the one *in* whom we live and move and have our being" (Acts 17:28). This, for me, entails what I can only call a Christian pan-*en*-theism. God is the Circumambient, Infinite Reality in whom we live, by whom we are given existence, and who works in and through us. We and the world are held in being and penetrated by God as a finite living sponge is held afloat and permeated by the endless sea (to use an image of Augustine). God works (instrumentally) in and through the processes of the world, thereby effecting God's purposes and ("symbolically") communicating Godself. (We could call this: "sacramental pan-en-theism.")

For me this insight involves taking absolutely seriously the affirmation in the Prologue to St. John's gospel that it was God as outgoing, expressive Word *(Logos)* in creation which was all the time present incognito in the world, which was "made flesh" in Jesus—that is, made explicit and manifest in a human person. Such a recovered emphasis of ancient insights could both preserve Christian perceptions of the uniqueness of Jesus the Christ and, at the same time, recognize fully that God's Word, God's Self-expression, could also be manifest historically "at sundry times and in diverse places" (Heb. 1:1) in other religions and cultures through their own symbolic and historical resources.

The stress on God's immanence at once also raises the issue of how we are now to conceive of God's interaction with the world and how God might influence some patterns of events to occur rather than others—as seems to be essential for understanding *inter alia* "revelation" and intercessory prayer. Scientific perspectives on divine action had been the focus of a series of state-of-the-art research consultations convened by the Vatican Observatory in conjunction with the Center for Theology and the Natural Sciences. Agreement still eludes these unique gatherings of theologians, scientists, and philosophers, though the issues have been identified and, to some extent, clarified—but will, I am sure, continue to be on the agenda as the new millennium begins.

God has traditionally been conceived of as transcending time and able to see past, present, and future together, holistically, "all at once," as it were. Certainly space and time, since Einstein, are now to be seen as relations within the created order and given their existence by the Creator God. But whether or not God can logically *know* completely the content of a future that does not exist is hotly debated. The classical view is now widely called in question, and the new perspectives of space and time of relativity theory are very pertinent to the debate and profoundly enrich our understanding of God and eternity

Biological evolution challenged received understandings of God's creative action when it showed that natural selection operates in living organisms whose form (phenotype) and functions have been modified by unconnected, random changes (mutations) occurring in its DNA. This role of chance led many Victorian thinkers to agnosticism. We, however, are now stimulated to see that chance and law together make not for an ossified universe, as in mechanistic pictures of the world, but one containing structures capable of change. God has to be conceived as creating through chance events operating in a law-like framework. This is a long way from the Artificer-Creator God, but perhaps nearer to a Composer-Creator God, weaving the fugue of evolving forms by exploring all the possible permutations of structure and processes inherent in the very stuff of the world, itself all the time being given existence by that same God. This generates significant new reflections on "natural evil," that is, on the nature of pain, suffering, and death, all of which are inevitable concomitants of an evolutionary, creative process that can elicit self-conscious, sensitive, aware *persons* capable of freely relating to the Creator God and cooperating in the work of creation.

Humanity

The evolved nature of human beings has generated particular problems for those who adhere to a literalistic interpretation of the Hebraic accounts of creation in Genesis in particular. (Is this a problem for Jews and Muslims too?) For human beings, who are a very late arrival on Earth compared with all other living organisms, never had, it now transpires, a paradisal past but are rising beasts rather than fallen angels. Moreover, contrary to the implications of Genesis, individual biological death, as the means of creative evolution, existed aeons before the appearance of humanity. Death certainly cannot be called, as St. Paul does, "the wages of sin" (Rom. 6:23) in any strict biological sense.

All of the foregoing, and much else, imposes on Western Christians, at least, the necessity to rethink those redemption theologies that are based on the postulate of a historical "Fall" (which was never actually propounded in the Hebrew Scriptures) and on Augustine's interpretation of "original sin." For if, as the scientific record now shows, human beings are creatures who have slowly, and sometimes painfully, emerged with self-consciousness and awareness of the values of truth, beauty, and goodness, and have developed community and mutual cooperation—that is, "rising beasts"—what significance can we now give to the particularity of the "Christ-event," that is, to the nature of Jesus of Nazareth and what he is supposed to have done for all humanity? In what sense can we today affirm with the Nicene Creed that he "died *for* us" in a way that can be transformative here and now, and eternally, of the possibilities and potentialities of human existence? In all of this the Eastern Christian church's emphasis on the effect of the "Christ-event," the "work of Christ," as being the enabling of humanity to be taken up into the life of God *(theosis)* is recovered and the profundity of Paul's emphasis of the significance of being "in Christ" is enhanced.

Furthermore, current advances in the neurosciences and cognitive sciences are showing how tightly linked are the subjective mental processes which constitute our personhood and consciousness to the physiological and biochemical processes of the human-brain-in-the-human-body. Christian anthropology has to return to the more Hebraic understanding of human beings as psychosomatic unities and not as the embodiment of naturally immortal souls—a notion imprinted on both academic and popular Christianity by centuries of the influence of Platonism on its philosophy.

These are profound questions, and many of us are searching for that rebirth of images which characterizes any truly vital community seeking human relationship with God. Christians have some problems special to their received traditions, but because it is the comprehensive perspectives on the world and humanity the sciences now afford which has generated these problems, they experience many of these challenges to received insights in company with the other great monotheistic Abrahamic religions. The world can now, with the aid of the sciences, be seen more convincingly than ever before as the creation of an ever-working, ever-present Ultimate Reality, who transcends and yet is immanent in it—and can also be present in and to us humans. That is our hope, reinforced by our new perspectives on the cosmic process.

I believe that if religious believers of any faith ignore the new challenges of the dazzling, exalting even, vista which the sciences continuously amplify and spread before our eyes, we shall all—Christians, Jews, and Muslims—simply be digging deeper and deeper holes and, as we go downwards, we shall be talking more and more to each other and less and less to the great human world up there—a world now bathed in the clearer light of the sciences describing God's creative work. As we enter the new millennium, that light on creation from the sciences will transpire more and more to constitute the first glint on the horizon of a wider and deeper illumination of the cosmic significance of many central, and sometimes forgotten, Christian affirmations which in that light become more and more capable of being integrated with those of the other Abrahamic religions and with our cosmic perspectives—but only if we are open to the endeavor at whatever cost to our preconceived notions. For after all, theology, like science, is a great enterprise of the human spirit.

EPILOGUE

CHAPTER 13

Wisdom in Science and Education

—and Robert Grosseteste, a Medieval Scientist-
Theologian and Educator

The Wisdom of God

An uncle of mine, who was in the police force and should therefore be expected to know, used to affirm that the way to live a harmonious, ordered life was to apply one principle which he labeled
"CS," common sense, a lack of which he noted in the clever and the
academic! There are many today who would stress CS and there certainly have been in the past, as witness the many proverbs of common
sense in the English language alone. The ancient Hebrews also collected them and they can be mined in the book of Proverbs. But
there is more to that exercise than first appears. For the very possibility of making generalizations about conduct and about the world in
general presupposes an ordered natural and social life, and the question arises, where does that order come from?

The book of Proverbs, and the whole corpus of ancient writings
we call "Wisdom literature" (Job, Proverbs, Ecclesiastes, Ecclesiasticus
[Sirach] and the Wisdom of Solomon, etc.) have no doubts. The ordered patterning of the natural and social world stems from the creative action of God. Human wisdom consists in not only knowing

The Grosseteste Festival Day Lecture delivered October 29, 2003, at Bishop Grosseteste (Higher Education) College, Lincoln, England.

how to cope, to succeed by "know-how," to "know the ropes," but also in discerning the signs of intelligibility and meaning in the world around. Thus Solomon thanks God for the gift of being able to have "unerring knowledge of what exists, to know the structure of the world and the activity of the elements; the beginning and end and middle of times . . . the natures of animals . . . and the thoughts of human beings" for, he says, "wisdom, the fashioner of all things, taught me" (Wis. 7:17ff). We hear in the eighth chapter of the book of Proverbs about this Wisdom, who is a feminine figure personifying God's creative activity in patterning and shaping all-that-is in creation. Wisdom says: "Ages ago I was set up, at the first, before the beginning of his work . . . when he [the Lord] marked out the foundations of the earth, then I was beside him, like a master worker, rejoicing before him always" (8:22ff).

One biblical scholar[1] has recently expressed her conclusions concerning this literature in the following terms:

> On the one hand, wisdom is the content of what one must know to understand the deep logic underlying the natural world and the social order alike. . . . By discerning that coherence . . . and by following the ethical "way" consistent with it, people could shape their lives in congruence with God's will. On the other hand, more than simply the content of God's creative acts, Wisdom is also God's working partner, or perhaps even the expression of God's own creative self. As the self-disclosure of Wisdom, then, creation is not simply something God has done, but a glimpse into the very heart and nature of God.

All such wisdom, imprinted as a pattern on the natural world and in the mind of the sage, is but a pale image of the divine Wisdom— that activity distinctive of God's relation to the world. In the present context, it is pertinent that this important concept of Wisdom (Sophia) unites intimately the divine activity of creation, human experience, and the processes of the natural world.

The world of science

It is just at this point that the sciences of our day deeply illuminate these ancient insights and, by their very discoveries, provoke new questions and ethical problems. For a significant element in these scientific perspectives is that human beings are inherently a part of nature, evolved out of the very stuff of the world. Scientific perceptions of what we are continually change in content and focus of interest, and this inevitably changes our understanding of the three-cornered relation of nature-humanity-God.

What, then, today is the vista that twenty-first-century science now unveils for our contemplation? How might the beginning of a "Bible for 2003" look?

Genesis for the twenty-first century

There was God. And God Was All-That-Was.

God's Love overflowed and God said: "Let Other be. And let it have the capacity to become what it might be, making it make itself—and let it explore its potentialities."

And there was Other in God, a field of energy, vibrating energy—but no matter, space, time, or form. Obeying its given laws and with one intensely hot surge of energy—a hot big bang—this Other exploded as the Universe from a point 12 or so billion years ago in our time, thereby making space.

Vibrating fundamental particles appeared, expanded and expanded, and cooled into clouds of gas, bathed in radiant light. Still the Universe went on expanding and condensing into swirling whirlpools of matter and light—a billion galaxies.

Five billion years ago, one star in one galaxy—our Sun—attracted round it matter as planets. One of them was our Earth. On Earth, the assembly of atoms and the temperature became just right to allow water and solid rock to form. Continents and mountains grew, and in some deep wet crevice, or pool, or deep in the sea, just over 3 billion years ago some molecules became large and complex enough to make copies of themselves and became the first specks of life.

Life multiplied in the seas, diversifying and becoming more and more complex. Five hundred million years ago, creatures with solid skeletons— the vertebrates—appeared. Algae in the sea and green plants on land changed the atmosphere by making oxygen. Then 300 million years ago, certain fish learned to crawl from the sea and live on the edge of land, breathing that oxygen from the air.

Now life burst into many forms—reptiles, mammals (and dinosaurs) on land—reptiles and birds in the air. Over millions of years the mammals began to develop complex brains that enabled them to learn. Among these were creatures who lived in trees. From these our first ancestors derived and then, only some sixty to eighty thousand years ago, the first men and women appeared. They began to know about themselves and what they were doing—they were not only conscious but also self-conscious. The first word, the first laugh was heard. The first paintings were made. The first sense of a destiny beyond—with the first signs of hope, for these people buried their dead with ritual. The first prayers were made to the One who made All-That-Is and All-That-Is-Becoming—the first experiences of goodness, beauty, and truth—but also of their opposites, for human beings were free.

Even those of you who are not scientists have, at least from television, a fairly broad apprehension of this vista—the whole is a seamless web and increasingly intelligible to the sciences. The energy and dust of the cosmos has become a Mozart, a Shakespeare, Jesus of Nazareth—and you and me!

Surely as we contemplate this extraordinary vista—which has only been vouchsafed to human beings in the last half-century as the fruit of scientific study—we cannot but be overcome by a sense of awe and wonder at the beauty, rational intricacies, and sheer creativity and fruitfulness of the natural world which the sciences have now revealed.

Educators know how to build on the sense of wonder and awe that can be elicited in quite small children at the fascinations of nature—and this should be the fertile soil and seedbed for the later maturation of the *spiritual* apprehension of the adult contemplating this world the sciences now reveal. I have deliberately introduced the word "spiritual" here, for there has long been a deep apprehension that there is a divine shaping and patterning of the world which expresses the inherent nature and creativity of God—what that literature I referred to earlier calls the Wisdom of God's very Self.

As you probably know, this college is named after one of the most fertile and original minds in medieval England, and Robert Grosseteste's whole approach is extremely pertinent at this juncture. For he was convinced that "knowledge, though it begins with sensation, must not end there but must rise to the spiritual."[2] Like many of us in the English tradition, his was fundamentally a theology of creation which he integrated with his deep appreciation of what he believed to be revealed in the Scriptures. It is notable that he took an immense interest in those works of Aristotle, newly arriving in Europe in the late eleventh and early twelfth centuries, that were concerned with the natural world. He was one of the earliest Western theologians to learn Greek to obtain an accurate understanding of these works. His lectures to the Franciscans at Oxford initiated in them, before he was made Bishop of Lincoln in 1235, a tradition of scientific study and experimentation which is too often overlooked today as the launching pad of modern science.

For Grosseteste, the deliverances of the senses were the necessary gateway to knowledge of the world which, for fallible, fallen humanity, can lead to divine illumination. He encouraged "the widest possible use of the senses in the process of knowing: they are the tools that make knowledge possible. They are like a walking stick for a lame man: it is not the cause of his ability to walk, but a *sine qua non* of his doing so."[3] He drew attention (in his own words) to ". . . the penetrating power of the mind in virtue of which the mind's eye does not rest on the outer surface of an object, but penetrates to something below the visual image . . . It . . . penetrates this structure until it detects the elemental qualities of which the structure is itself an effect."[4] As Sir Richard Southern,[5] his great biographer and expositor, says, "One cannot read these words without a thrill of recognition: is not this the way in which a historian comes to recognize the significance of a historical event? . . . What Grosseteste here describes is an experience of all enquirers who begin with the observation of particular events and aim at grasping the coherence which lies beneath the surface. This process has almost nothing in common with the scholastic method. It is a method of discovery, initiated by an observer looking at individual events and seeking to discover their nature and causes."

This is the basis of all science, and Grosseteste would have been thrilled with the scientific vista and perspectives on the world, including humanity, which I have been indicating. For he saw knowledge as needing and beginning with the aid of the senses, with sensation, but not ending there but rising to the spiritual. He saw ". . . sense knowledge as the foundation of all higher knowing dimensions,"[6] which sounds to me an echo of "learning through play"!

We can now provide a more richly articulated basis for all this by our acquaintance with the map of knowledge of the various levels of complexity of the world studied by the different sciences. For these now place humanity in a setting that is entirely new for our generation by distinguishing various levels of complexity, different foci of interest. The distinctive, holistic qualities of human persons depend on the operation of processes occurring at many levels of complexity, each one of which is the focus of interest of a particular scientific discipline.

Figure 1 shows these levels of interest, and so of analysis. (The levels are *not* intended as a grading according to any value judgments.) The following four focal "levels" can be distinguished:

(1) *the physical world*, everything is constituted of matter-energy in space-time, the focus of the physical sciences;

(2) *living organisms*, the focus of the biological sciences;

(3) *the behavior of living organisms*, the focus of the behavioral sciences;

(4) *human culture*. (Within any particular analytical level of this scheme of disciplines, there are often subdisciplines that form a bridge with an adjacent level by focusing on the same events or domains as does the next higher-level discipline. This allows for and shows the significance of interdisciplinary interactions. These "bridges" are indicated in the figure by the vertical, dashed arrows between levels.)

FIGURE 1. A Map of Knowledge

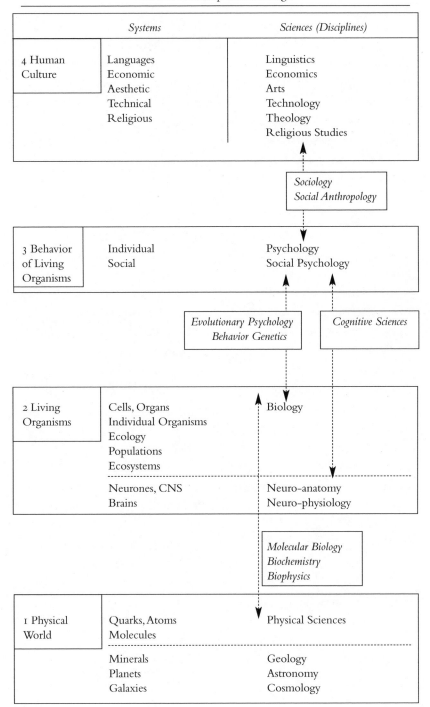

Structures, functions, and processes pertinent to human beings are to be found at focal levels (1) to (3) of this scheme, and they also span much of the part-whole sequences of structures in levels (1) and (2). No other part of the observed universe appears to include so many levels and to range over so much within these levels as do human beings (and level [4] refers only to human beings).

Humanity, we shall confirm, is indeed what Bishop Grosseteste and his contemporaries would have called a "microcosm" of the macrocosm, a miniature encapsulation of all-that-is.

The levels of the map of knowledge

Note that, as one proceeds up the hierarchy of complexity, new properties and new kinds of activities and functions emerge—and this is true whether one looks at the many levels of complexity in the world as it is today, in a kind of snapshot, or whether one has in mind those processes over time of cosmic and biological evolution that I outlined just now in that *Genesis for the twenty-first century*. Distinctive methods of study are needed to understand successive levels, and these generate concepts applicable only to those levels and their properties. In many cases these concepts and properties cannot be reduced logically to the terms of the concepts and properties pertinent to the simpler systems of which they are composed—so we see new realities emerging at higher levels and each requiring their own distinctive language. The evolutionary processes of the world are in themselves creative of new realities, the many levels of which we can still observe around us.

Biology is *not* "nothing but" physics and chemistry, *nor* is evolutionary biology "nothing but" biochemistry, *nor* is psychology "nothing but" neurophysiology, *nor* is sociology "nothing but" individual psychology, *nor* is education "nothing but" psychology and sociology, *nor* is mental life "nothing but" brain processes, *nor* is spiritual experience "nothing but" everyday mental processes.

Always we find "something more from nothing but."[7]

With all this in mind, let us look briefly at the perspectives on human beings from focusing on these different levels.

1. *Humanity: the physical basis*

From time immemorial human beings have known that they are made up of the same stuff as the rest of the world. Now we know that we are made up from atoms created in supernovae explosions aeons before the planet Earth was formed. We are stardust!—"dust thou art, and unto dust shalt thou return" (Gen. 3:19 AV). In living organisms this world-stuff has shown its inherent capacity to form self-copying structures and so to be living organisms—as revealed in the DNA story and the "bridge" science of molecular biology.

2. *Humanity: as living organisms*

All the biological sciences depicted in level (2) can include within their scope some aspects of human beings. This is not surprising in view of the evolutionary origins of humanity through natural selection, as manifested particularly in the fact that some 98 percent of human DNA is the same as that of the DNA of chimpanzees— and 50 percent, I hear, is the same as in bananas! Increase in self-organization, complexity, information processing and storage, consciousness, sensitivity to pain, and even self-consciousness can, under appropriate circumstances, all be advantageous in natural selection, so the emergence of self-conscious persons was "on the cards" and actually happened with us, relatively recent though our arrival on the planet is.

Between levels 2 and 3: bridging biology and the behavioral sciences

Cognitive science forms a bridge between the purely biological neurosciences and the sciences of *behavior*, and it is especially concerned with trying to understand how the mind-brain works, particularly in human beings. Cognitive scientists now recognize that they have to understand the intermediate levels of organization and processing of the brain and their interrelation to get the full picture. The emergent properties and functions at the more complex levels of organization and processing are new emergent *realities*.

Evolutionary psychology (formerly sociobiology) and *behavior genetics* are the systematic study of the biological, especially the genetic, basis of social and individual behavior. including that of human beings. We have now to recognize, far more explicitly than in the past, that some 50 percent of much in personal behavior, previously considered as conditioned by environment and culture, is genetically underpinned. However, our genetic heritage cannot in advance itself determine the *content* of our thinking and reasoning—for example, moral thinking —even if it is the prerequisite of the possession of these capacities.

Paradoxically, the biological endowment of human beings does not appear to be able to guarantee their *contented* adaptation to a dynamic environment. As human beings have widened their environmental horizons, they have come to experience a "gulf" between their biological past environment out of which they have evolved and that in which they conceive or wish themselves to be existing. I am thinking of such experiences as the contemplation—of death; of a sense of finitude; of suffering; of our inability to realize our potentialities; of the difficulties of steering a path through life to death. The spiritual needs of humanity soon manifest themselves—even in the youngest.

This engenders the further question of whether or not human beings have properly identified what their true "environment" really is—that "environment" in which human flourishing is possible. The need for wisdom certainly becomes apparent at this juncture, for the complexity and character of the human predicament clearly involves more subtle levels of human nature than we see at these levels (2/3).

3. Human behavior

The various forms of psychology have now undergone a "cognitive" or "mentalist" shift toward an interest into how it is to be a thinking and feeling human being. Instead of, on the one hand, a dualism of "body" and "mind" and, on the other, a reductive materialism, a new integrated view of human reality is emerging that accepts mental and spiritual qualities as causal realities, but at the same time denies they can exist separately in an disembodied state apart from the functioning brain. This gives increasing scientific credibility to what had never been doubted in the religions, and indeed in ordinary life—namely, the preeminence of the concept of the "personal." Indeed, as Philip Clayton has said,

> We have thoughts, wishes and desires that together constitute our character. We express these mental states through our bodies, which are simultaneously our organs of perception and our means of affecting other things and persons in the world . . . [The massive literature on theories of personhood] clearly points to the indispensability of embodiedness as the precondition for perception and action, moral agency, community and freedom—all aspects that philosophers take as indispensable to human personhood and that theologians have viewed as part of the *imago dei*.[8]

There is a strong case for designating the highest level, the whole, in that unique system which is the human-brain-in-the-human-body-in-social-relations as that of the "person." Furthermore a number of reflective psychologists remind us of the "mystery" and dynamic character of human personhood—". . . in our attempt to grasp personality scientifically, we experience something strange. As we reach out and are confronted by boundaries, we are filled with wonder at human personality, and we seem to touch mystery . . . We are not so much human beings as human becomings."[9]

Between levels 3 and 4: humanity in society

The social sciences form a bridge between the behavioral sciences and culture, and there is extremely strong evidence that the development of a being—a person—and of the sense of self-worth as a person depend acutely on our having fruitful interpersonal relations from the earliest moments of our lives.

4. Human culture and its products

Level 4 depicts the products of human creativity (for example, in the arts and sciences and in human relations and in relations to God) which are discernable and transmissible by their own distinctive

means through meaningful patterns created in what is received initially through our senses. These patterns of experience are the means
of communication both between human beings in personal relations
and between God and humanity, what we broadly call "spiritual."
They are generated through historical formation in continuous cultures which invest them with meaning for enabling such communication. They thereby have the unique power of inducting humanity
into an encounter with the transcendence in the "other," whether in
the form of a work of the creative, imaginative arts, or of another
human person, or of God the Beyond within our midst. This opens
up the dialogue between the human spiritual enterprise (with which
religion is concerned) and that of science in a way long barred by
the dominance of a mechanistic, reductionist naturalism of a kind
thought erroneously to have been warranted by science itself. The
human is undoubtedly biological, but what is distinctively human
transcends that out of which and in which it has emerged.

Wisdom from science?

So what is the new wisdom we may acquire about human beings
from these new perspectives of the map of the sciences? It will include the following

Human beings:

• are *a part of nature;*
• are *contingent,* notably with respect to their actual physical form
exemplifying the propensities in evolution to complexity, information processing, and so to consciousness and self-consciousness;
• *behave under the leash of their genes* more than was previously
thought, but are not determined by them;
• are *many-leveled,* indeed uniquely so, encompassing all the levels
1–4;
• are *conscious and self-conscious persons,* where "person" refers to
their unique integration of levels 1–4;
• *become integrated persons* through their interactions with other individuals and with society;

• have *mental and spiritual capacities* which *emerge* from the biophysical matrix of their brains-in-bodies-in-society.

Wisdom in education

will take account of these broad insights into the nature and origins of human capacities by paying attention to the educative implications of every level. Our flourishing as persons depends on our physical, mental, and spiritual health (dare I recall *mens sana in corpore sana?*), levels of human existence that are closely interlocked, one level often being the launching pad for the next. But the human being is really a human *becoming*—and think how often nature is the stimulus of spiritual experiences as are also the visual in art and sounds in music, both in children (especially in children?) and in adults.

Robert Grosseteste would not, I surmise, be at all surprised at such consequences of our newfound scientific understanding of the basis of the human. For was he not convinced, as I quoted earlier, that "knowledge, though it begins with sensation, must not end there but must rise to the spiritual," and did he not therefore encourage the widest possible use of the senses in the process of knowing, for they are the tools that make knowledge possible?

He saw education as nurturing the whole person—physically, mentally, and spiritually—and the essential quality in the teacher for this fruition to occur was what we can only call "educative love."[10] Grosseteste was convinced that love has a foundational role in education. He took a cue from St. Paul, who wrote to the Galatians (4:19), "My little children, whom I am in labor to bring forth again, until Christ be formed in you." Grosseteste pursued this metaphor of conceiving and childbearing to express his understanding of the role of the teacher (NOTE: In Latin *conceptus* is *both* a thought/idea *and* a growing human fetus.) Teaching was, for him, an expression of love that, as it were, procreates the word and idea in the mind of the pupil and brings it forth into the world of action. The teacher is like a father and a mother who in love gives birth to spiritual children. "This kind of begetting," he affirms, "is greater than physical generation, and the readiness of the teacher to beget should be proportionately greater." It is the painstaking and watchful love of the teacher in reprehending and rewarding that brings about and nurtures the process in the pupil whereby the idea is conceived through the teacher's words interacting with the pupil's memory and intelligence and brings forth new ideas and action. It is not without reason that he compares educative love with parental love. We need his wisdom in pursuing educational vocations.

Notes

Preface

1. Outlined in the introductory chapter of my *From DNA to Dean: Reflections and Explorations of a Priest-Scientist* (Norwich and London: SCM-Canterbury Press, 1996).

2. The most comprehensive being *Creation and the World of Science* (Oxford: Clarendon Press, 1979; 2nd paperback ed., Oxford: Oxford University Press, 2004); *Theology for a Scientific Age: Being and Becoming—Natural Divine and Human,* 2nd enlarged ed. (Minneapolis: Fortress Press; London: SCM Press, 1993); and *Paths from Science towards God: The End of All Our Exploring* (Oxford: Oneworld, 2001).

A Note on the Language

1. Cf. J. Z. Young's *An Introduction to the Study of Man* (Oxford: Clarendon Press, 1971), which is certainly as much, if not more, about female humanity as male humanity; and J. Bronowski's popular *The Ascent of Man* (London: BBC, 1973).

Chapter 1: God's Interaction with the World

1. "'Tis all in piecs, all cohaerance gone," John Donne, in his *Anatomie of the World, The First Anniversary* (1611).

2. There is also the possibility that some quantum events at the micro level can be amplified so as to have macroscopic consequences, for example, in the case of non-linear dynamic systems.

3. Donald T. Campbell, "'Downward Causation' in Hierarchically Organised Systems," in *Studies in the Philosophy of Biology: Reduction and Related Problems,* ed. F. J. Ayala and T. Dobzhansky (London: Macmillan, 1974), 179–86.

4. Roger Sperry, *Science and Moral Priority* (Oxford:, Blackwell, 1983), ch. 6.

5. The "downward/top-down causation" terminology can, I have found, be misleading since it is actually meant to denote an effect of the state of the system as a whole on its constituent parts, such as the constraints on the parts of the boundary conditions of the system as a whole—more broadly, the constraints of actually being in the interacting, co-operative network of that particular, whole system. The word "causation" is not really appropriate for describing such situations, so—in this paper—I have preferred the usage of "whole-part constraint," rather than that of "downward-" or "top-down causation," which I used more generally in *TSA*. Later I used the term "whole-part influence" to avoid any negative connotations.

6. Another example from another area of science, a computer programmed to re-

arrange its own circuitry through a robot that it itself controls, has been proposed by Paul Davies in *The Cosmic Blueprint* (London: Heinemann, 1987), 172–74 and fig. 32, as an instance of what he called "downward causation." In this hypothetical (but not at all impossible) system, changes in the information encoded in the computer's software (usually taken as the "higher" level) downwardly cause modifications in the computer's hardware (the "lower" level)—an example of software-hardware feedback.

7. As does M. Polanyi in *inter alia* "Life's Irreducible Structure," *Science* 160 (1968): 1308–12. See the account in my *God and the New Biology* (London: Dent, 1986; reprint, Magnolia, Mass.: Peter Smith, 1994), 23–25.

8. See Arthur Peacocke, *Intimations of Reality* (Notre Dame, Ind.: University of Notre Dame Press, 1984), ch. 1; see *TSA*, 11–19, for references to other authors.

9. This over-brief comment refers, of course, to the much debated issue of reductionism and the possibility of emergent realities at higher levels of complexity. My own views are expressed *inter alia* in *TSA*, 39–41, and in Peacocke, *God and the New Biology*, chs. 1, 2, where references to the extensive literature may be found. See also the next section.

10. Campbell, "Downward Causation," 181–82.

11. The relation between the different usages of "information" has been usefully clarified by J. C. Puddefoot (in "Information and Creation," *The Science and Theology of Information,* ed. C. Wassermann, R. Kirby, and B. Rordoff (Geneva: Labor et Fides, 1992), 15. He distinguishes three senses relevant to the present context (my numbering):

(i) "Information" in the physicists', communication engineers', and brain scientists' sense, that of C. E. Shannon—the sense in which "information" is related to the probability of one outcome, or case selected, out of many, equally probable, outcomes or cases. In this sense it is, in certain circumstances, the negative of entropy.

(ii) "Information" in the sense of the Latin *informo, -are,* meaning "to give shape or form to." Thus, "information" is "the action of informing with some active or essential quality [sense II]," as the noun corresponding to the transitive verb 'to inform', in the sense (II) of "To give 'form' or formative principle to; hence to stamp, impress, or imbue *with* some specific quality or attribute" (quotations from the Shorter Oxford English Dictionary [*O.E.D.*]).

(iii) "Information" in the ordinary sense of "that of which one is apprised or told" (Shorter *O.E.D.*, sense I.3).

Puddefoot points out that "information (i)" is necessary to shape or give form, as "information (ii)," to a receptor. If that receptor is the brain of a human being, then "information (iii)" is conveyed. In this paper the term "information" (and its associates) is being broadly used to represent this whole *process* of (i) becoming (ii)—and only modulating to (iii) when there is a specific reference to human brain processes.

Although in actual natural systems, there is never a flow of information without some transfer of energy, however small, the *concept* of "information" is clearly distinguishable from that of "energy."

12. D. M. Mackay, "The Interdependence of Mind and Brain," *Neuroscience* 5 (1980): 1389–91.

13. J. Searle, *Minds, Brains, and Science* (Cambridge, Mass.: Harvard University Press, 1984), 26 (emphasis added).

14. In a personal note, January 24, 1994. See also chapter 6 in this volume.

15. Here, and in what follows, by both "world" and "all-that-is" I intend to refer to everything apart from God, both terrestrially and cosmologically. I regard the "world"/"all-that-is," in this context, as an interconnected and interdependent system, but with, of course, great variation in the strength of mutual inter-coupling. All wave functions, for example, only go asymptotically to zero at infinity—and recall the effects of gravity from distant galaxies even on the collision of billiard balls, not to mention the ecological connectedness of terrestrial life within itself and with the state of the Earth.

16. This section represents an elucidation of *TSA*, 152–56, and a tightening up of the argument, by making more careful distinctions between "in principle" and "in practice" unpredictability with respect to deterministic chaos and quantum theory and to whether or not God or ourselves are under consideration.

17. In a paper in "Divine Action, Freedom, and the Laws of Nature," in *Quantum Cosmology and the Laws of Nature: Scientific Perspectives on Divine Action*, ed. R. J. Russell, N. Murphey, and C. J. Isham (Vatican City State: Vatican Observatory Publications, 1993), 185–207. W. P. Alston reverted to an earlier idea of W. F. Pollard, in *Chance and Providence* (New York: Charles Scribner's Sons, 1958), that God can act at the quantum level because quantum theory predicts only probabilities of particular outcomes of a given situation. He wrote, "God can, consistent with quantum theory, do something to bring about a physically improbable outcome in one or more instances without any violation of physical law" (189). For reasons outside the scope of this particular paper I am skeptical of this proposal.

Later (190) Alston argues that, at levels other than the quantum one—that is, at levels where there are genuinely deterministic laws relating outcomes to initial situations—God could be an additional factor, "a divine outside force," not previously allowed for by the science involved. But this is vulnerable to the criticism that such a "force" cannot but be in the natural order to be effective—and therefore amenable to scientific investigation. But it is these very investigations which unveil the deterministic laws which demonstrate that such arbitrary occurrences do not occur. So such "intervention" is an incoherent idea, as well as casting doubts on the foundations on which the very existence of a divine Creator can be postulated, namely the regularity of that ordering of the natural world which the sciences reveal and from which is inferred that it manifests and expresses an endowed rationality.

18. The positive evidence for the absence of, at least, *local* "hidden variables" is discussed in a way accessible to the general reader by J. C. Polkinghorne, *The Quantum World* (Harmondsworth: Penguin Books, 1986), ch. 7. Whether or not such "hidden variables" can, more generally, be regarded as absent is still a much-discussed question, though the majority view is against their existence.

19. See also *TSA*, 122, for a discussion of God's "self-limitation."

20. Ibid., 91–94, 121–23. In the latter passage (122), I included in the category of systems whose future states cannot be definitively known even to God (since they are in principle unknowable) not only the operation of human free will and (quantum)

systems in the "Heisenberg" range, but also "certain nonlinear systems at the microscopic level." I had in mind here (and was insufficiently precise in specifying) those nonlinear systems in which effects of *quantum* events can be amplified to the macroscopic level so that, in principle, knowledge only of the *probabilities* of occurrence of particular macroscopic states is possible—knowledge maximally available to God. If "quantum chaos," in the strict sense, proves to be possible, further reflection on God's knowledge of the future states of systems in which it occurs will be needed in the light of its precise epistemological character.

21. Ibid., 128–33, which gives references to other authors who also hold this view.

22. Note that the argument being pursued here does not depend on establishing that "quantum chaos," in the strict sense, actually occurs.

23. These would also include the future trajectories of systems displaying "chaotic" behavior if "quantum chaos" proves to be theoretically feasible.

24. As pointed out by R. J. Russell in this context, the notion of whole-part constraint does not depend critically on the idea of "boundary conditions" of a complex system, with its implicit phase-spatial connotations—and indeed the universe does not have a boundary in *that* sense. I am also indebted to him for some of the wording in the sentences that follow.

25. The interconnectedness and interdependence of all-that-is would be infinitely more apparent to God. For God holds it all in existence; is present to all space and time frameworks of reference; and all-that-is is ontologically "in God," on the, properly qualified, "pan-en-theistic" model which I espouse (see *TSA*, 370–72 n. 75, and associated text, as well as fig. 1).

26. A "pan-en-theistic" view, the sense of which I have explicated further, with references to other authors, in *TSA* (references in previous note) and in chapters in *In Whom We Live and Have Our Being: Panentheistic Reflections on God's Presence in a Scientific World*, ed. Philip Clayton and Arthur Peacocke (Grand Rapids and Cambridge, UK: Eerdmans, 2004).

27. For further elaboration of the understanding of God's relation to time assumed at this point, see *TSA*, 128–33. I there summarized my position in the following terms: "God is not 'timeless'; God is temporal in the sense that the divine life is successive in its relation to us—God is temporally related to us; God creates and is present to each instant of the (physical and, derivatively, psychological) time of the created world; God transcends past and present created time: God is eternal" (132), in the sense that there is no time at which God does not exist nor will there ever be a future time at which God does not exist.

For a discussion of the issues concerning the "block universe" model used in relativistic physics and their implications for the God-time relation, see the illuminating discussion of C. J. Isham and J. Polkinghorne in *Quantum Cosmology and the Laws of Nature Scientific Perspectives on Divine Action*, ed. R. J. Russell, N. Murphy, and C. J. Isham (Vatican Observatory and Center for Theology and the Natural Sciences; Notre Dame, Ind.: University of Notre Dame Press, 1993) 135–44). I take the view of the latter in this debate.

28. Both of the (for us) practical kind (e.g., chaotic systems) and of the in-principle, inherent kinds (e.g., certain quantum events).

29. I am indebted, at this point especially in this paper, to the wording of some illuminating comments by Philip Clayton.

30. See, *inter alia,* C. Blakemore, *The Mechanics of the Mind* (Cambridge: Cambridge University Press, 1976); the articles assembled in *Scientific American* publications, *The Brain* and *Mind and Brain* (San Francisco and Oxford: Freeman, 1979, 1992, respectively); and the comprehensive information in *The Oxford Companion to the Mind,* ed. Richard L. Gregory (Oxford: Oxford University Press, 1987).

31. With the qualification of the self-limitations of divine omniscience and divine omnipotence already made (cf. *TSA,* 121–23).

32. Do we have here one aspect of humanity as *imago dei?*

33. The "ontological gap at the causal joint"; see below.

34. To the best of my knowledge the first application of the concept of information to the interaction of God and the world was made by John Bowker in *The Sense of God* (Oxford: Clarendon Press, 1973), ch. 5, "Structural Accounts of Religion." See also the expression in similar terms of this idea, of God "informing" the world in a "downward/top-down" manner, by John Polkinghorne, *Science and Providence* (London: SPCK, 1989), 32 ff., and in *Reason and Reality* (London: SPCK, 1991), ch. 3; and *TSA,* 161, 164, 179, 207.

35. The consequences of this I have tried to develop in *TSA,* part 3.

36. Gordon D. Kaufman, *God the Problem* (Cambridge, Mass.: Harvard University Press, 1972).

37. Maurice Wiles, *God's Action in the World* (London: SCM Press, 1986).

38. See *TSA* (1993 ed.), part 3.

Chapter 2: Biological Evolution and Christian Theology

1. Gertrude Himmelfarb, *Darwin and the Darwinian Revolution* (New York: Norton Library, 1968).

2. S. Daecke, "Entwicklung," in *Theologische Realenzyklopädie* (Berlin: Walter de Gruyter, 1982), 710.

3. R. Seeberg, *Christliche Dogmatik* I (Leipzig: Erlangen, 1924).

4. J. Von Uexküll, *Theoretical Biology* (New York: Kegan Paul, Trench, Trubner & Co. Ltd., 1926).

5. Karl Heim, *Das Weltbild der Zukunft* (Berlin: C.A. Schwetschke, 1965).

6. W. Pannenberg, *Wissenschaftstheorie and Theologie* (Frankfurt am Main: Suhrkamp Verlag, 1973).

7. W. Pannenberg, "Theological Questions to Scientists," in *The Sciences and Theology in the Twentieth Century,* ed. A. R. Peacocke (Notre Dame, Ind.: University of Notre Dame Press; London: Oriel Press, 1981).

8. J. Moltmann, *The Future of Creation* (London: SCM Press, 1979).

9. Stephen Toulmin and June Goodfield, *The Discovery of Time* (London: Hutchinson, 1965), 214.

10. H. Bergson, *L'Evolution creatrice* [Creative evolution], trans. A. Mitchell (London: Macmillan, 1911).

11. P. Teilhard de Chardin, *The Phenomenon of Man,* trans. B. Wall (London: Collins, 1959).

12. Z. Alszeghi, "Development in the Doctrinal Formulations of the Church Concerning the Theory of Evolution," *Concilium* 6, no. 3 (1967): 14–17.

13. K. Rahner, "Christology within an Evolutionary View," in *Theological Investigations* V(III), trans. K.-H Kruger (London: Darton, Longman & Todd, 1966), ch. 8, 157–92.

14. J. R. Moore, *The Post-Darwinian Controversies* (Cambridge: Cambridge University Press, 1979).

15. A. L. Moore, *Science and Faith* (London: Kegan Paul, Trench & Co., 1889), 184.

16. A. L. Moore, "The Christian Doctrine of God," in *Lux Mundi,* 12th ed., ed. C. Gore (London: Murray, 1891), 73.

17. J. R. Illingworth, "The Incarnation in Relation to Development," in *Lux Mundi,* 12th ed., ed. C. Gore (London: Murray, 1891), 132, 151–52.

18. C. Gore, *The Incarnation of the Son of God*, Bampton Lectures (London: Murray, 1891), 32–33.

19. F. R. Tennant, *The Origin and Propagation of Sin*, Hulsean Lectures, Cambridge, 1901–2 (Cambridge: Cambridge University Press, 1902).

20. A. N. Whitehead, *Process and Reality* (New York: Macmillan; Cambridge: Cambridge University Press, 1929).

21. W. Temple, *Nature, Man, and God*, Gifford Lectures, 1932–33 and 1933–34 (London: Macmillan, 1934).

22. L. S. Thornton, *The Incarnate Lord* (London: Longmans, Green & Co., 1928).

23. F. W. Dillistone, *Charles Raven: Naturalist, Historian and Theologian* (London: Hodder & Stoughton, 1975).

24. C. E. Raven, *Natural Religion and Christian Theology*, vol. 1, *Science and Religion;* vol. 2, *Experience and Interpretation*, Gifford Lectures (Cambridge: Cambridge University Press, 1953).

25. A. R. Peacocke, *Creation and the World of Science,* Bampton Lectures 1978 (Oxford: Clarendon Press, 1979; new paperback ed., 2004), 125–27.

26. R. W. Burhoe, *Towards a Scientific Theology* (Belfast: Christian Journals, 1981), 21.

27. J. Monod, *Chance and Necessity* (London: Collins, 1972).

28. See A. R. Peacocke, *An Introduction to the Physical Chemistry of Biological Organization* (Oxford: Clarendon Press, 1983, 1989).

29. M. Eigen, "The Self-Organization of Matter and the Evolution of Biological Macromolecules," *Naturwissenschaften* 58 (1971): 519.

30. F. Jacob, "Molecular Tinkering in Evolution," in D. S. Bendall, ed., *Evolution from Molecules to Men* (Cambridge: Cambridge University Press, 1983), 131. See also F. Jacob, "Evolution and Tinkering," *Science* 196 (1977): 1161–66.

31. G. G. Simpson, *The Meaning of Evolution* (New Haven, Conn.: Yale University Press and Bantam Books, 1971), 258–59.

32. S. Brenner, "New Directions in Molecular Biology," *Nature* 248 (1974): 785–87.

33. F. H. C. Crick, *Of Molecules and Man* (Seattle: University of Washington Press, 1966), 10.

34. M. Beckner, "Reduction, Hierarchies, and Organism," in *Studies in the Philosophy of Biology*, ed. A. J. Ayala and T. Dobzhansky (London: Macmillan, 1974), 163–76.

35. A. R. Peacocke, "Reductionism: A Review of the Epistemological Issues and

Their Relevance to Biology and the Problem of Consciousness," *Zygon: Journal of Religion & Science* 11 (1976): 307–34.

36. W. R. Wimsatt, "Robustness, Reliability and Overdetermination," in *Scientific Inquiry and the Social Sciences*, ed. M. Brewer and B. Collins (San Francisco: Jossey-Bass, 1981), 124–63.

37. R. C. Lewontin, "Gene, Organism, and Environment," in *Evolution from Molecules to Men,* ed. D. S. Bendall (Cambridge: Cambridge University Press, 1983), 273–85.

38. Sir Alister Hardy, *The Living Stream* (London: Collins, 1965), 161ff., 189ff.

39. A. R. Peacocke, Introduction to *The Sciences and Theology in the Twentieth Century*, ed. A. R. Peacocke (London: Oriel Press; Notre Dame, Ind.: University of Notre Dame Press, 1981), ix–xviii.

40. A. R. Peacocke, *Intimations of Reality: Critical Realism in Science and Religion* (Notre Dame, Ind.: University of Notre Dame Press, 1984).

41. Doctrine Commission of the Church of England, *Christian Believing* (London: SPCK, 1976), 3.

42. D. J. Bartholomew, *God of Chance* (London: SCM Press, 1984).

43. W. Temple, *Nature, Man, and God.*

44. Moore, "The Christian Doctrine of God," 73.

Chapter 3: Chance, Potentiality, and God

1. J. Monod, *Chance and Necessity* (London: Collins, 1972).

2. Bertrand Russell, *Mysticism and Logic and Other Essays* (London: Allen & Lluwin, 1963 ed.), 41.

3. Cf. Stephen Toulmin, "French Toast," *New York Review of Books,* December 16, 1971, 17ff.; and Stuart Hampshire, "Molecular Philosophy," *Observer Review*, May 7, 1972.

4. E.g., Gen. 2:7: "And the Lord God formed man out of the dust of the ground and breathed into his nostrils the breath of life."

5. M. Polanyi, *Personal Knowledge* (London: Routledge & Kegan Paul, 1958).

6. M. Polanyi, *The Tacit Dimension* (London: Routledge & Kegan Paul, 1967), 47.

7. I. T. Ramsey, *Religious Language* (London: SCM Press, 1957), e.g., 67 and *passim*.

Chapter 4: Complexity, Emergence, and Divine Creativity

1. This term need not (*should* not) be taken to imply the operation of any influences, either external in the form of an "entelechy" or "life force" or internal in the sense of "top-down/whole-part" causative influences. It is, in my usage, a purely descriptive term for the observed phenomenon of the appearance of new capabilities, functions, and so on at greater levels of complexity. It is not intended to have any normative or evaluative connotations.

2. Francis H. C. Crick, *Of Molecules and Man* (Seattle: University of Washington Press, 1966), 10.

3. See *Studies in the Philosophy of Biology: Reduction and Related Problems,* ed. F. J. Ayala and T. Dobzhansky (London: Macmillan, 1974).

4. These distinctions were well delineated by F. J. Ayala in his introduction to *Studies in the Philosophy of Biology* (see previous note) and are elaborated in my *God and the*

New Biology (London: Dent, 1986; reprint, Gloucester, Mass.: Peter Smith, 1994), chs. 1 and 2.

5. Formal criteria for this have already been developed by Ernest Nagel, "Wholes, Sums, and Organic Unities," *Philosophical Studies* 3 (1952): 17–32.

6. These are conventionally said to run from the "lower," less complex to the "higher," more complex systems, from parts to wholes so that these wholes themselves constitute parts of more complex entities—rather like a series of Russian dolls. In the complex systems I have in mind here, the parts retain their identity and properties as isolated individual entities. The *internal* relations of such elements are not regarded as affected by their incorporation into the system.

7. See, e.g., Arthur Peacocke, *Theology for a Scientific Age: Being and Becoming—Natural Divine and Human,* 2nd enlarged ed. (Minneapolis: Fortress Press; London: SCM Press, 1993), 36–43, 214–18, and fig. 3, based on a scheme of W. Bechtel and A. Abrahamson. *Connectionism and the Mind* (Oxford: Blackwell, 1991), fig. 8.1.

8. For the subtle distinction between "theory" autonomy and "process" autonomy, concepts related to that of ontological reduction, see Arthur Peacocke, "The Sound of Sheer Silence: How Does God Communicate with Humanity?" in *Neuroscience and the Person: Scientific Perspective on Divine Action,* ed. R. J. Russell et al. (Vatican Observatory and Center for Theology and the Natural Sciences; Notre Dame, Ind.: University of Notre Dame Press, 1999), especially the appendix, 245–47, from which some of this text has been drawn.

9. S. Alexander, as quoted by J. Kim, "Non-Reductivism and Mental Causation," in *Mental Causation,* ed. J. Heil and A. Mele (Oxford: Clarendon Press, 1993), 204.

10. W. C. Wimsatt has elaborated criteria of "robustness" for such attributions of reality for emergent properties at the higher levels. These involve noting what is invariant under a variety of independent procedures (W. C. Wimsatt, "Robustness, Reliability and Multiple-Determination in Science," in *Knowing and Validating in the Social Sciences: A Tribute to Donald T. Campbell,* ed. M. Brewer and B. Collins (San Francisco: Jossey-Bass, 1981).

11. See Peacocke ("The Sound of Sheer Silence") and the discussion of Philip Clayton in the same volume (209–11).

12. D. T. Campbell, "'Downward Causation' in Hierarchically Organised Systems," in *Studies in the Philosophy of Biology: Reduction and Related Problems,* ed. Ayala and Dobzhansky.

13. I. Prigogine and I. Stengers, *Order out of Chaos* (London: Heinemann, 1984).

14. Niels Henrik Gregersen, "The Idea of Creation and the Theory of Autopoietic Processes," *Zygon* 33 (1998): 333–67; A. R. Peacocke, *The Physical Chemistry of Biological Organization* (Oxford: Clarendon Press, [1983] 1989); Prigogine and Stengers, *Order out of Chaos.*

15. F. Dretske, "Mental Events as Structuring Causes of Behavior," in *Mental Causation,* ed. Heil and Mele.

16. Karl Popper, *A World of Propensities* (Bristol, Eng.: Thoemmes, 1990), 12.

17. Ibid., 17.

18. M. Polanyi, "Life Transcending Physics and Chemistry," *Chemical and Engineering News,* August 21, 1967; "Life's Irreducible Structure," *Science* 160 (1968): 1308–12. In his discussion, and mine in this essay, the term "boundary condition" is *not* being

used, as it often is, to refer *either* to the initial (and in that sense "boundary") conditions of, say, a partial differential equation as applied in theoretical physics *or* to the physical, geometrical boundary of a system.

19. In *Chaos and Complexity: Scientific Perspectives on Divine Action*, ed. R. J. Russell, N. Murphy, and A. R. Peacocke (Vatican City State: Vatican Observatory and Center for Theology and the Natural Sciences; Notre Dame, Ind.: Notre Dame Press, 1995), 100.

20. D. Davidson, "Mental Events," in *Essays on Actions and Events* (Oxford: Clarendon Press, 1980).

21. J. Kim, "Epiphenomal and Supervenient Causation," *Midwest Studies in Philosophy* 9 (1984): 257–70. Reprinted in his *Supervenience and Mind: Selected Philosophical Essays* (Cambridge: Cambridge University Press, 1993).

22. Kim, *Supervenience and Mind*, 191.

23. T. J. Sejnowski, C. Koch, and P. Churchland, "Computational Neuroscience," *Science* 241 (1988): 1300.

24. J. Heil and A. Mele, eds., *Mental Causation* (Oxford: Clarendon Press, 1993).

25. E.g., Peacocke, "The Sound of Sheer Silence." It must be stressed that the "whole-part" relation is *not* regarded here necessarily, or frequently, as a spatial one. "Whole-part" is synonymous with "system-constituent."

26. The "nonreductive physicalist" view of the mental/physical relation of many philosophers has been summarized by Kim (see n. 21) as follows: "1. *(Physical Monism)*. All concrete particulars are physical. 2. *(Antireductionism)*. Mental properties are not reducible to physical properties. 3. *(The Physical Realization Thesis)*. All mental properties are physically realized; that is, whenever an organism, or system, instantiates a mental property *M*, it has some physical property *P* such that *P* realizes *M* in organisms of its kind. . . . 4. *(Mental Realism)*. Mental properties are real properties of objects and events; they are not merely useful aids in making predictions or fictitious manners of speech."

27. See Peacocke, "The Sound of Sheer Silence," 229–31.

28. Philip Clayton, "The Case for Christian Panentheism," *Dialog* 37, no. 3 (1998): 205.

29. See Gregersen, "The Idea of Creation."

30. For the only dualism acceptable to modern theology and consistent with science is the God-world one, with no fundamental dualities *within* the created world—bearing in mind the nuances and qualifications of the emergentist monism I developed above.

31. Augustine, *Confessions* 11.14, trans. R. S. Pine-Coffins (Harmondsworth: Penguin Classics, 1961).

32. Charles Kingsley, *The Water Babies* (London: Hodder & Stoughton, [1863] 1930), 248.

33. Frederick Temple, *The Relations between Religion and Science* (London: Macmillan, 1885), 115.

34. For a discussion of these ideas, see Arthur Peacocke, "Biology and a Theology of Evolution," *Zygon* 34 (1999): 695–712, and *Paths from Science towards God: The End of All Our Exploring* (Oxford: Oneworld, 2001), part 3.

35. Sharon H. Runge, *Wisdom's Friends* (Louisville, Ky.: Westminster John Knox

Press, 1999); Celia Deane-Drummond, *Creation through Wisdom: Theology and the New Biology* (Edinburgh: T & T Clark, 2000).

36. William Temple, *Nature, Man, and God* (London: Macmillan, [1934] 1964), ch. 19; Arthur Peacocke, "Nature as Sacrament," *Third Millennium* 2 (2000): 16–31.

37. Vladimir Lossky, *The Mystical Theology of the Eastern Church* (French ed., 1944; Cambridge: James Clark, 1991).

38. *The Work of Love: Creation as Kenosis*, ed. John C. Polkinghorne (Grand Rapids: Eerdmans; London: SPCK, 2000).

39. An interpretation of the Eucharist I originally suggested in "Matter in the Theological and Scientific Perspective," in *Thinking about the Eucharist*, a collection of essays by members of the Doctrine Commission of the Church of England (London: SCM Press, 1972), especially 32. It is entirely congruent with that recently expounded by Niels Henrik Gregersen, "God's Public Traffic: Holist versus Physicalist Supervenience," in *The Human Person and Theology*, ed. N. H. Gregersen, W. B. Drees, and U. Görman (Edinburgh: T & T Clark; Grand Rapids: Eerdmans, 2000), 180–82.

40. Gregersen, "God's Public Traffic."

41. An exemplification of God's nonintervening, but specific, "whole-part" influence on the world, which I have elaborated elsewhere (see Peacocke, "The Sound of Sheer Silence").

42. An approach I adumbrated in my Bampton Lectures of 1978—*Creation and the World of Science* (Oxford: Clarendon Press, 1979; new ed., 2004), appendix C, "Reductionism and Religion-and-Science: [Theology] 'the Queen of the Sciences'?" 367–71.

Chapter 5: Articulating God's Presence in and to the World Unveiled by the Sciences

1. Thomas Traherne, *Centuries: First Century (18)* (London: The Faith Press, [1670] 1963), 9.

2. J. Kim, "The Non-Reductivist's Troubles with Mental Causation," in *Mental Causation*, ed. J. Heil and A. Mele (Oxford: Clarendon Press, 1995), 189–210.

3. H. Wheeler Robinson, "Hebrew Psychology," in *The People and the Book*, ed. A. S. Peake (Oxford: Clarendon Press, 1925), 362.

4. S. Kaufmann, *At Home in the Universe: The Search for the Laws of Complexity* (London: Penguin, 1996); and for wider references see A. R. Peacocke, *The Physical Chemistry of Biological Organization* (Oxford: Clarendon Press, 1989), chs. 2, 4, and 5.

5. Kaufmann, *At Home in the Universe, passim*; P. Bak, *How Nature Works: The Science of Self-Organized Criticality* (Oxford: Oxford University Press, 1997); and I. Stewart, *Life's Other Secret: The New Mathematics of the Living World* (London: Penguin, 1998).

6. Karl Popper, *A World of Propensities* (Bristol, Eng.: Thoemmes, 1990); and Arthur Peacocke, "Biological Evolution—A Positive Theological Appraisal," in *Evolutionary and Molecular Biology: Scientific Perspectives on Divine Action*, ed. R. J. Russell, W. R. Stoeger, and F. J. Ayala (Vatican City State: Vatican Observatory and Center for Theology and the Natural Sciences; Notre Dame, Ind.: University of Notre Dame Press, 1998), 357–76.

7. A. R. Peacocke, *Creation and the World of Science* (Oxford: Clarendon Press, 1979), ch. 3.

8. T. W. Deacon, "Evolution and the Emergence of Spirit," paper given at the Science and the Spiritual Quest Boston Conference, October 21–23, 2001.

9. Ibid.

10. A. Moore, "The Christian Doctrine of God," in *Lux Mundi*, 12th ed., ed. C. Gore (London: Murray, 1891), 73.

11. C. Kingsley, *The Water Babies* (London: Hodder & Stoughton, [1863] 1930), 248.

12. H. van Till, "The Creation Intelligently Designed or Optimally Equipped?" *Theology Today* 55 (1988): 349, 351.

13. See the discussion below on this divine agency being analogous to *personal* agency.

14. G. R. Peterson, "Whither Panentheism?" *Zygon* 36 (September 2001): 395–405.

15. *The Oxford Dictionary of the Christian Church*, 2nd ed., ed. F. L. Cross and E. A. Livingstone (Oxford: Oxford University Press, 1974), 1027.

16. Acts 17:28 (AV and RSV).

17. J. Moltmann, *God in Creation* (London: SCM Press, 1985).

18. Augustine *Confessions* VII, trans. E. B. Pusey, in *Great Books of the Western World*, vol. 18, ed. R. M. Hutchins (Chicago: Encyclopaedia Britannica Inc., 1952), 45.

19. See the series of volumes on "Scientific Perspectives on Divine Action," which have resulted from the biennial discussions organized by the Vatican Observatory and Center for Theology and the Natural Sciences, Berkeley (general editor, R. J. Russell) and distributed through the University of Notre Dame Press, Notre Dame, Ind.

20. J. G. Dunn, *Christology in the Making* (London: SCM Press, 1986), 259, 262.

21. Celia Deane-Drummond, *Creation through Wisdom* (Edinburgh: T & T Clark, 2000), xv and *passim*.

22. John 1:1–4.

23. John 1:14.

24. W. Temple, *Nature, Man, and God* (London: Macmillan, 1934), ch. 19.

Chapter 6: Natural Being and Becoming

1. John Donne, "An Anatomie of the World: The First Anniversary," in C. A. Plerides, ed., *The Complete English Poems of John Donne* (London: Dent, 1985).

2. Herbert Butterfield, *The Origins of Modern Science, 1300–1800* (London: Bell, 1968), vii.

3. Jarrett Leplin, ed., *Scientific Realism* (Berkeley: University of California Press, 1984), 2.

4. Ernan McMullin, "A Case for Scientific Realism," in Leplin, ed., *Scientific Realism*, 26.

5. Francis H. C. Crick, *Of Molecules and Man* (Seattle: University of Washington Press, 1966), 10.

6. James P. Crutchfield, J. Doyne Farmer, Norman H. Packard, and Robert S. Shaw, "Chaos," *Scientific American,* December 1986, 38.

7. See, *inter alia,* Ilya Prigogine, *From Being to Becoming* (San Francisco: Freeman, 1980); Ilya Prigogine and Isabelle Stengers, *Order Out of Chaos* (London: Heinemann, 1984); and the exposition of these ideas given in Arthur R. Peacocke, *An Introduction*

to the Physical Chemistry of Biological Organization (Oxford: Clarendon Press, 1983), ch. 2.

8. Manfried Eigen and Peter Schuster, *The Hypercycle* (Berlin: Springer-Verlag, 1979); Manfried Eigen and Ruthild Winkler, *Laws of the Game* (New York: Knopf; London: Allen Lane, 1982); also expounded in Peacocke, *An Introduction to the Physical Chemistry of Biological Organization,* ch. 7.

9. Konrad Lorenz, *Behind the Mirror* (English trans., London: Methuen, 1977), ch. 7, 113ff.

10. Ian T. Ramsey, "Human Personality," in *Personality and Science: An Interdisciplinary Discussion,* ed. I. T. Ramsey and R. Porter (Edinburgh: Churchill Livingstone, 1971), 128.

11. Crutchfield et al., "Chaos," 49.

Chapter 7: The Nature and Purpose of Man in Science and Christian Theology

1. Michael Polanyi, *The Tacit Dimension* (London: Routledge & Kegan Paul, 1967), 47.

2. *Westminster Shorter Catechism* (1647).

3. A. Quinton, *Biology and Personality,* ed. I. T. Ramsey (Oxford: Blackwell, 1965), 107 ff.

4. See Michael Polanyi, *Personal Knowledge* (London: Routledge & Kegan Paul, 1958).

5. A. R. Peacocke, *Science and the Christian Experiment* (London: Oxford University Press, 1971), 84 ff.

6. See M. Grene, ed., *Interpretations of Life and Mind: Essays around the Problem of Reduction* (London: Routledge & Kegan Paul, 1971), which has a useful bibliography on this topic, 149–50.

7. See J. C. Eccles, "Cultural Evolution versus Biological Evolution," *Zygon* 3–4 (1972): 282–93.

8. Ervin Laszlo, "The Purpose of Mankind," *Zygon* 3–4 (1972): 310–24.

9. Alfred E. Emerson, "Some Biological Antecedents of Human Purpose," *Zygon* 3–4 (1972): 294–309.

10. Peacocke, *Science and the Christian Experiment,* 91–102, based on George Gaylord Simpson, *The Meaning of Evolution* (London: Oxford University Press, 1950), chs. 15, 17.

11. Julian Huxley, "The Evolutionary Process," in *Evolution as a Process,* ed. Julian Huxley, A. C. Hardy, and E. B. Ford (London: George Allen & Unwin, 1954), 13.

12. Polanyi, *Personal Knowledge,* 328–31; Polanyi, *The Tacit Dimension,* ch. 2.

13. J. A. T. Robinson, *The Body* (London: SCM Press, 1957), 11.

14. Wheeler Robinson, "Hebrew Psychology," in *The People and the Book,* ed. Arthur S. Peake (Oxford: Clarendon Press, 1925), 362.

15. W. Eichrodt, *Theology of the Old Testament,* trans. J. A. Baker (London: SCM Press, 1967), 2:124.

16. J. A. Baker, "Man: His Nature, Predicament and Hope (1), the Old Testament," in *Man, Fallen and Free,* ed. E. W. Kamp (London: Hodder & Stroughton, 1969), ch. 5.

17. J. L. Houlden, "Man: His Nature, Predicament and Hope (2), the New Testament," ibid., ch. 6.

18. Eichrodt, *Theology of the Old Testament,* 2:126

19. Peacocke, *Science and the Christian Experiment,* ch. 4.

20. Dante *Paradiso,* last line.

21. "Christ" is the Greek translation of the Hebrew "Messiah" and means literally "the Anointed One."

22. Irenaeus *Adversus Haereses* 5, *praef.*

23. 2 Cor. 5:17 (RV).

24. A. Richardson, *A Theological Word Book of the Bible* (London: SCM Press, 1957), paraphrasing Col. 3:9–11.

25. D. E. Jenkins, *The Glory of Man* (London: SCM Press, 1967), 53–55.

26. In fact into a discussion of the doctrines of "redemption" and "sanctification."

27. John 10:10 (NEB).

28. Cf. the use of the term "personalness" by Jenkins, *The Glory of Man.*

29. Luke 1:35; Mark 1:10; Rom. 1:4.

30. Rom. 5:5.

31. C. E. Raven, *Natural Science and Christian Theology,* Gifford Lectures, *Experience and Interpretation,* vol. 2 (Cambridge: Cambridge University Press, 1953), 157.

32. Peacocke, *Science and the Christian Experiment,* 124–32.

33. Philip Hefner, "The Self-Definition of Life and Human Purpose: Reflections upon the Divine Spirit and the Human Spirit," *Zygon* 3–4 (1972): 395–411.

34. See Eccles, "Cultural Evolution versus Biological Evolution."

35. Gal. 4:20 (NEB).

36. Peacocke, *Science and the Christian Experiment,* 174 ff.

37. Ibid., 194–96.

38. F. Hoyle, *The Nature of the Universe* (Oxford: Blackwell, 1960), 72.

39. Mark 1:15 (NEB).

Chapter 8: Science and the Future of Theology

1. John H. Brooke, *Science and Religion: Some Historical Perspectives* (Cambridge: Cambridge University Press, 1991), 1.

2. John Locke, *Essay Concerning Human Understanding,* 6th ed. (1690), Book IV, XVIII, 3.

3. Ibid., Book IV, XVIII, 10.

4. Joseph Butler, Introduction to *The Analogy of Religion* (1736), emphasis added.

5. Jarrett Leplin, *Scientific Realism* (Berkeley: University of California Press, 1984), 1; for a wider-ranging critique, see Paul R Gross and Norman Levitt, *Higher Superstition: The Academic Left and Its Quarrels with Science* (Baltimore: John Hopkins University Press, 1994).

6. Leplin, *Scientific Realism,* 26.

7. Ibid., 30.

8. J. Leplin, *A Novel Defence of Scientific Realism* (Oxford: Oxford University Press, 1997).

9. Ibid., 184.

10. Ibid.

11. Alan Sokal and Jean Bricmont, *Intellectual Imposture* (London: Profile Books, 1998).

12. Henry Harris, "Rationality in Science," in *Scientific Explanations*, ed. A. F. Heath (Oxford: Clarendon Press, 1981), 40.

13. Philip Kitcher, *The Advancement of Science: Science without Legend, Objectivity without Illusion* (New York: Oxford University Press, 1993), 3.

14. Ibid., 390.

15. "*Foundationalism*, as it is generally defined today, is the thesis that all our beliefs can be justified by appealing to some item of knowledge that is self-evident or indubitable. Foundationalism in this epistemological sense therefore always implies the holding of a position inflexibly and infallibly, because in the process of justifying our knowledge-claims, we are able to invoke ultimate foundations on which we construct the evidential support systems of our various convictional beliefs. These 'foundations' for our knowledge are accepted as 'given,' and therefore are treated as a privileged class of aristocratic beliefs that serve as ultimate terminating points in the argumentative justification for our views." J. Wentzel van Huyssteen, *Essays in Post-foundationalist Theology* (Grand Rapids: Eerdmans, 1997), 2, 3. An example follows.

One of the most recent thorough attempts to restore rationality to theological procedures is that of Nancey Murphy in her *Theology in the Age of Scientific Reasoning* (Ithaca, N.Y.: Cornell University Press, 1990; page numbers below refer to this work, with emphases sometimes added). Her transfer of the research program notion of Lakatos from science to theology runs the risk of reverting to the foundationalism many wish to eschew. For her, a Lakatosian research program starts with a "central organizing idea" as its hard core. This can be "the God of Jesus as the all-determining reality" (176) or "the trinitarian nature of God, God's holiness, and God's revelation in Jesus" (184). Such a research program should "develop theories (auxiliary hypotheses) concerning all the *traditional* theological loci" (176); it must be "faithful to any authoritative pronouncements *within the relevant communities*" (176) and "in many cases" to the "dogmas of a *particular communion*" (185). It must relate "the doctrines to available data" (176), as one would expect for any program described as "research," but these data are drawn from "revelation" or the Scriptures, or (in her own case) from this last and "the varied results of discernment" (188). All of which sounds to me not only as very foundationalist but also as very cultural-linguistic (à la G. Lindbeck in his *The Nature of Doctrine* [Philadelphia: Westminster, 1984])—falling within that explicating of the "grammar" within a particular faith community which would entail that theology had no public forum.

16. Arthur Peacocke, *Theology for a Scientific Age: Being and Becoming—Natural Divine and Human,* 2nd enlarged ed. (Minneapolis: Fortress Press; London: SCM Press, 1993), 73, 76, emphasis added.

17. Peter Munz, *Our Knowledge of the Growth of Knowledge* (London: Routledge & Kegan Paul, 1985); G. Radnitzky and W. W. Bartley II, eds., *Evolutionary Epistemology: Theory of Rationality and the Sociology of Knowledge* (LaSalle, Ill.: Open Court, 1987).

18. Konrad Lorenz, *Behind the Mirror: A Search for a Natural History of Human Knowledge* (London: Methuen, [1973] 1977), 113. He identifies these functions as: perception of form; representation of space, especially through sight; locomotion; memory, or storage of information; voluntary movement with feedback; exploratory be-

havior; imitation (and so learning); and transmission of individually acquired knowledge between the generations.

19. Sokal and Bricmont, *Intellectual Imposture*, 54.

20. J. Wentzel van Huyssteen, *Duet or Duel? Theology and Science in a Postmodern World* (London: SCM Press, 1998), 137.

21. The development of Popper's thought in this respect is well described by W. W. Bartley II (in G. Radnitzky and W. W. Bartley II. eds., *Evolutionary Epistemology*, 18–20. He dates Popper's public discussion of the role of biology in elucidating human cognition from 1960 and refers (20–23) to the key contributions of Lorenz *(Behind the Mirror)* and of D. T. Campbell, "Evolutionary Epistemology," in *The Philosophy of Karl Popper*, ed. P. A. Schilpp (LaSalle, Ill.: Open Court, 1974). The latter's key essay of 1974, "Evolutionary Epistemology," is reproduced in Radnitzky and Bartley II (*Evolutionary Epistemology*, ch. 2), and also goes back to an earlier 1960 essay of his, "Blind Variation and Selective Retention in Creative Thought as in Other Knowledge Processes" (ch. 3 in that volume).

22. Gross and Levitt, *Higher Superstition*.

23. Sokal and Bricmont, *Intellectual Imposture*.

24. Peter Lipton, *Inference to the Best Explanation* (London: Routledge & Kegan Paul, 1991), 58, 188.

25. See also Philip Clayton, "Inference to the Best Explanation," *Zygon* 32 (1997): 377–91, for a persuasive argument for its application to theology, especially in its interaction with science.

26. Paul R. Thagard, "The Best Explanation: Criteria for Theory Choice," *Journal of Philosophy* 75 (1978): 92.

27. Lipton, *Inference to the Best Explanation*, 186. He calls this the "loveliest" explanation, but what he calls the "likeliest" explanation—the one most warranted by the evidence—he rightly regards as not conducive to finding the best explanation, for the model can then tend to triviality.

28. Clayton, "Inference to the Best Explanation," 385.

29. See Philip Clayton, *Explanation from Physics to Theology* (New Haven, Conn.: Yale University Press, 1989), ch. 6.

30. Lipton, *Inference to the Best Explanation*, 121, 182ff., 188.

31. Compare the criteria proposed by Thagard ("The Best Explanation"): consilience, simplicity, and analogy. An explanation is better than another if it is more consilient (explains more classes of facts than the other); simpler (has fewer ad hoc auxiliary hypotheses); and can point to more plausible analogies.

32. John Wisdom, "Gods," *Proc. Aristotelian Soc.* (1944–45), quoted by Basil Mitchell in *The Justification of Righteous Belief* (London: Macmillan, 1973), 45.

33. Niels Henrik Gregersen, "A Contextual Coherence Theory for the Science-Theology Dialogue," in *Rethinking Theology and Science: Six Models for the Current Dialogue*, ed. N. H. Gregersen and J. W. van Huyssteen (Grand Rapids: Eerdmans, 1998), 181–231.

34. Clayton, "Inference to the Best Explanation," 387.

35. Kitcher, *The Advancement of Science*, 182.

36. Initially and explicitly in my *Creation and the World of Science* (Oxford: Clarendon Press, 1979), 21–23; then more fully in *Intimations of Reality: Critical Realism in*

Science and Theology (Notre Dame, Ind.: University of Notre Dame Press, 1984), ch. 1; and subsequently in other publications.

37. J. Wentzel van Huysteen, "Postfoundationalism in Theology and Science: Beyond Conflict and Consonance," in *Rethinking Theology and Science: Six Models for the Current Dialogue,* ed. N. H. Gregersen and J. W. van Huyssteen (Grand Rapids: Eerdmans, 1998), 13–49.

38. Hans Küng, *Theology for the Third Millennium—An Ecumenical View,* trans. P. Heinegy (New York: Doubleday; London: HarperCollins, 1991), 161–62.

39. George Lindbeck, *The Nature of Doctrine* (Philadelphia: Westminster, 1984).

40. Gerd Theissen, *A Theory of Primitive Christian Religion,* Speaker's Lectures, Oxford, 1998–99 (London: SCM Press, 1999), 2.

41. David Pailin, "What Game Is Being Played? The Need for Clarity about the Relationships between Scientific and Theological Understanding," *Zygon* 35 (2000): 149.

42. I have incorporated, with gratitude, some of the "Ten Commandments" of Willem Drees, expounded in his 1998 Idreos Lectures in Oxford and later published in *Science and Spirit* 4 (1998): 2–4.

43. Acts 17:28 (AV).

44. Rom. 6:23 (AV).

45. Peacocke, *Theology for a Scientific Age,* 77.

46. Ibid., 231–32, 252–53.

47. Thomas Chalmers, "The Power, Wisdom and Goodness of God," *First Bridgewater Treatise,* 1833, vol. 2, 3rd ed.; (London: William Pickering, 1834), 129–30.

48. Augustine, *Confessions* see new 1.1.1.

49. Matt. 17:7.

Chapter 9: Public Truth in Religion

1. *Correspondence of John Locke,* ed. E. S. Beer (Oxford: Clarendon Press, 1976), 6:294–95.

2. Leonard Hodgson, *For Faith and Freedom* (Oxford: Oxford University Press, 1956), x, where he posed the question as: "What must the truth have been and be if that is how it looked to men who thought and wrote like that?"

3. A. Sokal and J. Bricmont, *Intellectual Impostures* (London: Profile Books, 1998).

4. See chapter 8 in this volume.

5. Sokal and Bricmont, *Intellectual Impostures,* 54.

6. William Wordsworth, *Tintern Abbey* (1790), l. 93ff.

7. K. Jaspers, *The Origin and Goal of History* (London: Routledge & Kegan Paul, 1953), 2—on which this paragraph is based.

8. As developed in my *Theology for a Scientific Age: Being and Becoming—Natural Divine and Human,* 2nd enlarged ed. (Minneapolis: Fortress Press; London: SCM Press, 1993); *God & Science—A Quest for Christian Credibility* (London: SCM Press, 1996); and on the "Virgin Birth," "DNA of our DNA," in *The Birth of Jesus: Biblical and Theological Reflections,* ed. G. J. Brooke (Edinburgh: T & T Clark, 2000), 59–67. Chapter 11 in this volume.

9. In my *Paths from Science towards God: The End of All Our Exploring* (Oxford: Oneworld, 2001).

Chapter 10: *The Incarnation of the Informing Self-Expressive Word of God*

1. This essay was written while preparing *Theology for a Scientific Age: Being and Becoming—Natural Divine and Human,* 2nd enlarged ed. (Minneapolis: Fortress Press; London: SCM Press, 1993); hereafter *TSA*, and shares some material with its ch. 14, "Divine Being Becoming Human." References to that and other sections of *TSA* are provided in this essay for readers interested in more detail.

2. *TSA*, ch. 11.

3. The Chalcedonian Definition established boundary conditions within which christological reflection should proceed. It reads as follows: "Therefore, following the holy Fathers, we all with one accord teach men to acknowledge one and the same Son, our Lord Jesus Christ, at once complete in Godhead and complete in manhood, truly God and truly man, consisting also of a reasonable soul and body; of one substance *(homoousios)* with the Father as regards his Godhead, and at the same time of one substance with us as regards his manhood; like us in all respects, apart from sin; as regards his Godhead, begotten of the Father before all ages, but yet as regards his manhood begotten, for us men and for our salvation, of Mary the Virgin, the God-bearer *(Theotokos);* one and the same Christ, Son, Lord, Only-begotten, recognized in two natures, without confusion, without change, without division, without separation; the distinction of natures being in no way annulled by the union, but rather the characteristics of each nature being preserved and coming together to form one person and subsistence *(hypostasis),* not as parted or separated into two persons, but one and the same Son and Only-begotten God the Word, Lord Jesus Christ; even as the prophets from earliest times spoke of him, and our Lord Jesus Christ himself taught us, and the creed of the Fathers has handed down to us." H. Bettenson, *Documents of the Christian Church* (London: Oxford University Press, 1956), 73.

4. For an accessible and readable account, see John Macquarrie, *Jesus Christ in Modern Thought* (London: SCM Press, 1990).

5. Irenaeus, *Adversus Haereses,* trans. Dominic J. Unger (New York: Paulist Press, 1992), *v. praef.*

6. Wisdom was conceived of as "personification of divine action" in pre-Christian Judaism rather than as "a divine being in some sense independent of God," according to James D. G. Dunn, *Christology in the Making* (London: SCM Press, 1980), 262. Wisdom was especially conceived as being present at and in the divine action of creation.

7. Ibid., 258–59 (Dunn's emphasis).

8. Ibid., 262 (Dunn's emphasis).

9. Ibid. (Dunn's emphasis).

10. A. E. Harvey, *Jesus and the Constraints of History* (London: Duckworth, 1982), 157.

11. Something that Dunn disputes; see *Christology in the Making*, 38–45.

12. Harvey, *Jesus and the Constraints of History,* 178.

13. See Raymond E. Brown, *Jesus God and Man* (London: Collier Macmillan, 1967), 30–34.

14. For a brief discussion, see my *Creation and the World of Science* (Oxford: Clarendon Press, [1979] 2004), 222–27.

15. C. F. D. Moule, *The Origin of Christology* (Cambridge: Cambridge University Press, 1977), 2.

16. See W. O. Chadwick, *From Bossuet to Newman: The Idea of Doctrinal Development* (Cambridge: Cambridge University Press, 1957); N. Lash, "Development, Doctrinal," in *New Dictionary of Christian Theology* (Philadelphia: Westminster Press, 1983), 155–56; M. F. Wiles, *The Remaking of Christian Doctrine* (London: SCM Press, 1974).

17. Dunn, *Christology in the Making,* 266–67.

18. See James P. Mackay, "The Task of Systematic Theology," in James D. G. Dunn and James P. Mackay, *New Testament Theology in Dialogue* (London: SPCK, 1987), 27–53.

19. See Wiles, *The Remaking of Christian Doctrine*, especially ch. 1.

20. J. Hick, ed., *The Myth of God Incarnate* (London: SCM Press, 1977); M. Green, ed., *The Truth of God Incarnate* (London: Hodder & Stoughton, 1977); A. E. Harvey, ed., *God Incarnate: Story and Belief* (London: SPCK, 1981), and many other sequels. The debate was not confined to the English-speaking world, as witness the publication of, *inter alia*, W. Pannenberg, *Jesus—God and Man* (London: SCM Press, 1968 [originally in German, 1964]); and E. Schillebeeckx's *Jesus—An Experiment in Christology* (New York: Seabury Press, 1979) and *Christ—The Experience of Jesus as Lord* (New York: Seabury Press, 1980).

21. Dunn, *Christology in the Making,* 265 (emphasis omitted).

22. D. Nineham, in *The Myth of God Incarnate*, ed. Hick, 202–3.

23. Henceforth in this article we shall, for brevity, use the term "Resurrection" to denote *both* the "Resurrection" *and* the "exaltation" of Jesus the Christ.

24. See C. F. D. Moule's evidence that the individual Jesus of history turned out, after the resurrection, to be one who transcended individuality—an unconfined, unrestricted, inclusive personality, the universal "Christ" to all humanity—in his *The Phenomenon of the New Testament* (London: SCM Press, 1967), ch. 2; and Moule, *The Origin of Christology,* ch. 2.

25. This hermeneutical question is posed by Leonard Hodgson, *For Faith and Freedom* (Oxford: Oxford University Press, 1956), x.

26. See J. C. Puddefoot, "Information and Creation," in C. Wassermann, R. Kirby, and B. Rordoff, eds., *The Science and Theology of Information* (Geneva: Editions Labor et Fides, University of Geneva, 1991), 7–25.

27. *TSA,* ch. 9.

28. Ibid., sec. 4, p. 179; ch. 11, sections 2(a), 3(b), and 3(c).

29. Dunn, *Christology in the Making,* 262 (emphasis omitted).

30. Macquarrie, *Jesus Christ in Modern Thought,* 43–44, 108.

31. Ibid., 106–7 (verse numbers added).

32. John Bowker, *The Sense of God* (Oxford: Clarendon Press, 1973), 95.

33. John Bowker, *The Religious Imagination and the Sense of God* (Oxford: Clarendon Press, 1978), 187–88.

34. *TSA,* part 2, esp. ch. 8.

35. Ibid., ch. 3, section 3(a).

36. Ibid., ch. 4, section 3(a), and ch. 8, section 1(g).

37. See John A. T. Robinson, *Exploration into God* (London: SCM Press, 1967), 83, 97.

38. *TSA*, ch. 10, 187.

39. See Adrian Thatcher, *Truly a Person, Truly God* (London: SPCK, 1990), for an investigation emphasizing the centrality of the concept of the person for any adequate understanding of the incarnation. See also his "Christian Theism and the Concept of a Person," in Arthur Peacocke and Grant Gillett, eds., *Persons and Personality* (Oxford: Blackwell, 1987), 180–90.

40. Robinson, *Exploration into God,* 98–99 (numbers refer to the verses of John 1).

41. *TSA*, ch. 15.

42. Mark 15:34.

43. *TSA*, ch. 8, sec. 2(c).

44. For a fuller discussion, see Macquarrie, *Jesus Christ in Modern Thought,* 245–50.

45. Phil. 2:6–11; 2 Cor. 8:9.

46. See Macquarrie, *Jesus Christ in Modern Thought,* 388–92; Dunn, *Christology in the Making,* 114–21.

Chapter 11: DNA of Our DNA

1. Raymond E. Brown, *The Virginal Conception and Bodily Resurrection of Jesus* (New York: Paulist Press, 1973), 42.

2. Ibid., 42 n. 56, citing Ratzinger, *Introduction to Christianity* (New York: Herder and Herder, 1969), 208.

3. Michael J. Langford, *Providence* (London: SCM Press, 1981), 18–19.

4. Raymond E. Brown, *The Birth of the Messiah* (London: Geoffrey Chapman; New York: Macmillan, 1977), 527, emphasis in text.

5. Ibid., 527 n. 26a.

6. John Macquarrie, *Jesus Christ in Modern Thought* (London: SCM Press, 1990), 392–93.

7. C. J. Cadoux, *The Life of Jesus* (West Drayton, Middsex.: Penguin Books, 1948), 30.

8. Derek Stanesby, "Notes on Biology and Salvation," in *The Annual Review of St. George's House, Windsor,* 1990, 28; see also his article, "Nature of Jesus and His Genes," *The Times,* December 12, 1987, for a similar statement.

9. Stanesby, "Notes on Biology and Salvation." n. 8, above.

10. Macquarrie, *Jesus Christ in Modern Thought,* 393.

11. Gregory of Nazianzus, Ep. 101, *Nicene and Post-Nicene Fathers* (Parker, 1894), quoted in H. Bettenson, *Documents of the Christian Church* (London: Oxford University Press, 1943; reprint 1956), 64.

12. "Docetism (from Greek *dokeo* = I seem) refers to the doctrine that the manhood of Christ was apparent not real, that, as in some Greek myths, a divine being was dressed up as a man in order to communicate revelations, but was not really involved in the human state and withdrew before the passion." Frances Young, "Docetism," in *A New Dictionary of Christian Theology,* ed. A. Richardson and J. Bowden (London: SCM Press, 1983), 160. The adjective "docetic" is widely used to denote doctrines or views that tend in this direction, that is, which imply that the humanity of Jesus was not real.

13. Ironically, according to Raymond Brown, the credal statement "born of the virgin Mary" was intended, by shifting the emphasis to birth, to signal "that *part* of

the interest was now on the reality of Jesus' humanity against a docetic heresy: the proof of his humanity is that we know the agents of his birth (Mary) and death (Pontius Pilate)" (*A New Dictionary of Christian Theology,* 598). Today, in the light of biology—and of historical studies—it has an opposite, docetic, tendency.

Chapter 12: The Challenges and Possibilities for Western Monotheism—Christianity

1. Quoted by J. H. Brooke, *Science and Religion: Some Historical Perspectives* (Cambridge: Cambridge University Press, 1991), 1.

2. Sir Richard Livingstone, *The Pageant of Greece* (Oxford: Clarendon Press, 1923; reprint, 1945), 414.

3. Gerd Theissen, Lecture at Oxford, February 23, 1998; in *A Theory of Primitive Religion* (London: SCM Press, 1999), 2.

Chapter 13: Wisdom in Science and Education

1. Sharon H. Ringe, *Wisdom's Friends* (Louisville, Ky.: Westminster John Knox Press, 1999), 44.

2. J. McEvoy, *Robert Grosseteste* (Oxford: Oxford University Press, 2000), 84.

3. R. W. Southern, *Robert Grosseteste: The Growth of an English Mind in Medieval Europe* (Oxford: Clarendon Press, 1986), 165.

4. Ibid., 168.

5. Southern, *Robert Grosseteste.*

6. McEvoy, *Robert Grosseteste.*

7. Ursula Goodenough, personal communication.

8. Philip Clayton, "The Case for Christian Panentheism," *Dialog* 37, no. 3 (summer 1998): 201–8 (quotation on 205); see also his *God and Contemporary Science* (Edinburgh: Edinburgh University Press, 1997), ch. 4.

9. Peter Morea, *Personality: An Introduction to the Theories of Psychology* (London: Penguin Books, 1990), 170–71.

10. This section is indebted to the exposition of this aspect of Grosseteste's thought by McEvoy, *Robert Grosseteste,* 137–38, 189–91.

Index